The Top UK Soap and Detergent Manufacturers

Profiles of the leading 650 companies

John D Blackburn

Editor

dp

First Edition

Summer 2019

ISBN-13: 978-1-912736-30-0

ISBN-10: 1-912736-30-6

All rights reserved. No part of this publication may be reproduced, distributed, or transmitted in any form or by any means, including photocopying, recording, or other electronic or mechanical methods, without our prior written permission, except in the case of brief quotations embodied in critical reviews and certain other non-commercial uses permitted by copyright law. For permission requests, please write to us.

Copyright © 2019 Dellam Publishing Limited

Printed in 8pt Nimbus Sans L

Designed by URW++ Design and Development GmbH

Dellam Publishing Limited

2 Heath Drive, Sutton, Surrey, SM2 5RP

Fax: 020 8770 7478   email: enquiries@dellam.com

SAN: 0177881   EAN/GLN: 5030670177882

Table of Contents

1 Acknowledgements ... iv

2 Introduction ... v

3 Total Assets League Table ... 1
- As a measure of size, total assets is preferable to turnover which is influenced by profit margins and whether companies are capital or labour intensive.

4 Age of Companies ... 5
- Each company is ranked by its date of incorporation. Newcomers are defined as those registered since 2017.

5 Geographic Distribution ... 11
- Each company is classed by county.

6 Company Profiles ... 17
- Full company name, date incorporated, net worth, total assets, registered office, activities, shareholders and parent company, directors (with date of birth, nationality and occupation) and number of employees (if available).

7 Index of Directorships ... 57
- Alphabetical list of directors showing their directorships. If several directors have identical names then their date of birth is shown.

8 Standard Industrial Classification ... 73
- These codes are used to classify businesses by the type of economic activity in which they are engaged.

9 *finis* ... 79

Acknowledgements

This is a long and detailed publication containing thousands of facts and figures. It is only to be expected, despite continuous and repeated editing and checking, that errors may occur. In such cases, once we are aware of any, we publish a correction on our website.

Readers are encouraged to check regularly at www.dellam.com/books for any corrections and updates.

Although we take extreme care to ensure accuracy and being up-to-date, we cannot accept responsibility for any errors or omissions.

Contains public sector information licensed under Open Government Licence v3.0. from The Charity Commission (England and Wales) and The Charity Commission for Northern Ireland. © Crown Copyright and database right (2018).

Contains information from the Scottish Charity Register supplied by the Office of the Scottish Charity Regulator and licensed under the Open Government Licence v.2.0. © Crown Copyright and database right (2018).

Contains OS data © Crown copyright and database right (2018)

Contains Royal Mail data © Royal Mail copyright and database right (2018)

Contains National Statistics data © Crown copyright and database right (2018)

Contains Office for National Statistics © Crown copyright and database right (2018)

Maps based on those produced by the Office for National Statistics Geography GIS & Mapping Unit (2012 and 2018).

Contains HM Land Registry data © Crown copyright and database right (2018).

Contains Parliamentary information licensed under the Open Parliament Licence v3.0.

House of Commons Library Briefing Papers licensed under the Open Parliament Licence v3.0.

Contains Food Standards Agency data © Crown copyright and database right (2018).

Contains Eurostat data, 1995-2018, copyright European Commission by the Decision of 12 December 2011.

Maps based on produced by ONS Geography GIS & Mapping Unit.

Contains Companies House data supplied under section 47 and 50 of the Copyright, Designs and Patents Act 1988 and Schedule 1 of the Database Regulations (SI 1997/3032).

We appreciate your interest in our publications, and your comments and suggestions are always welcome. Please contact us at enquiries@dellam.com.

Introduction

This study looks at all companies registered in the United Kingdom where they identify themselves as manufacturers of soap and detergents.

This study includes companies that are dormant or non-trading some of which might be latent while others may operate under their owners' names but incorporate to protect the business name. In addition, all newly incorporated companies are included. The study will exclude those companies that do not specifically identify themselves as manufacturers of soap and detergents.

The aim of this study is to provide an overview of the key movers and shakers in the UK manufacture of soap and detergents sector. Only key data has been isolated, particularly the company's net worth and total assets, but also its full name, date incorporated, registered office, other activities, shareholders, directors (with date of birth, occupation and nationality) and number of employees.

Two indicators of size are used: net worth and total assets. These are preferable to turnover which is influenced by profit margins and whether the companies are capital or labour intensive.

In the years 2016, 2017 and 2018, new company incorporations in the manufacture of soap and detergents sector were 32, 108 and 174 respectively.

The index of production for 2010-2018 was as follows: -0.5, 15.1, 8.1, 3.7, 0.1, -2.3, -6.3, 5.7 and 5.0 respectively.

The UK Cleaning Products Industry Association (UKCPI) is the leading trade association representing UK producers of cleaning and hygiene products. It represents companies that manufacture or market cleaning products in the UK and its membership includes over 98% of UK consumer product manufacturers and over 60% of UK industrial and institutional product manufacturers.

The UK sector generates over £4.5 billion in sales annually and directly employs over 30,000 people.

Soap, detergents and other cleaning products make up a fifth of chemical exports.

L'Association Internationale de la Savonnerie, de la Detergence et des Produits d'Entretien (AISE) based in Brussels, represents the industry in the EU. Its members are the 29 national associations in Europe. It represents over 900 companies supplying household and professional cleaning products and services across Europe.

72% of UK consumers use liquid soap regularly, compared with just 55% using bar soap. However, more consumers are becoming concerned about single-use plastic. In 2018, sales of bar soap was £68.3 million, up £2 million. Sales are growing at 3%, faster than liquid soaps and shower gel products.

Standard cataloguing guidelines for company names in the profile section have been used, but there will be occurrences when the name may not be strictly alphabetical. A certain licence was adopted where it was felt that strictly alphabetical could lead to improper cataloguing. Some company names have been shortened in the league tables for aesthetic reasons.

John D Blackburn
Editor

This page is intentionally left blank

Total Assets League Table

The Top UK Soap and Detergent Manufacturers

Company	Revenue
Unilever UK Limited	£1,671,614,976
Procter & Gamble Product Supply (U.K.) Limited	£432,592,992
Dimex Limited	£332,260,992
Robert McBride Ltd	£158,680,000
Ecolab Limited	£145,591,008
Diversey Limited	£90,623,000
Diversey Holdings Limited	£73,196,000
SC Johnson Professional Limited	£62,328,000
Molton Brown Limited	£55,077,000
Stepan UK Limited	£51,685,000
Industrial Chemicals Limited	£48,816,096
Zenith Hygiene Group Limited	£47,140,000
Arch UK Biocides Limited	£42,653,000
Holt Lloyd International Limited	£37,460,000
The Holchem Group Limited	£37,337,000
Zenith Hygiene Systems Limited	£32,489,000
Christeyns UK Ltd	£30,519,140
NCH (UK) Limited	£30,053,000
Holchem Laboratories Limited	£28,292,000
Evonik Goldschmidt UK Limited	£20,582,184
Evans Vanodine International PLC	£20,189,306
Selden Research Limited	£19,214,784
Autosmart Holdings Limited	£16,947,212
Shorrock Trichem Limited	£16,001,280
Adam Investment Company Limited	£15,958,523
Fillcare Limited	£15,329,000
Diversey UK Production Limited	£15,156,000
Libra Speciality Chemicals Limited	£13,247,113
Coventry Chemicals Limited	£12,446,000
Acdoco Limited	£10,814,428
Royal Sanders (UK) Limited	£10,738,000
GEA Farm Technologies (UK) Ltd	£10,718,982
Star Brands (Holdings) Limited	£10,583,399
Star Brands Limited	£10,309,552
The Coventry Group Limited	£10,154,000
Stephenson Group Ltd	£9,778,523
R P Adam Limited	£9,748,482
Zep UK Limited	£9,409,107
Dri-Pak Limited	£9,362,620
Pangaea Laboratories Limited	£8,474,315
Pluswipes Limited	£7,709,593
Malibu Health Products Limited	£7,536,565
Pilling Trading Limited	£6,115,209
Cleenol Group Limited	£6,027,567
Rutpen Limited	£5,982,748
ERH Propack Limited	£5,522,000
Christeyns Food Hygiene Ltd	£5,347,209
Medichem Manufacturing Ltd	£5,051,155
Clover Chemicals Limited	£4,944,551
3M UK Trading Limited	£4,662,671
Fisher Research Ltd	£4,362,538
Freshorize Ltd	£4,209,926
Superfine Manufacturing Limited	£4,200,140
Carvansons Ltd	£4,007,118
Totem Properties Limited	£3,717,022
Scottish Fine Soaps Limited	£3,429,628
Pure Solve UK Limited	£3,395,000
Astley Dye and Chemical Company Limited	£3,330,467
Itaconix (U.K.) Limited	£3,310,000
Springdawn Bolton Limited	£3,214,154
Soapworks Limited	£3,110,872
The Proton Group Limited	£2,773,480
Dasic International Limited	£2,756,788
Datesand Limited	£2,698,093
Kitchenmaster (N.I.) Limited	£2,497,036
Aromatic Flavours & Fragrances Europe Limited	£2,450,243
Merlin Chemicals Limited	£2,378,341
Melpass Limited	£2,312,102
Decon Laboratories Limited	£2,258,096
John Drury & Co. Limited	£2,252,378
Lankem Ltd.	£2,130,363
Denykem Limited	£2,089,161
Ideal Manufacturing Limited	£2,007,665
Quill International Group Limited	£1,970,767
Serchem Limited	£1,953,030
Universal Toiletries Corporation Limited	£1,933,357
Sechelle Manufacturing Limited	£1,929,081
Sycamore (UK) Limited	£1,805,902
Prime Industries Ltd	£1,798,181
Omnova Performance Chemicals Limited	£1,761,000
John Drury Holdings Limited	£1,752,498
Techtron Limited	£1,696,945
Millchem (UK) Limited	£1,423,789
William Clements (Chemicals) Ltd	£1,411,109
Spectrum Industrial Limited	£1,240,598
ZOK International Group Limited	£1,239,409
Bonasystems Europe Ltd	£1,167,684
Apex Industrial Chemicals Limited	£1,122,528
MSH Chemical Manufacturing Limited	£1,121,021
Christina May Limited	£964,391
Powerclean Chemicals Limited	£962,367
Chemisphere UK Limited	£896,611
Safe Solutions (Safe4) Limited	£864,871
Residual Barrier Technology Limited	£841,910
Delf (UK) Limited	£838,675
Specialised Aerosols Company Limited	£837,709
Larragard Limited	£755,636
Quill International Chemicals Limited	£719,551
Midland Chemicals Limited	£702,480
Best-Chem Limited	£700,861

The Top UK Soap and Detergent Manufacturers

dellam

Company	Value	Company	Value
Revert Limited	£669,704	The Soap Shop Ltd	£123,931
Future Developments (Manufacturing) Limited	£638,869	Aventual Ltd	£120,318
X.R.O. Chemical Services Limited	£607,515	ICP Direct Limited	£111,235
Greener Solutions Ltd	£596,972	Chemiclean Products Limited	£111,227
Chela Ltd	£591,784	The Soap Story Limited	£108,590
Stockcare Limited	£590,150	Cares Laboratory Limited	£108,247
Little Soap Company Limited	£569,896	Eden Classics Limited	£93,934
Portland Janitorial Products Limited	£567,171	Field International UK Limited	£93,667
R-MC Power Recovery Limited	£544,903	Splosh Limited	£89,054
Trichem Scotland Limited	£526,209	Bramchem Ltd.	£88,821
Silk Detergent Limited	£500,256	Handmade Naturals Ltd	£88,006
Syntec Manufacturing Limited	£491,538	Nimble Babies Limited	£87,912
Paragon PE Ltd	£467,082	Calman Enterprise Limited	£87,880
Hygenol Cleaning Supplies Ltd	£460,982	Arulabeauty Ltd	£87,496
A-Chem Plant & Equipment Limited	£455,704	Friendly Soap Limited	£85,586
Afco C & S Limited	£441,016	Newry Chemicals Ltd	£72,562
Scorcher Idea Limited	£419,000	Murray-Smith Consulting Limited	£71,401
Total Liquid Solutions Ltd	£417,052	Industrial Chemical Experts Limited	£71,166
Capricorn Detergents Limited	£415,459	Paramount Chemicals Limited	£69,467
Droyt Products Limited	£413,473	You're Gorgeous Handmade Soap Limited	£69,323
K C Butler & Son Limited	£411,926	De Montfort Marketing Limited	£66,131
Steri-7 Worldwide Limited	£400,000	Globemeth Limited	£66,000
Travik Chemicals (UK) Limited	£380,966	SAS Environmental Services Ltd	£65,918
Academy Hair and Beauty (UK) Ltd	£376,876	Nathalie Bond Limited	£61,754
MSL Limited	£355,537	Purdie's of Argyll Ltd	£60,500
The Bio-D Holdings (UK) Limited	£342,855	Lower Swell Chemicals Limited	£60,366
The Chemical Hut Ltd	£340,641	Proskin Europe Ltd	£59,762
London Soap and Chemical Co. Limited	£329,151	Lamella Structures Limited	£58,162
Bayer-Wood Technologies Limited	£325,675	Kirkwood Chemicals Ltd	£57,281
The Highland Soap Co. Limited	£294,882	4th Floor Products Limited	£53,656
Paul McCaffrey Systems Ltd	£275,418	Washworks Bodycare Limited	£51,509
Texatherm Systems Limited	£253,807	All Natural Cosmetics Ltd	£49,925
Ottimo Supplies Limited	£248,284	OC Transformation Limited	£49,471
Saanro International Limited	£243,597	Azure Liquid Solutions Limited	£47,860
Ian Mitchell Distribution Limited	£241,511	Marble Hill Soaps Limited	£46,854
Cole & Wilson,Limited	£241,380	Dizziak Ltd	£44,072
PRSS Solutions (UK) Limited	£234,443	Love To B Skincare Ltd	£44,064
Main Chemical Co Limited	£228,986	Tersus Niteo Limited	£42,793
Bloom and Blossom Limited	£225,391	The Little Goat Soap Company Limited	£41,716
James Law (Chemicals) Limited	£220,872	Soap School Ltd	£40,194
Chemex (North West) Limited	£213,888	RBL Laboratories Ltd	£38,309
AMB Hygiene Limited	£212,958	Origin Pet Products Limited	£37,711
Zamo Household Products Limited	£208,480	Holistic Plant Technologies Ltd	£35,000
Ecosearch Limited	£192,686	Eucaderm Limited	£34,893
Hebridean Soap Company Ltd	£180,689	Piesse and Kinney Limited	£33,715
PH Direct Limited	£176,810	Bespro Chemicals Ltd	£33,682
Apvodo Ltd.	£157,888	Chimera UK Chemical Solutions Limited	£33,101
MDCO Ltd	£145,720	The Natural Soap Company Limited	£30,984
Rapid Washrooms Limited	£142,476	Universal Chemicals Limited	£29,102
Archem (N.I.) Ltd	£133,839	Sevin London Limited	£29,075

Tony Maleedy Hair Ltd.	£27,412	Ora-Heal Ltd	£2,508
International Maintenance Chemicals Ltd	£26,341	Lemon Spring Ltd	£2,444
Soapsmith Limited	£25,275	Savage Alchemy Limited	£2,436
Dynamic Chemicals Limited	£24,966	Edinburgh Natural Skincare Co (Retail Shops) Ltd	£2,100
Ochil Skincare Company Ltd	£24,315	Emollience Ltd	£2,000
Unitor Limited	£24,044	Aromatherapy Infusions Ltd	£1,721
Natural British Limited	£23,236	Windy Mill Ltd	£1,627
Yess Essentials Limited	£22,355	Anahita Limited	£1,472
Grassroots Health Ltd	£20,254	Cut from The Wild Limited	£1,447
Cliffe House (Organics) Limited	£19,005	Sikania Ltd	£1,447
Wild Planet Products Ltd	£16,763	Luvly Bubbly Limited	£1,149
Spirit of The Isle Ltd.	£14,584	Clean Sciences Limited	£1,043
Soapy Skin Limited	£13,866	Newton Formulations Limited	£1,000
Dee Doo Limited	£13,766	LJSP Ltd	£1,000
Ian Greenwood Engineering Limited	£13,617	Chromasol Limited	£971
CClear Limited	£12,798	Elimin8 Limited	£962
Levant Soap Limited	£11,064	Lathersmith Ltd	£929
Inter Bio Chemicals Ltd	£10,581	Hutrade Ltd.	£871
Essential Spirit Limited	£9,652	Dalton Luxury Ltd	£800
Born To Be Natural Ltd	£9,166	So.Soap Company Limited	£720
Mbikudi Ltd	£9,015	Old Park Farm Estate Limited	£707
Wagonwash Limited	£8,970	Ebiox Limited	£704
Yeardeal Limited	£6,881	Dagarti CIC	£646
Ultimate Car Care Ltd	£6,151	Mitcheldean Soap Ltd	£611
Hunca Munka Limited	£6,125	Madalyn and Rose Ltd	£599
Golden Soaps Ltd	£5,885	Freestyle Beauty Products Limited	£598
Arize and Dazzle Limited	£5,628	Gently Handcrafted Ltd	£516
Butter Bar Soapery Ltd	£5,197	Wordsworth Handcrafted Soap Co. Ltd.	£500
Seren Soaps Limited	£4,721	NS Industries Ltd	£389
Decontamin8 (Europe) Limited	£4,666	The Soap Souk Ltd	£370
Humble Bee Botanica Ltd.	£4,624	Langhedge Limited	£347
Sheabynature Ltd	£4,000	Nuts About Soap Limited	£255
The Austonley Soap Company Ltd	£3,982	Mazu Seaweed Limited	£184
The Happy Bee Company Ltd	£3,859	Bubble Shack Ltd	£113
Funkydz Ltd	£3,812	The Colhoon Corporation Limited	£100
Hydrophilic Ltd	£3,800	Bristol Soap Limited	£100
Oooh Skincare Ltd	£3,680	Pembrokeshire Seaweeds Ltd	£100
Ghastly Games Limited	£3,647	Simply Ewe Limited	£69
Enchanted Plants Ltd	£3,442	Leum Skin Care Ltd	£35
The Waterside Soap Company Limited	£3,135	Glamour Natural Cosmetics Ltd	£6
Dogbreath Brewery Ltd	£3,062	Daisy Gordon Limited	£3
Everfolk Limited	£3,054	Gard Chemicals Limited	£2
Kallisti Ltd	£2,959	Decontamin8 Limited	£1
CKC Aromatherapy Beauty Products Limited	£2,890	Naturali360 Limited	£1
Spartisan Ltd	£2,853	Nature Native Limited	£1
Macob Online Shopping Ltd.	£2,764		

Age of Companies

The Top UK Soap and Detergent Manufacturers

1900-1909
Stephenson Group Ltd

1920-1929
Astley Dye and Chemical Co Ltd
Cole & Wilson, Limited
Robert McBride Ltd

1930-1939
Droyt Products Limited
James Law (Chemicals) Limited
Unilever UK Limited

1940-1949
John Drury Holdings Limited
ERH Propack Limited
SC Johnson Professional Ltd

1950-1959
Cleenol Group Limited
Evans Vanodine International PLC

1960-1969 [8]
Christeyns UK Ltd
Decon Laboratories Limited
Dri-Pak Limited
John Drury & Co. Limited
Ecolab Limited
NCH (UK) Limited
Scottish Fine Soaps Limited
Superfine Manufacturing Ltd

1970-1979 [15]
Adam Investment Co Ltd
Coventry Chemicals Limited
Denykem Limited
Evonik Goldschmidt UK Limited
GEA Farm Technologies (UK) Ltd
Holt Lloyd International Ltd
Larragard Limited
Libra Speciality Chemicals Ltd
Lower Swell Chemicals Limited
Proton Group Limited
Quill International Group Ltd
Selden Research Limited
Specialised Aerosols Co Ltd
Spectrum Industrial Limited
Zep UK Limited

1980-1989 [34]
AMB Hygiene Limited
Apex Industrial Chemicals Ltd
Aromatic Flavours & Fragrances Europe
Cater-Lyne Limited
Chemisphere UK Limited
Christeyns Food Hygiene Ltd
William Clements (Chemicals) Ltd
Dasic International Limited
Datesand Limited
Dimex Limited
Diversey Industrial Limited
Diversey UK Production Limited
Fillcare Limited
Fisher Research Ltd
Ian Greenwood Engineering Ltd
Holchem Laboratories Limited
Ideal Manufacturing Limited
International Maintenance Chemicals Ltd
Kitchenmaster (N.I.) Limited

London Soap and Chemical Co. Ltd
MSL Limited
Main Chemical Co Limited
Paul McCaffrey Systems Ltd
Melpass Limited
Molton Brown Limited
Ottimo Supplies Limited
Paramount Chemicals Limited
Powerclean Chemicals Limited
Serchem Limited
Stockcare Limited
Syntec Manufacturing Limited
Techtron Limited
Totem Properties Limited
Universal Chemicals Limited

1990-1994 [21]
R P Adam Limited
Aqua Chemicals Limited
Bayer-Wood Technologies Ltd
Chela Ltd
Clover Chemicals Limited
Cut from The Wild Limited
Delf (UK) Limited
Dynamic Chemicals Limited
Ecosearch Limited
Eucaderm Limited
Future Developments (Manufacturing)
Klenzan Direct Limited
Merlin Chemicals Limited
Midland Chemicals Limited
Millchem (UK) Limited
Portland Janitorial Products Ltd
Rite Solution Limited
Rutpen Limited
Unitor Limited
X.R.O. Chemical Services Ltd
Yeardeal Limited

1995
MSH Chemical Manufacturing Ltd
Ian Mitchell Distribution Ltd
Procter & Gamble Product Supply (U.K.)
Zamo Household Products Ltd

1996 [7]
Friendly Soap Limited
Pure Solve UK Limited
Stepan UK Limited
Texatherm Systems Limited
Trichem Scotland Limited
ZOK International Group Ltd
Zenith Hygiene Systems Limited

1997 [7]
Academy Hair and Beauty (UK) Ltd
Bio-Clean Limited
Diversey Limited
Hebridean Soap Co Ltd
Saanro International Limited
Sechelle Manufacturing Limited
Sycamore (UK) Limited

1998 [5]
Ebiox Limited
McIntyre Group Ltd.
PH Direct Limited
Smartic Truckwash Ltd
Zok Group Limited

1999 [9]
Best-Chem Limited
Coventry Group Limited
Freestyle Beauty Products Ltd
Industrial Chemicals Limited
Lankem Ltd.
Malibu Health Products Limited
Omnova Performance Chemicals Ltd
Pangaea Laboratories Limited
Universal Toiletries Corporation Ltd

2000 [5]
Essential Spirit Limited
Hygenol Cleaning Supplies Ltd
Christina May Limited
Natural Soap Co Ltd
Quill International Chemicals Ltd

2001 [9]
3M UK Trading Limited
K C Butler & Son Limited
Capricorn Detergents Limited
Diversey Holdings Limited
Field International UK Limited
R-MC Power Recovery Limited
Shorrock Trichem Limited
Star Brands Limited
Yess Essentials Limited

2002 [9]
4th Floor Products Limited
Bespro Chemicals Ltd
Freshorize Ltd
Lamella Structures Limited
Momar Limited
Pluswipes Limited
Revert Limited
SAS Environmental Services Ltd
Scorcher Idea Limited

2003 [7]
Apvodo Ltd.
Arch UK Biocides Limited
Archem (N.I.) Ltd
Autosmart Group Limited
Chemex (North West) Limited
Enchanted Plants Ltd
Gard Chemicals Limited

2004 [9]
De Montfort Marketing Limited
Dee Doo Limited
Dogbreath Brewery Ltd
PRSS Solutions (UK) Limited
Paragon PE Ltd
Prime Industries Ltd
Safe Solutions (Safe4) Limited
Star Brands (Holdings) Limited
Strathpeffer Spa Soap Co Ltd

2005 [6]
Autosmart Holdings Limited
Chemiclean Products Limited
Itaconix (U.K.) Limited
Marble Hill Soaps Limited
Old Park Farm Estate Limited
Mimi Pisano Limited

The Top UK Soap and Detergent Manufacturers

2006 [6]
Eden Classics Limited
Golden Soaps Ltd
Highland Soap Co. Limited
Holchem Group Limited
Montague Lloyd Limited
Steri-7 Worldwide Limited

2007 [8]
Acdoco Limited
Anahita Limited
Chemical Hut Ltd
Newry Chemicals Ltd
Newton Formulations Limited
Ora-Heal Ltd
Pilling Trading Limited
Springdawn Bolton Limited

2008 [10]
A-Chem Plant & Equipment Ltd
Bloom and Blossom Limited
Bonasystems Europe Ltd
Food Tech Hygiene Limited
Langhedge Limited
Little Soap Co Ltd
Mitcheldean Soap Ltd
OC Transformation Limited
Royal Sanders (UK) Limited
Zenith Hygiene Group Limited

2009 [9]
Bio-D Holdings (UK) Limited
Born To Be Natural Ltd
CClear Limited
Handmade Naturals Ltd
Kush Moma Limited
Renbow Haircare Limited
Residual Barrier Technology Ltd
Splosh Limited
Vehicle Cleaning Products Ltd

January-June 2010 [7]
Colhoon Corporation Limited
Elimin8 Limited
Eurotank Limited
Origin Pet Products Limited
Wagonwash Limited
Wild Planet Products Ltd
You're Gorgeous Handmade Soap Ltd

July-December 2010 [8]
Calman Enterprise Limited
Edinburgh Natural Skincare Company (Retail Shops)
Greener Solutions Ltd
Heavenly Fragrance (UK) Ltd
Nuts About Soap Limited
Soapsmith Limited
Soapworks Limited
Travik Chemicals (UK) Limited

January-June 2011
Crafty Lady Ltd
W & J Global Ltd.

July-December 2011 [9]
Arulabeauty Ltd
Bonasystems Worldwide Ltd
Dagarti CIC
Globemeth Limited
London Cosmetics (UK) Limited
Luvly Bubbly Limited
Oooh Skincare Ltd
Piesse and Kinney Limited
West Trading Ltd

April-June 2012
Love To B Skincare Ltd
Shea Life Limited
Spartisan Ltd

July-September 2012 [5]
Bramchem Ltd.
Chimera UK Chemical Solutions Ltd
Gently Handcrafted Ltd
Oleonix Solutions Limited
SKC Resources Ltd

October-December 2012
Clean Sciences Limited
Happy Bee Co Ltd

January-March 2013
Lathersmith Ltd
MDCO Ltd
Soap School Ltd
Spirit of The Isle Ltd.

April-June 2013 [8]
2J's Medical Supplies Ltd
Azure Liquid Solutions Limited
Hutrade Ltd.
Ideation Solutions Limited
Little Goat Soap Co Ltd
Soap Arcade Limited
Soapy Skin Limited
Washworks Bodycare Limited

July-September 2013 [6]
Businotech Limited
Carvansons Ltd
Chromasol Limited
Decontamin8 Limited
Ennebee Ltd
Soap Shop Ltd

October-December 2013
Nathalie Bond Limited
Decontamin8 (Europe) Limited

January-March 2014
Afco C & S Limited
Nimble Babies Limited
Tersus Niteo Limited

April-June 2014 [6]
ICP Direct Limited
Lana-Rae Ltd Ltd
Leum Skin Care Ltd
Mazu Seaweed Limited
Rowanhays Ltd
Steri-7 Brazil Limited

July-September 2014 [6]
All Natural Cosmetics Ltd
Cliffe House (Organics) Ltd
Meadow Farm Friends Ltd
Ultimate Car Care Ltd
Vanillin Limited
Windy Mill Ltd

October-December 2014
Black and Silver Equestrian Ltd
Soap & Soak Limited
Soapnsoak Limited

January 2015
Aventual Ltd
Ochil Skincare Co Ltd

February 2015
Austonley Soap Co Ltd

March 2015
TRU Products Limited

April 2015
Bristol Soap Limited
Murray-Smith Consulting Ltd

May 2015
Chemtrading Limited

June 2015
Funkydz Ltd

July 2015
Check You Limited
Madalyn and Rose Ltd

September 2015
Lemon Spring Ltd

October 2015
Conatural Ltd
Tony Maleedy Hair Ltd.
RBL Laboratories Ltd
So.Soap Co Ltd

November 2015
Aromatherapy Infusions Ltd
Holistic Plant Technologies Ltd

December 2015
Medichem Manufacturing Ltd
Savon Paradis Ltd

January 2016
Jackanoryjones Limited
Sevin London Limited

February 2016
Proskin Europe Ltd

March 2016
Candy & Mischief Ltd
Cares Laboratory Limited
Mbikudi Ltd

April 2016
Levant Soap Limited

May 2016
Alkleen Ltd
Rapid Washrooms Limited

June 2016
Fysha Ltd

July 2016
Arize and Dazzle Limited
Soap Cellar Limited

August 2016
Dijon Soaps Limited
LJSP Ltd
NS Industries Ltd

September 2016
Ghastly Games Limited
Grassroots Health Ltd
Inter Bio Chemicals Ltd
Koorax Ltd

October 2016 [7]
Butter Bar Soapery Ltd
Fairy Treats Ltd
Daisy Gordon Limited
Green Housekeeper Ltd
Ohana CBD Limited
Seren Soaps Limited
Waterside Soap Co Ltd

November 2016
Hunam Limited
Macob Online Shopping Ltd.
Mayde Essence Ltd
Vienne Luca Limited

December 2016
Puddlemud Ltd.
Silk Detergent Limited

January 2017 [6]
Completely Conkers Limited
MOL Soap Ltd.
Mano Pack Limited
Purdie's of Argyll Ltd
Sikania Ltd
Total Liquid Solutions Ltd

February 2017 [5]
Glamour Natural Cosmetics Ltd
Meaningful Earth Soap Co Ltd
Naturali360 Limited
Sani Professional Limited
Soap Story Limited

March 2017 [6]
Bubble Shack Ltd
CKC Aromatherapy Beauty Products Ltd
Carzel Limited
Easy Newco Limited
Hydrophilic Ltd
Sheabynature Ltd

April 2017 [8]
Aromatic Scents Ltd
Dalton Luxury Ltd
Felicity Solutions Ltd
Hunca Munka Limited
Kallisti Ltd
SE & SA Limited
Simply Ewe Limited
Willis Doyle Limited

May 2017 [15]
Danchemtech Ltd
Dizziak Ltd
Everfolk Limited
Humble Bee Botanica Ltd.
Kirkwood Chemicals Ltd
Nature Native Limited
Paragon Technical PE Services Ltd
Pure Purpose Cosmetics Ltd
SC567361 Ltd.
Saltaire Soap Ltd
Samola Industries Limited
Sanofi International Biotech Co Ltd.
Supreme Wax Limited
Wren and Willow Limited
Wrinkly Elephant Co Ltd

June 2017 [10]
Cosmetic Hooligans Ltd
Dales Heritage Soap Co Ltd
Dales Natural Soap Co Ltd
Get The Scent Limited
Harmonious Brown Limited
Industrial Chemical Experts Ltd
Kokoa UK Limited
M.A. Industries Limited
Rustic Blends Limited
Yorkshire Dales Soap Co Ltd

July 2017 [5]
Azara Beautique Ltd
Kindness Collective Limited
Nature Reflects Limited
Pretty Little Treat Company (Yorkshire)
Salopian Ltd

August 2017 [13]
Anastaz Beverly Hills Ltd
Bonham Soaps Limited
Brush Europe Limited
CB Services Limited
Ersag UK Limited
Evocativ Limited
Fresh from Nature Limited
Goats on the Coast Ltd
Greatest of All Time Soapworks Ltd
Making Scents Ltd
Sisi Cosmetics Ltd
Soap Souk Ltd
Soapy Goat Ltd

September 2017 [14]
21 Road Limited
CS Holistic Therapy Products Ltd
Cleanux Chemicals Ltd
Driftwood Shaper Ltd
Emollience Ltd
Gemini Cosmetics Ltd
Gondar Soaps Ltd
Home of The Green Gobblin Ltd
Irae Limited
Natural British Limited
Pembrokeshire Seaweeds Ltd
Smellifiscent Ltd
Tiger Lily Soapery Ltd
Wordsworth Handcrafted Soap Co Ltd

October 2017 [8]
Diamond (Edibles) Limited
Dino-Mite Ltd
Maribella London Limited
Nature B Limited
SGHP Ltd
Sankofa Heritage Ltd
Scent By Hand Ltd
Sweet Orange Soapery Ltd

November 2017 [12]
Ayurveda Wellness Ltd
Edinburgh Soap Co Ltd
GoodNaturedSkincare Ltd
Island Soapery Ltd
Pampered Me Ltd
Pebble Soap Ltd
Savon de V Ltd
Scinn Limited
Shrieking Soap Shack Limited
Soap Lab Limited
T. & Toff Ltd
Wash Bomb Ltd

December 2017 [6]
Aromabar (Scotland) Ltd
Makin' Scents Ltd
Molecula Ltd
Kathryn Tilly Limited
Von Bons Bath Bombs Limited
Wholesome Toiletries Ltd

January 2018 [15]
All Naturals Beauty Limited
Anuvaayum Ltd
Axwood Limited
Elegant Soap Co Ltd
Fernandez Cosmetics Ltd
Fysifarm Limited
Goatally Soaps Ltd
Kalabash Limited
Marsh Valley Ltd
Natural Jem Limited
OCD Finish Limited
Rural Skills Centre Limited
Safeway Wood Care Limited
Savage Alchemy Limited
TWA Production Ltd.

February 2018 [17]
Belkor Bay Limited
Biologico Cosmetics Limited
Body Candy Ltd.
Carapoll Chemicals Ltd
Clensure Global Ltd
Cocoa Lime Limited
Eco Earth Limited
Elinor-UK Ltd
Italist Skincare Ltd
Ko. Essentials Ltd.
LU Aromatherapy Ltd
Madcow Brand Limited
Poppy Products Limited
Relax Candle and Bath Co Ltd
TAC Perfumes & Cosmetics (UK) Ltd
Winchester Soap Co Ltd
Yogi Fresh Limited

The Top UK Soap and Detergent Manufacturers dellam

March 2018 [14]
Adamy Cosmetics Ltd
Blok Soap Ltd
Bloomtown Ltd
Coco Timyal Limited
Cueball Cosmetics Ltd
Dandy Gent Manufactory Ltd
Exterin Ltd
Java Coffee Co Ltd
KA Shere-Khan Limited
Lady Smidgeton's Apothecary Ltd
Lather Cute Soap Limited
Mauchit Ltd
Shinerite Solutions Limited
Springer Soap Co Ltd

April 2018 [11]
Annael Ltd
Cahercon Group Limited
Sarah Ireland Perfumes Ltd
Little Green Beehive Ltd
Little Wax Workshop Limited
Narauli Ltd
Ohana Soaps and More Limited
Soapberries Ltd
Therapy Factory Ltd
United Company Specialty Chemicals & Mineral Oils
Zenken Limited

May 2018 [13]
Caley's of Exeter Ltd
Detergents Ltd
Elizabeth Vintage Soap Ltd
Ethicalsoap Limited
Gio Natura Ltd
Harmony Bodycare Limited
Letlalo Ltd
Mama Bee Soaps Ltd
Natural By Nature Limited
Northumbrian Botanicals Ltd
Soap Legacy Ltd
Ultima Direct Limited
Wildcraft Ltd

June 2018 [17]
Auto. B Limited
Bare & Bloom Works Handmade Bath and Body Treats
Emilia's Handmade Bath and Body Ltd
Farasha-Cosmetics Ltd
HGH Trading Ltd
Naked Cosmetics Ltd
Nomad Soapery Limited
Oryza Naturale Limited
Red Cottage Industries Ltd
Refresh Tea & Soap Co Ltd
Roots & Paradise Ltd
Rutherford Bambury Ltd
Spiritual Cleanse Ltd
Swan Lake Candle Ltd
UK Better Cleaner Industry Co., Ltd
UK Nuduun Personal-Care Supply Co.,
Ultra Bien Limited

July 2018 [15]
47 Skin Ltd
Antifoaming Agents Ltd
Berry Inc Ltd
Cornwall Soapbox (Mevagissey) Ltd
Deliciously Me Ltd
Evbioo Ltd
Firecraft Ltd
Glametuber Ltd
Kleos Naturals Ltd
Let It Bee Ltd
Nana's Studio Ltd
Original Soapchair Co Ltd
Soapaffection Ltd
Suds & Salve Ltd
Zomi Ltd

August 2018 [15]
24 Cures Limited
Chinese Gentry Limited
D'lishx0x0 Limited
Duchess Naturals Limited
Eljay Group Ltd
Filthy Kids Ltd
Halritt Ltd
Haromatic Ltd
Hocktester Ltd
Mild + Wild Ltd
Paisley Soap Co Ltd
Perboscolo Ltd
Seadpearl Ltd
Team Titan Performance Ltd
Very Good Vegan Co Ltd

September 2018 [14]
Amita Cosmetics Ltd
Bar.None Limited
Estela Dermocosmetics Ltd
Green Spa Therapy Ltd
Greener Good Ltd
London Soap Co Ltd
Magpie's Ocean Ltd
Polka Lab Limited
Season Clean Ltd
Soul of Ayurveda Ltd
Sustain Global Limited
Toilet Safe UK Limited
Touch of Nature Limited
Wild Stem Soaps Limited

October 2018 [16]
B.Me Skincare Ltd
Biggin Bees Limited
Buypolar Ltd
E-Sensual Oil Soap By Farah Ltd
Forward Chemicals Ltd
Hempia Limited
Icilda's Ltd
Innoscent Ltd
Lick Labs Limited
Lofty Gardens Ltd
Naturally Nourishing Ltd
Sheer Bliss Retail Ltd
Soap People Ltd
Soap Sensations Ltd
Thornton Baron Ltd
Wizard Soap Co Ltd

November 2018 [13]
Body Station Limited
Earth's Naturals Ltd
Fragrance Tree Ltd
Fragrant Alchemy Ltd
La Boulle Ltd
Lamina Animal Limited
Peak Soap Ltd
Respect Soaps Limited
Seilich Limited
Shifting London Ltd
Soaps By Stacey Limited
Touch Soap Ltd
Vuitton Group Ltd

December 2018 [14]
Aglow Limited
Amira Products Ltd
Eco-Point Laboratories Limited
Genten Skincare Ltd
Ginchiest Artisan Soap Co Ltd
Insensed Ltd
Locks in Goodness Ltd
Loveve. Ltd
MWK Cosmetics (UK) Ltd
R & T Natural Cosmetics Ltd
Reesoaps.co.uk Ltd
Spa Mommy Limited
Times Capital Industry Limited
UK Pandora Fairy Skin Beautiyfying Co.,

January 2019 [24]
Amsar Soap Co Ltd
Anyki Ltd
Autosheen Ltd
Beardog and Roo Ltd
Boweasel Ltd
Dook Ltd
Durabond Chemicals Limited
Emily's Soap Shop Limited
Emma Victoria Cosmetics Ltd
Goat Soap Co Ltd
Jared Gonzalez Ltd
Grumpy Gorilla Ltd
Hitchin Soap Co Ltd
Kalula Cosmetics Ltd
KrUde Cosmetics Ltd
Little Lodge Bees Ltd
Elizabeth Martin Creative Studio Ltd
Nu-E55ence Ltd
Orikii Naturals Ltd
P & H Natural Skincare Ltd
Peaceful Potager Limited
St Andrews Soap Co Ltd
Thistle & Berry Ltd
Zyzven Naturals Cosmetics Ltd

February 2019 [20]
Bean and Boy Ltd
Clean Bidco Limited
Clean Topco Limited
Diamond Fizzles Ltd
Ed N' Grace Ltd
GM Globalhealth Ltd
Good Soap Co Ltd
Gosling Soap Ltd
Mrs Whelan Ltd
Paws and Unwind Limited
Pur Natural Soaps Ltd
Purealba Limited
Quint Essence Lab Ltd
Smelliz Ltd
Soap Collection Limited
Soap Foundry Limited
Thebubblebar Ltd
Vegan Soap Co Ltd
Welsh Valley Soapery Ltd
Deloris White Limited

This page is intentionally left blank

Geographic Distribution by County

Co Antrim [5]
Ayurveda Wellness Ltd
Bespro Chemicals Ltd
CB Services Limited
William Clements (Chemicals) Ltd
Soap Story Limited

Co Down [6]
Archem (N.I.) Ltd
Hempia Limited
Kirkwood Chemicals Ltd
Kitchenmaster (N.I.) Limited
Makin' Scents Ltd
Newry Chemicals Ltd

Co Fermanagh
Shinerite Solutions Limited

Co Londonderry
Marble Hill Soaps Limited

Co Tyrone
CKC Aromatherapy Beauty Products Ltd

Aberdeenshire
Apex Industrial Chemicals Ltd
Check You Limited

Angus
Fairy Treats Ltd
Superfine Manufacturing Ltd

Argyll & Bute
Purdie's of Argyll Ltd

Ayrshire
Emollience Ltd
Portland Janitorial Products Ltd

Clackmannanshire
Ochil Skincare Co Ltd

Dumfries-shire
Essential Spirit Limited

Dumfries & Galloway
Purealba Limited

Dunbartonshire
Sheer Bliss Retail Ltd

Fife
St Andrews Soap Co Ltd

Highland
Highland Soap Co. Limited
Waterside Soap Co Ltd

Inverness-shire
Calman Enterprise Limited

Lanarkshire [10]
Dynamic Chemicals Limited
HGH Trading Ltd
MSL Limited
Mbikudi Ltd
Paisley Soap Co Ltd
SC567361 Ltd.
Sanofi International Biotech Co Ltd.
Soapworks Limited
Syntec Manufacturing Limited
Thistle & Berry Ltd

Perthshire
Mauchit Ltd

Renfrewshire
Aromabar (Scotland) Ltd
MWK Cosmetics (UK) Ltd
Renbow Haircare Limited

Ross & Cromarty
Strathpeffer Spa Soap Co Ltd

Roxburghshire
Narauli Ltd

Selkirkshire
Adam Investment Co Ltd
R P Adam Limited

Stirlingshire
Montague Lloyd Limited

Anglesey
Spirit of The Isle Ltd.

Bedfordshire [5]
Anuvaayum Ltd
Ghastly Games Limited
Rite Solution Limited
Soap Shop Ltd
Spa Mommy Limited

Berkshire [7]
3M UK Trading Limited
ERH Propack Limited
Peaceful Potager Limited
Mimi Pisano Limited
Rutpen Limited
Sycamore (UK) Limited
Windy Mill Ltd

Buckinghamshire [7]
Candy & Mischief Ltd
Evonik Goldschmidt UK Limited
International Maintenance Chemicals Ltd
Jackanoryjones Limited
MOL Soap Ltd.
Tersus Niteo Limited
Toilet Safe UK Limited

Cambridgeshire [6]
Businotech Limited
Emma Victoria Cosmetics Ltd
London Cosmetics (UK) Limited
Madcow Brand Limited
Mano Pack Limited
Scorcher Idea Limited

Cardiganshire
Exterin Ltd
Pur Natural Soaps Ltd

Carmarthenshire
2J's Medical Supplies Ltd

Cheshire [15]
Amsar Soap Co Ltd
Blok Soap Ltd
Chemex (North West) Limited
Christeyns Food Hygiene Ltd
Ecolab Limited
Hunca Munka Limited
Hygenol Cleaning Supplies Ltd
Klenzan Direct Limited
Kokoa UK Limited
Lankem Ltd.
Paragon Technical PE Services Ltd
Safe Solutions (Safe4) Limited
Spartisan Ltd
Stepan UK Limited
Zep UK Limited

Cleveland
NS Industries Ltd
Respect Soaps Limited
Smellifiscent Ltd

Clwyd [5]
Prime Industries Ltd
Soap Arcade Limited
Ultima Direct Limited
Wizard Soap Co Ltd
You're Gorgeous Handmade Soap Ltd

Cornwall [5]
Bloomtown Ltd
Cornwall Soapbox (Mevagissey) Ltd
Lick Labs Limited
Soap & Soak Limited
Soapnsoak Limited

Cumbria
Get The Scent Limited
Green Housekeeper Ltd
Ian Mitchell Distribution Ltd

Denbighshire
Polka Lab Limited

Derbyshire [16]
A-Chem Plant & Equipment Ltd
Best-Chem Limited
Clover Chemicals Limited
Dandy Gent Manufactory Ltd
Dri-Pak Limited
Driftwood Shaper Ltd
Grumpy Gorilla Ltd
Naturally Nourishing Ltd
PH Direct Limited
Peak Soap Ltd
Quill International Chemicals Ltd
Quill International Group Ltd
SC Johnson Professional Ltd
Selden Research Limited
Ultimate Car Care Ltd
X.R.O. Chemical Services Ltd

The Top UK Soap and Detergent Manufacturers

dellam

Devon [8]

Caley's of Exeter Ltd
Ennebee Ltd
Goats on the Coast Ltd
Little Lodge Bees Ltd
Meaningful Earth Soap Co Ltd
Rowanhays Ltd
Savon Paradis Ltd
Soap Cellar Limited

Dorset

Enchanted Plants Ltd
Wash Bomb Ltd

Essex [18]

Adamy Cosmetics Ltd
Arulabeauty Ltd
Bare & Bloom Works Handmade Bath and Body Treats
Bean and Boy Ltd
CS Holistic Therapy Products Ltd
Decontamin8 (Europe) Limited
Decontamin8 Limited
Dimex Limited
Dino-Mite Ltd
Ebiox Limited
Eljay Group Ltd
Golden Soaps Ltd
Industrial Chemicals Limited
KA Shere-Khan Limited
Luvly Bubbly Limited
Orikii Naturals Ltd
Samola Industries Limited
Wren and Willow Limited

Flintshire

Aglow Limited

Glamorgan [13]

CClear Limited
Chinese Gentry Limited
Cut from The Wild Limited
Elizabeth Martin Creative Studio Ltd
Mazu Seaweed Limited
Mrs Whelan Ltd
Omnova Performance Chemicals Ltd
Rural Skills Centre Limited
Seren Soaps Limited
UK Pandora Fairy Skin Beautiyfying Co.,
Universal Chemicals Limited
Welsh Valley Soapery Ltd
Wildcraft Ltd

Gloucestershire [5]

Aqua Chemicals Limited
Lower Swell Chemicals Limited
Mitcheldean Soap Ltd
Original Soapchair Co Ltd
Paramount Chemicals Limited

Gwent

Bar.None Limited

Hampshire [16]

24 Cures Limited
Born To Be Natural Ltd
Chemtrading Limited
Dasic International Limited
Dijon Soaps Limited
Emilia's Handmade Bath and Body Ltd
Field International UK Limited
Filthy Kids Ltd
Glamour Natural Cosmetics Ltd
Love To B Skincare Ltd
Rapid Washrooms Limited
Sikania Ltd
Swan Lake Candle Ltd
Team Titan Performance Ltd
Very Good Vegan Co Ltd
Winchester Soap Co Ltd

Herefordshire

Elizabeth Vintage Soap Ltd
Gently Handcrafted Ltd
Splosh Limited

Hertfordshire [16]

Bonasystems Europe Ltd
Bonasystems Worldwide Ltd
Cater-Lyne Limited
Eden Classics Limited
Freestyle Beauty Products Ltd
Gemini Cosmetics Ltd
Glametuber Ltd
Gondar Soaps Ltd
Halritt Ltd
Hitchin Soap Co Ltd
La Boulle Ltd
McIntyre Group Ltd.
Nature Native Limited
Universal Toiletries Corporation Ltd
Zenith Hygiene Group Limited
Zenith Hygiene Systems Limited

Kent [17]

Anahita Limited
Apvodo Ltd.
Biggin Bees Limited
Globemeth Limited
Goatally Soaps Ltd
Greener Solutions Ltd
Happy Bee Co Ltd
Little Wax Workshop Limited
London Soap and Chemical Co. Ltd
Medichem Manufacturing Ltd
Murray-Smith Consulting Ltd
Nature Reflects Limited
Pure Purpose Cosmetics Ltd
Shifting London Ltd
Soap Lab Limited
Totem Properties Limited
Wild Planet Products Ltd

Lancashire [47]

Acdoco Limited
Afco C & S Limited
Aromatherapy Infusions Ltd
Aromatic Scents Ltd
Astley Dye and Chemical Co Ltd
Auto. B Limited
Carvansons Ltd
Chemisphere UK Limited
Colhoon Corporation Limited
Completely Conkers Limited
Datesand Limited
Droyt Products Limited
Duchess Naturals Limited
Earth's Naturals Ltd
Emily's Soap Shop Limited
Evans Vanodine International PLC
Daisy Gordon Limited
Green Spa Therapy Ltd
Holchem Group Limited
Holchem Laboratories Limited
Holt Lloyd International Ltd
ICP Direct Limited
James Law (Chemicals) Limited
Lofty Gardens Ltd
Robert McBride Ltd
Melpass Limited
Merlin Chemicals Limited
Mild + Wild Ltd
Millchem (UK) Limited
Newton Formulations Limited
PRSS Solutions (UK) Limited
Paws and Unwind Limited
Piesse and Kinney Limited
Pilling Trading Limited
Relax Candle and Bath Co Ltd
Royal Sanders (UK) Limited
SKC Resources Ltd
Saanro International Limited
Scent By Hand Ltd
Shorrock Trichem Limited
Smelliz Ltd
So.Soap Co Ltd
Soap Legacy Ltd
Soapy Skin Limited
Springdawn Bolton Limited
Touch Soap Ltd
Wagonwash Limited

Leicestershire [5]

Alkleen Ltd
K C Butler & Son Limited
De Montfort Marketing Limited
Gio Natura Ltd
Total Liquid Solutions Ltd

Lincolnshire

Black and Silver Equestrian Ltd
Pebble Soap Ltd
R-MC Power Recovery Limited
Soap Foundry Limited

London [124]
21 Road Limited
Amira Products Ltd
Amita Cosmetics Ltd
Anastaz Beverly Hills Ltd
Annael Ltd
Antifoaming Agents Ltd
Anyki Ltd
Autosheen Ltd
Aventual Ltd
Axwood Limited
Azara Beautique Ltd
Belkor Bay Limited
Berry Inc Ltd
Bloom and Blossom Limited
Body Candy Ltd.
Body Station Limited
Boweasel Ltd
Brush Europe Limited
Butter Bar Soapery Ltd
Cahercon Group Limited
Capricorn Detergents Limited
Clensure Global Ltd
Danchemtech Ltd
Dizziak Ltd
Ed N' Grace Ltd
Elegant Soap Co Ltd
Elinor-UK Ltd
Estela Dermocosmetics Ltd
Ethicalsoap Limited
Eurotank Limited
Evbioo Ltd
Evocativ Limited
Farasha-Cosmetics Ltd
Felicity Solutions Ltd
Firecraft Ltd
Forward Chemicals Ltd
Freshorize Ltd
Funkydz Ltd
Fysha Ltd
Fysifarm Limited
GM Globalhealth Ltd
Genten Skincare Ltd
Good Soap Co Ltd
GoodNaturedSkincare Ltd
Heavenly Fragrance (UK) Ltd
Holistic Plant Technologies Ltd
Hunam Limited
Icilda's Ltd
Industrial Chemical Experts Ltd
Inter Bio Chemicals Ltd
Sarah Ireland Perfumes Ltd
Itaconix (U.K.) Limited
Italist Skincare Ltd
Kalabash Limited
Kindness Collective Limited
Kleos Naturals Ltd
Kush Moma Limited
LJSP Ltd
Lady Smidgeton's Apothecary Ltd
Lamina Animal Limited
Lana-Rae Ltd Ltd
Lather Cute Soap Limited
Lathersmith Ltd
Leum Skin Care Ltd
Levant Soap Limited
Locks in Goodness Ltd
London Soap Co Ltd
Loveve. Ltd
Macob Online Shopping Ltd.
Madalyn and Rose Ltd
Mama Bee Soaps Ltd

Maribella London Limited
Molecula Ltd
Molton Brown Limited
Natural Jem Limited
Naturali360 Limited
Nature B Limited
Nu-E55ence Ltd
Nuts About Soap Limited
Ohana CBD Limited
Old Park Farm Estate Limited
Origin Pet Products Limited
Oryza Naturale Limited
P & H Natural Skincare Ltd
Pampered Me Ltd
Pangaea Laboratories Limited
Poppy Products Limited
Proskin Europe Ltd
Puddlemud Ltd.
R & T Natural Cosmetics Ltd
Refresh Tea & Soap Co Ltd
Roots & Paradise Ltd
Rustic Blends Limited
SE & SA Limited
SGHP Ltd
Safeway Wood Care Limited
Sankofa Heritage Ltd
Scottish Fine Soaps Limited
Sechelle Manufacturing Limited
Sevin London Limited
Shea Life Limited
Soapaffection Ltd
Soapberries Ltd
Soapsmith Limited
Soul of Ayurveda Ltd
Spiritual Cleanse Ltd
TAC Perfumes & Cosmetics (UK) Ltd
Therapy Factory Ltd
Times Capital Industry Limited
Touch of Nature Limited
UK Better Cleaner Industry Co., Ltd
UK Nuduun Personal-Care Supply Co.,
United Company Specialty Chemicals & Mineral Oils
Vuitton Group Ltd
Washworks Bodycare Limited
West Trading Ltd
Deloris White Limited
Wholesome Toiletries Ltd
Wild Stem Soaps Limited
Yeardeal Limited
Yess Essentials Limited
Yogi Fresh Limited
Zamo Household Products Ltd
Zomi Ltd

Lothian [5]
Edinburgh Natural Skincare Company (Retail Shops)
Edinburgh Soap Co Ltd
SAS Environmental Services Ltd
Seilich Limited
Trichem Scotland Limited

Merseyside [9]
Azure Liquid Solutions Limited
Crafty Lady Ltd
Delf (UK) Limited
Fernandez Cosmetics Ltd
Hocktester Ltd
LU Aromatherapy Ltd
Paragon PE Ltd

Perboscolo Ltd
Vanillin Limited

Middlesex [11]
47 Skin Ltd
Arize and Dazzle Limited
Chela Ltd
Cleanux Chemicals Ltd
Eco-Point Laboratories Limited
Ecosearch Limited
Fisher Research Ltd
Hydrophilic Ltd
Ideation Solutions Limited
Langhedge Limited
Malibu Health Products Limited

Midlothian [6]
Biologico Cosmetics Limited
Dook Ltd
Grassroots Health Ltd
KrUde Cosmetics Ltd
Sisi Cosmetics Ltd
Supreme Wax Limited

Monmouthshire
E-Sensual Oil Soap By Farah Ltd
Insensed Ltd
Lamella Structures Limited
Von Bons Bath Bombs Limited

Norfolk [6]
Easy Newco Limited
Natural Soap Co Ltd
Oleonix Solutions Limited
Suds & Salve Ltd
Sweet Orange Soapery Ltd
Tiger Lily Soapery Ltd

Northamptonshire [17]
AMB Hygiene Limited
D'lishx0x0 Limited
Dagarti CIC
Dee Doo Limited
Diversey Holdings Limited
Diversey Industrial Limited
Diversey Limited
Diversey UK Production Limited
Ginchiest Artisan Soap Co Ltd
Ideal Manufacturing Limited
Kallisti Ltd
Nana's Studio Ltd
Pluswipes Limited
Residual Barrier Technology Ltd
Sani Professional Limited
Shrieking Soap Shack Limited
Soaps By Stacey Limited

Northumberland
Ersag UK Limited
Northumbrian Botanicals Ltd
Revert Limited
Wordsworth Handcrafted Soap Co Ltd

Nottinghamshire [7]
All Natural Cosmetics Ltd
All Naturals Beauty Limited
Beardog and Roo Ltd
Carapoll Chemicals Ltd
Natural British Limited
Savage Alchemy Limited
Vehicle Cleaning Products Ltd

The Top UK Soap and Detergent Manufacturers

Oxfordshire [5]
Cleenol Group Limited
Diamond Fizzles Ltd
Little Goat Soap Co Ltd
Nomad Soapery Limited
Vienne Luca Limited

Pembrokeshire
Pembrokeshire Seaweeds Ltd

Rhondda Cynon Taf
Fillcare Limited

Shropshire [7]
Cocoa Lime Limited
Greatest of All Time Soapworks Ltd
Haromatic Ltd
Salopian Ltd
Serchem Limited
Soapy Goat Ltd
Techtron Limited

Somerset [11]
B.Me Skincare Ltd
Fragrant Alchemy Ltd
Jared Gonzalez Ltd
Harmony Bodycare Limited
Humble Bee Botanica Ltd.
Meadow Farm Friends Ltd
Savon de V Ltd
Soap Collection Limited
TRU Products Limited
Texatherm Systems Limited
Zenken Limited

Staffordshire [10]
Autosmart Group Limited
Autosmart Holdings Limited
Chemical Hut Ltd
Dogbreath Brewery Ltd
Future Developments (Manufacturing)
Goat Soap Co Ltd
Handmade Naturals Ltd
Magpie's Ocean Ltd
Natural By Nature Limited
Reesoaps.co.uk Ltd

Suffolk [6]
Aromatic Flavours & Fragrances Europe
Kalula Cosmetics Ltd
Paul McCaffrey Systems Ltd
Powerclean Chemicals Limited
Silk Detergent Limited
Travik Chemicals (UK) Limited

Surrey [22]
4th Floor Products Limited
Academy Hair and Beauty (UK) Ltd
Bio-Clean Limited
Carzel Limited
Coco Timyal Limited
Conatural Ltd
Harmonious Brown Limited
Innoscent Ltd
OC Transformation Limited
Ohana Soaps and More Limited
Ora-Heal Ltd
Procter & Gamble Product Supply (U.K.)

Red Cottage Industries Ltd
Soap Sensations Ltd
Steri-7 Brazil Limited
Steri-7 Worldwide Limited
Ultra Bien Limited
Unilever UK Limited
Vegan Soap Co Ltd
W & J Global Ltd.
Willis Doyle Limited
Zyzven Naturals Cosmetics Ltd

Sussex [14]
Cueball Cosmetics Ltd
Decon Laboratories Limited
Eucaderm Limited
Gosling Soap Ltd
Greener Good Ltd
Letlalo Ltd
Christina May Limited
Naked Cosmetics Ltd
Quint Essence Lab Ltd
Rutherford Bambury Ltd
Soap People Ltd
Unitor Limited
ZOK International Group Ltd
Zok Group Limited

Tyne & Wear
Spectrum Industrial Limited

Warwickshire [10]
Coventry Chemicals Limited
Coventry Group Limited
Eco Earth Limited
Little Green Beehive Ltd
Midland Chemicals Limited
Nimble Babies Limited
Soap Souk Ltd
T. & Toff Ltd
TWA Production Ltd.
Thebubblebar Ltd

West Midlands [19]
Bubble Shack Ltd
Chemiclean Products Limited
Chimera UK Chemical Solutions Ltd
Cosmetic Hooligans Ltd
Fragrance Tree Ltd
Fresh from Nature Limited
Hebridean Soap Co Ltd
Hutrade Ltd.
Irae Limited
Let It Bee Ltd
MDCO Ltd
MSH Chemical Manufacturing Ltd
Mayde Essence Ltd
Momar Limited
NCH (UK) Limited
OCD Finish Limited
Oooh Skincare Ltd
Pure Solve UK Limited
Seadpearl Ltd

Wiltshire [7]
Bristol Soap Limited
Deliciously Me Ltd
Everfolk Limited
GEA Farm Technologies (UK) Ltd
Island Soapery Ltd
Season Clean Ltd
Simply Ewe Limited

Worcestershire [6]
Bayer-Wood Technologies Ltd
Ian Greenwood Engineering Ltd
Little Soap Co Ltd
Smartic Truckwash Ltd
Sustain Global Limited
Wrinkly Elephant Co Ltd

Yorkshire [57]
Arch UK Biocides Limited
Austonley Soap Co Ltd
Bio-D Holdings (UK) Limited
Nathalie Bond Limited
Bonham Soaps Limited
Bramchem Ltd.
Buypolar Ltd
Cares Laboratory Limited
Christeyns UK Ltd
Chromasol Limited
Clean Bidco Limited
Clean Sciences Limited
Clean Topco Limited
Cliffe House (Organics) Ltd
Cole & Wilson, Limited
Dales Heritage Soap Co Ltd
Dales Natural Soap Co Ltd
Dalton Luxury Ltd
Denykem Limited
Detergents Ltd
Diamond (Edibles) Limited
John Drury & Co. Limited
John Drury Holdings Limited
Durabond Chemicals Limited
Elimin8 Limited
Food Tech Hygiene Limited
Friendly Soap Limited
Gard Chemicals Limited
Home of The Green Gobblin Ltd
Java Coffee Co Ltd
Ko. Essentials Ltd.
Koorax Ltd
Larragard Limited
Lemon Spring Ltd
Libra Speciality Chemicals Ltd
M.A. Industries Limited
Main Chemical Co Limited
Making Scents Ltd
Tony Maleedy Hair Ltd.
Marsh Valley Ltd
Ottimo Supplies Limited
Pretty Little Treat Company (Yorkshire)
Proton Group Limited
RBL Laboratories Ltd
Saltaire Soap Ltd
Scinn Limited
Sheabynature Ltd
Soap School Ltd
Specialised Aerosols Co Ltd
Springer Soap Co Ltd
Star Brands (Holdings) Limited
Star Brands Limited
Stephenson Group Ltd
Stockcare Limited
Thornton Baron Ltd
Kathryn Tilly Limited
Yorkshire Dales Soap Co Ltd

This page is intentionally left blank

Company Profiles

21 Road Limited
Incorporated: 12 September 2017
Registered Office: 134 Putney Bridge Road, London, SW15 2NQ
Major Shareholder: Nnenna Onuba
Officers: Nnenna Onuba [1980] Director/Banker

24 Cures Limited
Incorporated: 21 August 2018
Registered Office: 22 Adams Close, Hedge End, Southampton, SO30 2NB
Officers: Anna Collins [1976] Director

2J's Medical Supplies Ltd
Incorporated: 1 May 2013
Registered Office: 7 Conduit Lane, Carmarthen, SA31 1LD
Officers: Steven Andrew Jenkins [1979] Director/Consultant

3M UK Trading Limited
Incorporated: 9 March 2001 *Employees:* 7
Net Worth: £3,727,109 *Total Assets:* £4,662,671
Registered Office: 3M Centre, Cain Road, Bracknell, Berks, RG12 8HT
Officers: Ian Richard Brown, Secretary; David James Ashley [1968] Director/General Counsel; Mohammad Irfan Malik [1965] Director [Pakistani]; Simla Semerciyan [1973] Director/Finance Manager [Turkish]

47 Skin Ltd
Incorporated: 20 July 2018
Registered Office: 2nd Floor, College House, 17 King Edwards Road, Ruislip, Middlesex, HA4 7AE
Major Shareholder: Nicholas Taylor
Officers: Jessica Taylor [1989] Director/Cosmetics

4th Floor Products Limited
Incorporated: 14 August 2002 *Employees:* 1
Net Worth: £2,843 *Total Assets:* £53,656
Registered Office: 73a High Street, Egham, Surrey, TW20 9HE
Shareholders: Richard Ian Stepney; Pamela Stepney
Officers: Richard Ian Stepney, Secretary; Pamela Stepney [1960] Director/Hairdresser; Richard Ian Stepney [1959] Director/Hairdresser

A-Chem Plant & Equipment Limited
Incorporated: 16 April 2008
Net Worth: £306,475 *Total Assets:* £455,704
Registered Office: Meadow Lane Industrial Estate, Dunsford Road, Alfreton, Derbys, DE55 7RH
Shareholders: Sharon Davis; Andrew Charles Davis
Officers: Sharon Davis, Secretary/Director; Andrew Charles Davis [1962] Director; Ashleigh Victoria Davis [1990] Director; James Davis [1992] Director; Sharon Davis [1962] Director

Academy Hair and Beauty (UK) Ltd
Incorporated: 2 May 1997
Net Worth: £188,029 *Total Assets:* £376,876
Registered Office: Doshi Accountants Ltd, 6th Floor, Amp House, Dingwall Road, Croydon, Surrey, CR0 2LX
Shareholders: Mohsin Janmohamed; Fidahusein Gulamali Asharia
Officers: Fidahusein Gulamali Asharia, Secretary; Mohsin Janmohamed [1961] Director/Businessman

Acdoco Limited
Incorporated: 21 March 2007 *Employees:* 27
Net Worth: £1,999,270 *Total Assets:* £10,814,428
Registered Office: Mallison Street, Bolton, Lancs, BL1 8PP
Shareholders: Heinrich Kurt Beckmann; Johann Gerhard Krauss
Officers: Nigel Drinkwater, Secretary; Heinrich Kurt Beckman [1947] Director/General Manager [German]; Nils Beckmann [1983] Director/Managing Partner [German]; Gareth William James Edwards [1958] Managing Director; Johann Gerhard Krauss [1961] Director/General Manager [German]; Brandon Pilling [1962] Director

Adam Investment Company Limited
Incorporated: 12 April 1978 *Employees:* 116
Net Worth: £9,261,248 *Total Assets:* £15,958,523
Registered Office: Arpal Works, Riverside Road, Selkirk, TD7 5DU
Parent: Ecolab (U.K.) Holdings Limited
Officers: Wendy Annette Joyce, Secretary; Carl Richmond Lee [1963] Director/Chartered Accountant; Paul Rawding [1971] Director/General Manager

R P Adam Limited
Incorporated: 5 January 1994 *Employees:* 87
Net Worth: £2,719,265 *Total Assets:* £9,748,482
Registered Office: Arpal Works, Riverside Road, Selkirk, TD7 5DU
Parent: Adam Investment Company Ltd
Officers: Wendy Annette Joyce, Secretary; Carl Richmond Lee [1963] Director/Chartered Accountant; Paul Rawding [1971] Director/General Manager

Adamy Cosmetics Ltd
Incorporated: 15 March 2018
Registered Office: 117 Wedderburn Road, Barking, Essex, IG11 7XF
Officers: Beatrice Mariana Mihut [1980] Director [Romanian]

Afco C & S Limited
Incorporated: 8 January 2014 *Employees:* 9
Net Worth Deficit: £2,539,504 *Total Assets:* £441,016
Registered Office: New Bridge Chemical Works, York Street, Radcliffe, Manchester, M26 2GL
Officers: Thomas Andrew Curtis, Secretary; Michael K Hinkle [1957] Director/President [American]

Aglow Limited
Incorporated: 21 December 2018
Registered Office: Yew Tree, Bryn-Sannan, Brynford, Holywell, Flintshire, CH8 8AX
Major Shareholder: Rachel Nadine Jones
Officers: Rachel Nadine Jones [1979] Director

Alkleen Ltd
Incorporated: 26 May 2016
Registered Office: 46 Cardinals Walk, Leicester, LE5 1LF
Shareholder: Ardian Ukmata
Officers: Valdet Teneqja [1978] Director/Chemist [Kosovan]; Ardian Ukmata [1971] Director/Chemist [American]

All Natural Cosmetics Ltd
Incorporated: 4 September 2014
Net Worth Deficit: £55,488 *Total Assets:* £49,925
Registered Office: MediCity, D6 Building, West Thane Road, Nottingham, NG90 6BH
Major Shareholder: Julita Joanna Geary
Officers: Dr Julita Joanna Geary, Secretary; Dr Julita Joanna Geary [1973] Managing Director [Polish]

The Top UK Soap and Detergent Manufacturers

All Naturals Beauty Limited
Incorporated: 11 January 2018
Registered Office: Medicity D6 Building West, Thane Road, Nottingham, NG90 6BH
Major Shareholder: Julita Joanna Geary
Officers: Dr Julita Geary, Secretary; Dr Julita Joanna Geary [1973] Managing Director [Polish]

AMB Hygiene Limited
Incorporated: 4 February 1985 *Employees:* 18
Net Worth: £65,392 *Total Assets:* £212,958
Registered Office: 3 Weekley Wood Close, Kettering, Northants, NN14 1UQ
Shareholder: Alan Baillie
Officers: Jason Alan Baillie, Secretary; Jason Alan Baillie [1973] Director/Operations Manager

Amira Products Ltd
Incorporated: 14 December 2018
Registered Office: 28d Colville Terrace, London, W11 2BU
Major Shareholder: Charlotte Irene Mensah
Officers: Charlotte Irene Mensah [1970] Director/Hairdresser

Amita Cosmetics Ltd
Incorporated: 28 September 2018
Registered Office: Kemp House, 160 City Road, London, EC1V 2NX
Shareholders: Beatrice Moore; Nana Aggrey-Fynn
Officers: Nana Aggrey-Fynn, Secretary; Beatrice Moore, Secretary; Nana Aggrey-Fynn [1996] Director/Student [Ghanaian]; Beatrice Moore [1975] Director/Student

Amsar Soap Company Ltd
Incorporated: 28 January 2019
Registered Office: 94 West Street, Hoole, Chester, CH2 3PT
Major Shareholder: Amber Marie Rose
Officers: Amber Marie Rose [1976] Director/Soap Maker

Anahita Limited
Incorporated: 10 May 2007 *Employees:* 1
Net Worth Deficit: £40,504 *Total Assets:* £1,472
Registered Office: The Cearne, Kent Hatch, Crockham Hill, Edenbridge, Kent, TN8 6SZ
Major Shareholder: Georgina Grace Kirkwood
Officers: Alexandra Kirkwood, Secretary; Georgina Grace Kirkwood [1969] Director

Anastaz Beverly Hills Ltd
Incorporated: 30 August 2017
Registered Office: Kemp House, 160 City Road, London, EC1V 2NX
Major Shareholder: Schoinopoulos Anestis
Officers: Schoinopoulos Anestis, Secretary; Schoinopoulos Anestis [1973] Director [Greek]

Annael Ltd
Incorporated: 25 April 2018
Registered Office: Ground Floor, 2 Woodberry Grove, London, N12 0DR
Shareholders: Joanne Navaresi; Francis Navaresi
Officers: Francis Navaresi [1953] Director [French]; Joanne Navaresi [1959] Director [Australian]

The Antifoaming Agents Ltd
Incorporated: 5 July 2018
Registered Office: 20-22 Wenlock Road, London, N1 7GU
Major Shareholder: Stewart Campbell
Officers: Stewart Campbell [1988] Director

Anuvaayum Ltd
Incorporated: 15 January 2018
Registered Office: 17 Falconers Road, Luton, Beds, LU2 9ET
Major Shareholder: Karunakaran Subramaniam
Officers: Karunakaran Subramaniam [1978] Director/Consultant

Anyki Ltd
Incorporated: 22 January 2019
Registered Office: 20-22 Wenlock Road, London, N1 7GU
Shareholders: Anya Kruger; Kim Brown
Officers: Kim Brown [1963] Director/Project Consultant; Anya Kruger [1978] Director/Consultant [South African]

Apex Industrial Chemicals Limited
Incorporated: 12 February 1985 *Employees:* 26
Net Worth: £811,126 *Total Assets:* £1,122,528
Registered Office: Commercial House, 2 Rubislaw Terrace, Aberdeen, AB10 1XE
Parent: ECS Investment Property Limited
Officers: Edward Cameron Singer [1957] Director

Apvodo Ltd.
Incorporated: 13 November 2003
Net Worth: £12,277 *Total Assets:* £157,888
Registered Office: 80 Sidney Street, Folkestone, Kent, CT19 6HQ
Major Shareholder: John Otto Eduard Pronk
Officers: John Otto Eduard Pronk [1949] Director/Manager [Dutch]

Aqua Chemicals Limited
Incorporated: 9 November 1994
Registered Office: Lock Stock and Barrel GB, No 6, Unit 3 Newent Business Park, Newent, Glos, GL18 1DZ
Shareholder: Frings Limited
Officers: Charles Kalopungi [1966] Director/Manager [Ni-Vanuatu]

Arch UK Biocides Limited
Incorporated: 8 December 2003 *Employees:* 80
Net Worth: £28,066,000 *Total Assets:* £42,653,000
Registered Office: Wheldon Road, Castleford, W Yorks, WF10 2JT
Officers: Nicholas Thomas Carter, Secretary; Nicholas Thomas Carter [1981] Director/Financial Accountant; Alexander Henry Hoy [1966] Director; Gregor Keil [1974] Director/Head of Commercial Operations [German]; Anthony William Kelly [1963] Director; Jordan Todorov Petkov [1966] Global Head R&D Consumer Care CPI Director; Astrid Schnidrig [1968] Director/SVP BU Head Coating & Composites [Swiss]; Peter Jozef Van Aken [1968] Director/Head of Material Protection Europe [Belgian]

Archem (N.I.) Ltd
Incorporated: 9 July 2003
Net Worth: £57,931 *Total Assets:* £133,839
Registered Office: 158 High Street, Holywood, Co Down, BT18 9HT
Shareholders: Brian Alexander Hunniford; Lynne Diane Dorothy Joan Hunniford
Officers: Brian Alexander Hunniford, Secretary; Brian Alexander Hunniford [1952] Director; Lynne Diane Dorothy Joan Hunniford [1953] Director

Arize and Dazzle Limited
Incorporated: 8 July 2016
Net Worth: £3,628 *Total Assets:* £5,628
Registered Office: 15 Cohen Court, 5 Burnt Oak Broadway, Edgware, Middlesex, HA8 5FB
Major Shareholder: Gladys Gladys Mouyokolo
Officers: Gladys Gladys Mouyokolo [1974] Director/Skincare, Haircare and Beauty [French]

Aromabar (Scotland) Ltd
Incorporated: 5 December 2017
Registered Office: Unit 9-11 Robertson Street, Barrhead, E Renfrewshire, G78 1QW
Shareholders: Alan Grant; Catherine Grant
Officers: Alan Grant [1963] Director; Catherine Grant [1964] Director

Aromatherapy Infusions Ltd
Incorporated: 13 November 2015
Net Worth Deficit: £3,571 *Total Assets:* £1,721
Registered Office: 83 Ducie Street, Manchester, M1 2JQ
Major Shareholder: Ginina Houghton
Officers: Ginina Houghton [1972] Director/Manager

Aromatic Flavours & Fragrances Europe Limited
Incorporated: 29 September 1987 *Employees:* 30
Net Worth: £753,909 *Total Assets:* £2,450,243
Registered Office: AFF House, Station Road, Elmswell, Bury St Edmunds, Suffolk, IP30 9HD
Major Shareholder: Cherine Fanous
Officers: Cherine Adel Fanous, Secretary; Cherine Adel Fanous [1965] Director [Egyptian]; Marie Nadia Fanous [1940] Director [Egyptian]

Aromatic Scents Ltd
Incorporated: 20 April 2017
Registered Office: 18 Hall Street, Bury, Lancs, BL8 1RY
Shareholder: Barbara Allen
Officers: Barbara Allen, Secretary; Paul Mainwaring [1958] Director

Arulabeauty Ltd
Incorporated: 25 July 2011
Previous: Tamali Limited
Net Worth: £87,496 *Total Assets:* £87,496
Registered Office: The Crawler Shed, Housham Hall Farm, Harlow Road, Matching Tye, Harlow, Essex, CM17 0PB
Major Shareholder: Junior Everton Allijohn
Officers: Yvonne Ann Marie Allijohn, Secretary; Junior Everton Allijohn [1966] Director/Real Estate; Symone Marie Allijohn [1996] Director/Student

Astley Dye and Chemical Company Limited
Incorporated: 8 May 1929 *Employees:* 3
Net Worth: £2,821,972 *Total Assets:* £3,330,467
Registered Office: Mallison Street, Bolton, Lancs, BL1 8PP
Officers: Nigel Drinkwater, Secretary; Jeremy Guy Nicholas Bird [1961] Director/Management Consultant; Brandon Pilling [1962] Managing Director; Elizabeth Pilling [1962] Director/H R Manager

The Austonley Soap Company Ltd
Incorporated: 24 February 2015
Net Worth Deficit: £9,511 *Total Assets:* £3,982
Registered Office: Stoneygate House, 2 Greenfield Road, Holmfirth, W Yorks, HD9 2JT
Major Shareholder: Fiona Hinchliffe
Officers: Fiona Hinchliffe [1958] Director

Auto. B Limited
Incorporated: 5 June 2018
Registered Office: Apartment 8, Block A, Petal Court, Worsley, Salford, M28 3YN
Major Shareholder: Callum Tuckey
Officers: Callum Tuckey [1991] Managing Director

Autosheen Ltd
Incorporated: 7 January 2019
Registered Office: 20-22 Wenlock Road, London, N1 7GU
Major Shareholder: Ian Guest
Officers: Ian Guest [1955] Director

Autosmart Group Limited
Incorporated: 19 July 2003
Registered Office: Lynn Lane, Shenstone, Lichfield, Staffs, WS14 0DH
Parent: Autosmart Holdings Ltd
Officers: Christopher Anthony Ashton [1963] Sales Director; Sophie Atkinson [1964] Director; Christopher Keith Brain [1967] Technical Director

Autosmart Holdings Limited
Incorporated: 22 April 2005 *Employees:* 148
Net Worth: £13,329,867 *Total Assets:* £16,947,212
Registered Office: Lynn Lane, Shenstone, Lichfield, Staffs, WS14 0DH
Major Shareholder: Sophie Atkinson
Officers: Christopher Anthony Ashton [1963] Sales Director; Sophie Atkinson [1964] Director; Christopher Keith Brain [1967] Technical Director

Aventual Ltd
Incorporated: 9 January 2015
Net Worth Deficit: £47,705 *Total Assets:* £120,318
Registered Office: 38 Ermine Road, London, SE13 7JS
Shareholder: Lillian Amoah
Officers: Lillian Amoah [1962] Director

Axwood Limited
Incorporated: 29 January 2018
Registered Office: Kemp House, 160 City Road, London, EC1V 2NX
Major Shareholder: Alexandre Seewald-Butzerin
Officers: Alexandre Seewald-Butzerin, Secretary; Alexandre Seewald-Butzerin [1979] Director/Manager [French]

Ayurveda Wellness Ltd
Incorporated: 3 November 2017
Registered Office: Office 9 & 10, Anna House, Dunmurry Office Park, 37a Upper Dunmurry Lane, Dunmurry, Belfast, BT17 0AA
Major Shareholder: Upendra Shenoy Umesh Vijayam
Officers: Veena Gopalakini [1978] Director/Supervisor; Upendra Shenoy Umesh Vijayam [1971] Director/Self Employed

Azara Beautique Ltd
Incorporated: 12 July 2017
Registered Office: 3rd Floor, 207 Regent Street, Mayfair, London, W1B 3HH
Officers: Mona Alyedreessy [1985] Director/Entrepreneur

Azure Liquid Solutions Limited
Incorporated: 13 June 2013 *Employees:* 2
Net Worth: £1,470 *Total Assets:* £47,860
Registered Office: 10 Bahama Road, Haydock, Merseyside, WA11 9XB
Shareholder: Sarah Singleton
Officers: Sarah Singleton [1987] Sales Director

B.Me Skincare Ltd
Incorporated: 12 October 2018
Registered Office: Meriton Foundry, Meriton Street, Bristol, BS2 0SZ
Major Shareholder: Veronika Korytakova
Officers: Veronika Korytakova [1981] Director/Administrator [Czech]

Bar.None Limited
Incorporated: 26 September 2018
Registered Office: Unit 33 Flex Business Park, Western Trading Estate, Caerphilly, Gwent, CF83 1BE
Major Shareholder: Jonathan David Shipman
Officers: Jonathan David Shipman [1969] Director

Bare & Bloom Works Handmade Bath and Body Treats Ltd
Incorporated: 18 June 2018
Registered Office: 13 Furlongs, Basildon, Essex, SS16 4BW
Major Shareholder: Charissa Salvacion Simangan Lim
Officers: Roldan Abarra Lim, Secretary; Charissa Salvacion Simangan Lim [1972] Director/Manufacturer

Bayer-Wood Technologies Limited
Incorporated: 18 May 1992
Net Worth: £176,657 *Total Assets:* £325,675
Registered Office: Strensham Farmhouse, Upper Strensham, Worcs, WR8 9AH
Shareholders: Roderick Charles Rowland Wood; Laura Wood
Officers: Timothy George Harman, Secretary/Local Government Officer; Laura Wood [1959] Managing Director; Roderick Charles Rowland Wood [1953] Director/General Manager

Bean and Boy Ltd
Incorporated: 6 February 2019
Registered Office: 21 Durham Road, Southend on Sea, Essex, SS2 4LT
Major Shareholder: Stacey Siddons
Officers: Stacey Siddons [1985] Director/Soap Maker

Beardog and Roo Ltd
Incorporated: 29 January 2019
Registered Office: Copper Harvest, Main Street, Bleasby, Notts, NG14 7GH
Major Shareholder: Faye Leanora Simpson-White
Officers: Faye Leanora Simpson-White [1964] Director

Belkor Bay Limited
Incorporated: 27 February 2018
Registered Office: 111 King's Cross Road, London, WC1X 9LR
Officers: Emma McGuinness [1992] Director/Human Resource

Berry Inc Ltd
Incorporated: 30 July 2018
Registered Office: Kemp House, 160 City Road, London, EC1V 2NX
Major Shareholder: Evbi O'Sullivan
Officers: Evbi O'Sullivan, Secretary; Evbi O'Sullivan [1972] Director/Consultant

Bespro Chemicals Ltd
Incorporated: 21 January 2002
Net Worth: £4,390 *Total Assets:* £33,682
Registered Office: Unit 10 Springbank Industrial Estate, Pembroke Loop Road, Dunmurry, Belfast, BT17 0FE
Major Shareholder: Ian McComish
Officers: McComish Ms Noreen, Secretary; Ian McComish [1966] Director/Chemical Manufacturer [Irish]

Best-Chem Limited
Incorporated: 17 May 1999
Net Worth: £420,736 *Total Assets:* £700,861
Registered Office: Unit K, Westminster Industrial Estate, Measham, Derbys, DE12 7DS
Shareholder: Rajesh S Naik
Officers: Kalpana Rajesh Naik, Secretary; Kalpana Rajesh Naik [1960] Sales Director; Rajesh S Naik [1956] Director/Accountant

Biggin Bees Limited
Incorporated: 14 October 2018
Registered Office: 111a Sunningvale Avenue, Biggin Hill, Westerham, Kent, TN16 3TS
Major Shareholder: Melanie Susan Vaughan
Officers: Melanie Susan Vaughan [1978] Director/Businesswoman

Bio-Clean Limited
Incorporated: 20 August 1997
Registered Office: Waterhouse, Greenfields Road, Horley, Surrey, RH6 8HW
Major Shareholder: Lawrence James Baggs
Officers: Averil Baggs, Secretary; Lawrence James Baggs [1949] Director/Sales Engineer

The Bio-D Holdings (UK) Limited
Incorporated: 14 October 2009
Net Worth: £48,382 *Total Assets:* £342,855
Registered Office: 31 Bergen Way, Sutton Fields, Hull, HU7 0YQ
Officers: Lloyd Spencer Atkin, Secretary; Joanne Elizabeth Atkin [1981] Director/Senior HR Officer; Lloyd Spencer Atkin [1975] Director

Biologico Cosmetics Limited
Incorporated: 14 February 2018
Registered Office: 3rd Floor, Citypoint, 65 Haymarket Terrace, Edinburgh, EH12 5HD
Major Shareholder: Craig McKay
Officers: Craig McKay [1983] Director

Black and Silver Equestrian Ltd
Incorporated: 30 October 2014
Registered Office: Office G2, Enterprise Village, Prince Albert Gardens, Grimsby, N E Lincs, DN31 3AT
Major Shareholder: Jonathan Paul Sedman
Officers: Jonathan Paul Sedman [1966] Director/Accountant

Blok Soap Ltd
Incorporated: 23 March 2018
Registered Office: 49 Bramshill Close, Birchwood, Warrington, Cheshire, WA3 6TY
Shareholders: Tania Bains; Mohamed Abdelhamid
Officers: Mohamed Abdelhamid [1991] Director; Tania Bains [1986] Director

Bloom and Blossom Limited
Incorporated: 11 March 2008 *Employees:* 3
Net Worth: £169,036 *Total Assets:* £225,391
Registered Office: 45 Pall Mall, London, SW1Y 5JG
Shareholders: Richard Tufft; Caroline Maria Tufft; Julia Yule; Christina Moss
Officers: Ross Yule, Secretary; Christina Moss [1980] Director; Julia Yule [1976] Director

Bloomtown Ltd
Incorporated: 8 March 2018
Registered Office: Bloomtown Ltd, Unit 3 Empire Way, Tregoniggie Industrial Estate, Falmouth, Cornwall, TR11 4RX
Shareholders: Medwin John Culmer; Preyanka Jayanti Clark Prakash
Officers: Preyanka Jayanti Clark Prakash [1982] Director [American]; Medwin John Culmer [1977] Managing Director

Body Candy Ltd.
Incorporated: 15 February 2018
Registered Office: Kemp House, 160 City Road, London, EC1V 2NX
Officers: Michal Gasior [1982] Director [Polish]

Body Station Limited
Incorporated: 6 November 2018
Registered Office: 71-75 Shelton Street, London, WC2H 9JQ
Major Shareholder: Thomas Hadleigh
Officers: Thomas Hadleigh [1974] Director

dellam   The Top UK Soap and Detergent Manufacturers

Bonasystems Europe Ltd
Incorporated: 8 December 2008   *Employees:* 14
Net Worth: £238,070   *Total Assets:* £1,167,684
Registered Office: Hurshens, Unit 2 Station Close, Potters Bar, Herts, EN6 1TL
Shareholder: Steven Phillips
Officers: Nigel Anthony Geach [1952] Director; Stephen David Moss [1952] Director; Steven Phillips [1954] Director; Nicholas Howard Thomlinson [1953] Director

Bonasystems Worldwide Ltd
Incorporated: 2 August 2011
Registered Office: Unit 2, 32-34 Station Close, Potters Bar, Herts, EN6 1TL
Major Shareholder: Steven Philips
Officers: Philips Stephen [1954] Director/Manager

Nathalie Bond Limited
Incorporated: 2 October 2013
Net Worth Deficit: £16,523   *Total Assets:* £61,754
Registered Office: 38 Wood Lane, Sheffield, S6 5HE
Officers: Andrew Bond [1977] Director; Natalie Bond [1983] Director [Dutch]

Bonham Soaps Limited
Incorporated: 7 August 2017
Registered Office: 9 Bonham Court, 108a Queen Street, Morley, Leeds, LS27 9EB
Major Shareholder: Karen Nichola Reilly
Officers: Karen Nichola Reilly [1978] Director

Born To Be Natural Ltd
Incorporated: 26 February 2009
Net Worth Deficit: £23,784   *Total Assets:* £9,166
Registered Office: 237 Manor Farm Road, Bitterne Park, Southampton, SO18 1NY
Shareholder: Malcolm James Pascoe
Officers: Gloria Pascoe [1958] Operations Director; Malcolm James Pascoe [1956] Managing Director

Boweasel Ltd
Incorporated: 10 January 2019
Registered Office: 1 Albion Court, 72 Christchurch Road, London, SW2 3DE
Major Shareholder: Christopher Bodragon
Officers: Francisca Vazquez, Secretary; Christopher Bodragon [1962] Director

Bramchem Ltd.
Incorporated: 5 September 2012
Net Worth: £1,469   *Total Assets:* £88,821
Registered Office: Bramley House, Bath Lane, Bramley, Leeds, LS13 3BB
Shareholders: Eamonn Ceannt McCarron; Michael Steven Bentley; Adrian Aynsley
Officers: Michael Steven Bentley, Secretary; Adrian Aynsley [1960] Director; Michael Steven Bentley [1948] Director

Bristol Soap Limited
Incorporated: 22 April 2015
Net Worth: £100   *Total Assets:* £100
Registered Office: Unit 3 Atworth Business Park, Bath Road, Atworth, Melksham, Wilts, SN12 8SB
Major Shareholder: Kevin Shaun Stevens
Officers: Kevin Shaun Stevens [1965] Director

Brush Europe Limited
Incorporated: 2 August 2017
Registered Office: Flat 50, Albert Bigg Point, Godfrey Street, London, E15 2SF
Officers: Baby Davies Asuoha [1971] Director/Civil Servant; Chukwudi Asuoha [1972] Director/Teacher

Bubble Shack Ltd
Incorporated: 13 March 2017
Net Worth Deficit: £7   *Total Assets:* £113
Registered Office: 89 Wakeford Road, Birmingham, B31 3LN
Major Shareholder: James Parker
Officers: James Parker [1988] Director/Cosmetics

Businotech Limited
Incorporated: 14 August 2013
Registered Office: 185 The Sycamores, Milton, Cambridge, CB24 6ZH
Major Shareholder: Mirza Yousaf Baig
Officers: Mirza Yousaf Baig [1970] Director/IT Engineer

K C Butler & Son Limited
Incorporated: 25 January 2001   *Employees:* 2
Net Worth: £392,131   *Total Assets:* £411,926
Registered Office: 19 Warren Park Way, Enderby, Leicester, LE19 4SA
Shareholders: Ashley Charles Butler; Keith Charles Butler
Officers: Keith Charles Butler, Secretary; Ashley Charles Butler [1969] Director; Jane Butler [1969] Director

Butter Bar Soapery Ltd
Incorporated: 4 October 2016
Net Worth Deficit: £6,099   *Total Assets:* £5,197
Registered Office: 84 Aldermans Hill, London, N13 4PP
Major Shareholder: Christina Clements
Officers: Christina Clements [1983] Director/Manufacture and Retail of Cosmetics

Buypolar Ltd
Incorporated: 26 October 2018
Registered Office: 7 Finkle Court, Market Weighton, York, YO43 3LZ
Shareholders: Grant Allman; Sarah Danville
Officers: Grant Allman, Secretary; Grant Allman [1985] Director; Sarah Danville [1984] Director

Cahercon Group Limited
Incorporated: 11 April 2018
Registered Office: 19 Brandon Mews, London, EC2Y 8BE
Major Shareholder: Daniel Williams Williams
Officers: Daniel Williams [1976] Director, Cahercon Group

Caley's of Exeter Ltd
Incorporated: 10 May 2018
Registered Office: Flat 1, 78 Longbrook Street, Exeter, Devon, EX4 6AP
Major Shareholder: Judy Caley
Officers: Judy Caley [1988] Director/Manufacturer

Calman Enterprise Limited
Incorporated: 11 August 2010
Net Worth: £50,629   *Total Assets:* £87,880
Registered Office: 7 Strothers Lane, Inverness, IV1 1LR
Parent: Calman Trust
Officers: Dr Isobel Grigor, Secretary; Fiona Anne Brown [1953] Director/Housewife; David John Fraser [1948] Director/Retired; Mairi Lisa Fraser [1976] Director/Self Employed Retail Business; Sheila Fraser [1962] Director; Stephen Laurie [1981] Director/Business Executive; Gordon Henry McIntosh [1960] Director/Chartered Manager

The Top UK Soap and Detergent Manufacturers

Candy & Mischief Ltd
Incorporated: 29 March 2016
Registered Office: Caretakers Flat, Shardeloes, Missenden Road, Amersham, Bucks, HP7 0RL
Major Shareholder: Andrea Weber
Officers: Andrea Weber [1966] Director/Handmade Cosmetics [Hungarian]

Capricorn Detergents Limited
Incorporated: 31 July 2001 *Employees:* 7
Net Worth: £64,863 *Total Assets:* £415,459
Registered Office: Unit B1, Angel Road Works, Advent Way, London, N18 3AH
Shareholders: Joan Ahmet; Nureddin Ahmet; Joan Ahmet
Officers: Joan Ahmet, Secretary; Joan Ahmet [1945] Director; Nureddin Ahmet [1944] Director/Consultant

Carapoll Chemicals Ltd
Incorporated: 2 February 2018
Registered Office: 19 The Hawthorns, Kirkby in Ashfield, Notts, NG17 8NL
Officers: Andrew Harpham Dennis Harpham [1966] Company Secretary/Director

Cares Laboratory Limited
Incorporated: 16 March 2016 *Employees:* 2
Net Worth Deficit: £128,498 *Total Assets:* £108,247
Registered Office: Unit 3 Dodworth Business Park, Dodworth, Barnsley, S Yorks, S75 3SP
Major Shareholder: Thomas James Abbey
Officers: Alison Kay Woodward, Secretary; Thomas James Abbey [1967] Managing Director; David Toms [1965] Director

Carvansons Ltd
Incorporated: 19 August 2013 *Employees:* 53
Previous: Carvansons Exports Ltd
Net Worth: £1,251,895 *Total Assets:* £4,007,118
Registered Office: Alex House, 260-268 Chapel Street, Salford, M3 5JZ
Major Shareholder: Luke Whowell
Officers: Leanne Yvonne Dudley [1972] Financial Director; John Luke Whowell [1968] Director

Carzel Limited
Incorporated: 21 March 2017
Registered Office: 12 Courtleas, Cobham, Surrey, KT11 2PW
Major Shareholder: Akis Akis Tzortzis
Officers: Akis Zafirios Tzortzis [1965] Director

Cater-Lyne Limited
Incorporated: 12 December 1986
Registered Office: Zenith House, Dixons Hill Road, Welham Green, North Mymms, Hatfield, Herts, AL9 7JE
Parent: Zenith Hygiene Food and Beverage Limited
Officers: Simon Peter Bower [1964] Director/Accountant; James Duncan Hannaway [1976] Director/Sales Manager; Alison Jane Pettitt [1967] Finance Director

CB Services Limited
Incorporated: 7 August 2017
Registered Office: Unit 5 Building 14, Central Park, Mallusk, Newtownabbey, Co Antrim, BT36 4FS
Major Shareholder: Iain Malcolm Collins
Officers: Iain Malcolm Collins [1968] Director

CClear Limited
Incorporated: 6 March 2009
Net Worth Deficit: £892 *Total Assets:* £12,798
Registered Office: Unit 2 St Anne's, Old Port Road, Wenvoe, Vale of Glamorgan, CF5 6AB
Major Shareholder: John Damon Withey
Officers: John Damon Withey, Secretary; John Damon Withey [1946] Director/Surveyor; Sandra Lynn Eunice Withey [1947] Director/Consultant

Check You Limited
Incorporated: 2 July 2015
Registered Office: Mart House, Market Terrace, Strichen, Fraserburgh, Aberdeenshire, AB43 6TS
Major Shareholder: Amy Alexander
Officers: Amy Alexander [1971] Director/Soap Maker

Chela Ltd
Incorporated: 27 November 1992 *Employees:* 5
Net Worth: £334,097 *Total Assets:* £591,784
Registered Office: 68 Bilton Way, Enfield, Middlesex, EN3 7NH
Major Shareholder: Anthony Clive Umfreville Fisher
Officers: Valerie Margaret Elizabeth Darville, Secretary; Valerie Margaret Elizabeth Darville [1945] Director; Anthony Clive Umfreville Fisher [1943] Director/Chairman; Iwan Clive Umfreville Fisher [1969] Managing Director; Michael Fouracre [1943] Director; Antony Philippou [1980] Director/Sales and Marketing

Chemex (North West) Limited
Incorporated: 4 April 2003
Net Worth: £132,808 *Total Assets:* £213,888
Registered Office: Foxcroft, Pentre Lane, Ashton, Chester, CH3 8BX
Major Shareholder: Charles Edwin Williams
Officers: Donna Elizabeth Lewis Williams, Secretary; Charles Edwin Williams [1959] Director/Wholesaler

The Chemical Hut Ltd
Incorporated: 16 May 2007 *Employees:* 7
Previous: Cleanex Chemical Solutions Limited
Net Worth: £37,738 *Total Assets:* £340,641
Registered Office: Unit 5 Chadwick Street, Stoke on Trent, Staffs, ST3 1PJ
Officers: Paul Roscoe, Secretary; Jason Paul Ridge [1976] Director; Paul William Ridge [1953] Director

Chemiclean Products Limited
Incorporated: 18 July 2005
Net Worth: £27,108 *Total Assets:* £111,227
Registered Office: P O Box 2487, 365-369 Park Road, Hockley, Birmingham, B18 5JN
Major Shareholder: John Carr
Officers: John Carr [1952] Director/Chemical Distributor

Chemisphere UK Limited
Incorporated: 10 October 1986 *Employees:* 13
Net Worth: £642,679 *Total Assets:* £896,611
Registered Office: Unit 4 Richmond Road, Trafford Park, Manchester, M17 1RE
Parent: Chemisphere UK Holdings Limited
Officers: Rachael Jane Bowhay-Singer [1973] Director; Jan Kristian [1984] Director [Czech]; Glyn Robert McCracken [1961] Director; Marie Ruth Perrin [1972] Director; John Taylor [1957] Director/Service Manager; Wilfred Paul Worsley [1960] Director

Chemtrading Limited
Incorporated: 19 May 2015
Registered Office: Unit 16 Highcroft Industrial Estate, Enterprise Road, Waterlooville, Hants, PO8 0BT
Major Shareholder: Roberto Avondo
Officers: Roberto Avondo [1963] Director [Italian]

Chimera UK Chemical Solutions Limited
Incorporated: 14 September 2012
Net Worth Deficit: £10,502 *Total Assets:* £33,101
Registered Office: 23 Swynnerton Drive, Essington, Wolverhampton, W Midlands, WV11 2TA
Major Shareholder: Clinton James Evans
Officers: Clinton James Evans [1959] Director/Electrician

Chinese Gentry Limited
Incorporated: 8 August 2018
Registered Office: 9 Pantygraigwen Road, Pontypridd, Mid Glamorgan, CF37 2RR
Shareholders: Lili Ge; Xuepei Liu
Officers: Lili GE [1988] Director [Chinese]

Christeyns Food Hygiene Ltd
Incorporated: 29 December 1989 *Employees:* 66
Previous: Klenzan Limited
Net Worth: £3,456,426 *Total Assets:* £5,347,209
Registered Office: 2 Cameron Court, Winwick Quay, Warrington, Cheshire, WA2 8RE
Officers: Andrew Bethel [1969] Operations Director; Nicholas James Garthwaite [1957] Director; Graham Nigel Hunneman [1963] Sales Director; Jozef Wittouck [1962] Director [Belgian]

Christeyns UK Ltd
Incorporated: 6 May 1965 *Employees:* 128
Net Worth: £22,950,100 *Total Assets:* £30,519,140
Registered Office: Rutland Street, East Bowling, Bradford, W Yorks, BD4 7EA
Major Shareholder: Alain Joseph Andre Bostoen
Officers: Julie Susan Roberts, Secretary; David Peter Aveyard [1963] Director; Paul Gerrard Victor Camiel Bostoen [1939] Director [Belgian]; Elisabeth Josepha Margaretha Ghislenus Devos [1941] Director [Belgian]; Nicholas James Garthwaite [1957] Director; Daniel John Kilgallon [1956] Director Sales; Julie Susan Roberts [1969] Director/Chartered Accountant; Scott Alan Grant Wilson [1969] Sales Director; Jozef Maria Jaak Wittouck [1962] Director [Belgian]

Chromasol Limited
Incorporated: 26 July 2013
Net Worth Deficit: £181 *Total Assets:* £971
Registered Office: 44 Bridge Road, Bishopthorpe, York, YO23 2RR
Major Shareholder: Peter Richard Stubbs
Officers: Peter Richard Stubbs [1968] Director/Business Consultant

CKC Aromatherapy Beauty Products Limited
Incorporated: 14 March 2017
Net Worth: £96 *Total Assets:* £2,890
Registered Office: 25 Crosscavanagh Road, Galbally, Dungannon, Co Tyrone, BT70 3BJ
Officers: Christina Kelly [1975] Director/Beauty Therapist

Clean Bidco Limited
Incorporated: 15 February 2019
Registered Office: Floor 3, 100 Wellington Street, Leeds, LS1 4LT
Parent: Clean Midco Limited
Officers: Ashley Dan Broomberg [1969] Director/Investment Manager; Henrik Nygaard Pade [1962] Director [Danish]

Clean Sciences Limited
Incorporated: 11 December 2012
Net Worth Deficit: £10,373 *Total Assets:* £1,043
Registered Office: Unit 3 Inspire Business Park, Newlands Way, Bradford, W Yorks, BD10 0JE
Major Shareholder: Nigel Patrick Silcox
Officers: Nigel Patrick Silcox [1955] Director

Clean Topco Limited
Incorporated: 25 February 2019
Registered Office: Floor 3, 100 Wellington Street, Leeds, LS1 4LT
Major Shareholder: Henrik Nygaard Pade
Officers: Ashley Dan Broomberg [1969] Director/Investment Manager; Henrik Nygaard Pade [1962] Director [Danish]

Cleanux Chemicals Ltd
Incorporated: 11 September 2017
Registered Office: 20 Whitebutts Road, Ruislip, Middlesex, HA4 0NB
Officers: Himanshu Patel, Secretary; Himanshu Patel [1966] Director

Cleenol Group Limited
Incorporated: 26 August 1959 *Employees:* 101
Net Worth: £1,836,114 *Total Assets:* £6,027,567
Registered Office: Beaumont Road, Banbury, Oxon, OX16 1RB
Parent: Cleenol Holdings Limited
Officers: Jeremy Martin Childerstone, Secretary; Richard John Armitage [1956] Director; Jeremy Martin Childerstone [1963] Finance Director; Richard Stephen Greaves [1953] Director; Samuel Charles Greaves [1984] Director

William Clements (Chemicals) Ltd
Incorporated: 21 February 1989 *Employees:* 14
Net Worth: £1,205,850 *Total Assets:* £1,411,109
Registered Office: c/o Flannigan Edmonds Bannon, Pearl Assurance House, 2 Donegall Square East, Belfast, BT1 5HB
Shareholders: Mary Patricia Farley; Raymond Scott Farley
Officers: Raymond Scott Farley, Secretary; Victoria Jayne Duffy [1986] Director; Mary Patricia Farley [1957] Director; Raymond Scott Farley [1953] Director; Michael Patrick Thomas Rooney [1946] Director/Sales

Clensure Global Ltd
Incorporated: 12 February 2018
Registered Office: 113 Cumberland House, 80 Scrubs Lane, London, NW10 6RF
Major Shareholder: Saba Yussouf
Officers: Saba Yussouf [1988] Director

Cliffe House (Organics) Limited
Incorporated: 9 September 2014
Net Worth Deficit: £14,422 *Total Assets:* £19,005
Registered Office: Cliffe House, Thirstin Road, Honley, Holmfirth, W Yorks, HD9 6JG
Shareholders: Peter Andrew Royle; Thomas Michael Royle; Debra Royle
Officers: Debra Royle [1963] Director; Peter Andrew Royle [1961] Director; Thomas Michael Royle [1988] Director

Clover Chemicals Limited
Incorporated: 1 March 1990 *Employees:* 80
Net Worth: £3,770,953 *Total Assets:* £4,944,551
Registered Office: Clover House, Macclesfield Road, Whaley Bridge, High Peak, Derbys, SK23 7DQ
Parent: Christeyns UK Ltd
Officers: Julie Susan Roberts, Secretary; Desmond Charles Eustace [1956] Managing Director; Nicholas James Garthwaite [1957] Director; Julie Susan Roberts [1969] Director; James Mark Tobias [1967] Director; Jozef Maria Jaak Wittouck [1962] Director [Belgian]

The Top UK Soap and Detergent Manufacturers

Coco Timyal Limited
Incorporated: 6 March 2018
Registered Office: Flat 32, 47 Cherry Orchard Road, Croydon, Surrey, CR0 6FJ
Officers: Dee Hinds [1974] Manufacturing Director; Lord Tidiane M'baye [1992] Marketing Director [French]

Cocoa Lime Limited
Incorporated: 2 February 2018
Registered Office: 44 Cornflower Grove, Ketley, Telford, Salop, TF1 5ZH
Major Shareholder: Helen Baines
Officers: Helen Baines, Secretary; Helen Baines [1968] Director/Senior Manager

Cole & Wilson, Limited
Incorporated: 11 July 1927 *Employees:* 8
Net Worth: £104,736 *Total Assets:* £241,380
Registered Office: Nabbs Lane Chemical Works, Slaithwaite, Huddersfield, W Yorks, HD7 5AT
Major Shareholder: Alain Joseph Bostoen
Officers: Richard Anthony Cole [1968] Director; Nicholas James Garthwaite [1957] Director

The Colhoon Corporation Limited
Incorporated: 7 April 2010
Net Worth: £100 *Total Assets:* £100
Registered Office: Unit 3a, rear of Unit 3 Brookside, Red Marsh Industrial Estate, Thornton-Cleveleys, Lancs, FY5 4EZ
Major Shareholder: Alan William Reilly
Officers: Alan William Reilly, Secretary; Alan William Reilly [1959] Director

Completely Conkers Limited
Incorporated: 13 January 2017
Registered Office: 32-36 Chorley New Road, Bolton, Lancs, BL1 4AP
Shareholders: Mark Anthony Lyth; Janina Blackburn
Officers: Janina Blackburn [1968] Director; Mark Anthony Lyth [1962] Director

Conatural Ltd
Incorporated: 26 October 2015
Registered Office: 115 London Road, Morden, Surrey, SM4 5HP
Major Shareholder: Myra Husain Qureshi
Officers: Myra Husain Qureshi [1983] Director/Entrepreneur

Cornwall Soapbox (Mevagissey) Ltd
Incorporated: 6 July 2018
Registered Office: 2 Gramscatho Buildings, Marsh Lane Industrial Estate, Hayle, Cornwall, TR27 5JR
Shareholders: Michael John Sowden; Suzanne Eileen Sowden
Officers: Michael John Sowden, Secretary; Michael John Sowden [1962] Director; Suzanne Eileen Sowden [1956] Director

Cosmetic Hooligans Ltd
Incorporated: 29 June 2017
Registered Office: 153 Caledonia Road, Wolverhampton, W Midlands, WV2 1JA
Officers: Patrycja Kalkowska [1995] Director/Cosmetic Production [Polish]

Coventry Chemicals Limited
Incorporated: 3 April 1975 *Employees:* 135
Net Worth: £1,093,000 *Total Assets:* £12,446,000
Registered Office: Woodhams Road, Siskin Drive, Coventry, Warwicks, CV3 4FX
Shareholder: Michael Scott Underdown
Officers: Stephen Quinlan, Secretary; Peter John Bridge [1955] Director; Darren Paul Langdon [1977] Operations Director; Paul Marsh [1967] Finance Director; Stephen Quinlan [1961] Managing Director; Michael Montgomery Scott-Underdown [1945] Director; Paul Starkey [1959] Operations Director

The Coventry Group Limited
Incorporated: 14 July 1999 *Employees:* 139
Net Worth Deficit: £1,318,000 *Total Assets:* £10,154,000
Registered Office: Woodhams Road, Siskin Drive, Coventry, Warwicks, CV3 4FX
Shareholders: Stephen Quinlan; Stephen Quinlan; Michael Scott Underdown
Officers: Stephen Quinlan, Secretary; Peter John Bridge [1955] Director; Darren Paul Langdon [1977] Operations Director; Paul Marsh [1967] Finance Director; Stephen Quinlan [1961] Managing Director; Michael Montgomery Scott-Underdown [1945] Director/Chairman

Crafty Lady Ltd
Incorporated: 12 April 2011
Registered Office: 65 Pitsmead Road, Kirkby, Merseyside, L32 9QW
Officers: Kelly Ann Avis [1985] Director

CS Holistic Therapy Products Limited
Incorporated: 18 September 2017
Registered Office: 2 Victoria Court, Victoria Road, Romford, Essex, RM1 2NU
Major Shareholder: Catarina Scaramuzza
Officers: Catarina Scaramuzza [1963] Director/Holistic Therapy Products

Cueball Cosmetics Ltd
Incorporated: 6 March 2018
Registered Office: 3 Grand Crescent, Brighton, BN2 7GL
Major Shareholder: John Kemeny
Officers: John Kemeny [1982] Director/Engineer

Cut from The Wild Limited
Incorporated: 7 October 1994
Net Worth: £847 *Total Assets:* £1,447
Registered Office: Astral Court, Central Avenue, Baglan Energy Park, Port Talbot, SA12 7AX
Shareholders: Medical Express (UK) Ltd; Gregory Butcher
Officers: Robert Stanley Lucas [1965] Director/Graphic Designer

D'lishx0x0 Limited
Incorporated: 6 August 2018
Registered Office: 149 Wordsworth Road, Daventry, Northants, NN11 9BG
Officers: Michaela Leanne Ashby, Secretary; Michaela Leanne Ashby [1990] Director/Housewife

Dagarti CIC
Incorporated: 21 July 2011
Net Worth Deficit: £13,937 *Total Assets:* £646
Registered Office: 76 Flaxwell Court, Northampton, NN3 9DF
Officers: Haja Nana Salifu [1977] Director [German]

The Dales Heritage Soap Company Limited
Incorporated: 26 June 2017
Registered Office: 11 Little Studley Road, Ripon, N Yorks, HG4 1HD
Major Shareholder: Jonathan Scott Forsyth
Officers: Jonathan Scott Forsyth, Secretary; Jonathan Scott Forsyth [1962] Director/Pilot

The Dales Natural Soap Company Limited
Incorporated: 26 June 2017
Registered Office: 11 Little Studley Road, Ripon, N Yorks, HG4 1HD
Major Shareholder: Jonathan Scott Forsyth
Officers: Jonathan Scott Forsyth, Secretary; Jonathan Scott Forsyth [1962] Director/Pilot

Dalton Luxury Ltd
Incorporated: 24 April 2017
Net Worth: £800 *Total Assets:* £800
Registered Office: 2 Stock Close, Norton, Malton, N Yorks, YO17 8BE
Shareholders: Tracey Mattinson; George Mattinson
Officers: Tracey Mattinson [1984] Managing Director

Danchemtech Ltd
Incorporated: 8 May 2017
Registered Office: Niddry Lodge, 51 Holland Street, Kensington, London, W8 7JB
Major Shareholder: Mariusz Walczak
Officers: Mariusz Walczak [1960] Director [Polish]

The Dandy Gent Manufactory Ltd
Incorporated: 22 March 2018
Registered Office: Nesco, Bedford Street, Derby, DE22 3PE
Shareholders: Shane O'Shaughnessy; Sherri O'Shaughnessy
Officers: Shane O'Shaughnessy [1970] Director/Barber; Sherri O'Shaughnessy [1982] Director/Manufacturer

Dasic International Limited
Incorporated: 1 April 1986 *Employees:* 15
Net Worth: £2,558,659 *Total Assets:* £2,756,788
Registered Office: Winchester Hill, Romsey, Hants, SO51 7YD
Shareholders: Stephen James Thomas; John Leonard Belk
Officers: Annette Susan Belk, Secretary; John Leonard Belk [1955] Managing Director; Stephen James Thomas [1962] Director

Datesand Limited
Incorporated: 1 April 1980 *Employees:* 29
Net Worth: £1,343,510 *Total Assets:* £2,698,093
Registered Office: Freedom House, Units 9-12 Edwin Road, Manchester, M11 3ER
Shareholders: Jonathon Richard Wood; Claire Wood
Officers: Simon James Thorp [1954] Director; Claire Wood [1973] Director/Manager; Jonathon Richard Wood [1974] Managing Director; Nicholas Andrew Wood [1972] Sales Director

De Montfort Marketing Limited
Incorporated: 22 January 2004 *Employees:* 2
Net Worth: £31,598 *Total Assets:* £66,131
Registered Office: Linwood, St Peters Road, Arnesby, Leicester, LE8 5WJ
Shareholders: Graham Sawyer; Maria Louise Sawyer
Officers: Graham Sawyer, Company Secretary; Graham Sawyer [1964] Director; Maria Louise Sawyer [1967] Director

Decon Laboratories Limited
Incorporated: 23 July 1969 *Employees:* 10
Net Worth: £2,180,648 *Total Assets:* £2,258,096
Registered Office: Conway Street, Hove, E Sussex, BN3 3LY
Officers: Peter Ian Johnson, Secretary; Barbara Izabella Taylor [1954] Sales Director; Robert Nicholas Taylor [1947] Director

Decontamin8 (Europe) Limited
Incorporated: 10 December 2013
Net Worth Deficit: £1,014 *Total Assets:* £4,666
Registered Office: 76 Helena Road, Rayleigh, Essex, SS6 8LQ
Officers: Brian Ronald Mansfield, Secretary; Anthony Brian Mansfield [1967] Director [Australian]

Decontamin8 Limited
Incorporated: 17 September 2013
Net Worth: £1 *Total Assets:* £1
Registered Office: 76 Helena Road, Rayleigh, Essex, SS6 8LQ
Officers: Brian Ronald Mansfield, Secretary; Anthony Brian Mansfield [1967] Director/Marketing Consultant [Australian]

Dee Doo Limited
Incorporated: 11 June 2004
Net Worth Deficit: £52,441 *Total Assets:* £13,766
Registered Office: Unit E, Edison Courtyard, Brunel Road, Earlstrees Industrial Estate, Corby, Northants, NN17 4LS
Shareholders: Simon Timothy Rhodes; Suzan Rhodes
Officers: Simon Timothy Rhodes, Secretary; Simon Timothy Rhodes [1969] Director; Suzan Rhodes [1965] Director

Delf (UK) Limited
Incorporated: 13 March 1990 *Employees:* 17
Net Worth: £356,660 *Total Assets:* £838,675
Registered Office: Enterprise House, The Courtyard, Old Courthouse Road, Bromborough, Wirral, Merseyside, CH62 4UE
Shareholders: Jane Jones; Christopher Glyn Jones
Officers: Christopher Glyn Jones [1960] Director/Operations Manager; Dr Jane Jones [1961] Director/Consultancy

Deliciously Me Ltd
Incorporated: 30 July 2018
Registered Office: 9 Arnell Crescent, Swindon, Wilts, SN25 2NY
Major Shareholder: Claire Amy Mangan
Officers: Claire Amy Mangan [1976] Director/Self Employed

Denykem Limited
Incorporated: 22 May 1973 *Employees:* 14
Net Worth: £1,808,699 *Total Assets:* £2,089,161
Registered Office: 67 Station Road, Ossett, W Yorks, WF5 8AY
Shareholders: Amanda Jane Stoner; Paul Stoner; Michelle McGee
Officers: Amanda Jane Stoner, Secretary; Michelle McGee [1968] Director/Financial Controller; Amanda Jane Stoner [1966] Director/Financial Controller; Paul Stoner [1969] Sales Director

Detergents Ltd
Incorporated: 30 May 2018
Registered Office: Impulse House, Westgate Hill Street, Tong, Bradford, W Yorks, BD4 0SJ
Officers: Samina Quaddus [1971] Director

Diamond (Edibles) Limited
Incorporated: 2 October 2017
Registered Office: 19 Buttershaw Lane, Bradford, BD6 2DD
Major Shareholder: Kasam Rasool
Officers: Kasam Rasool [1992] Director

Diamond Fizzles Ltd
Incorporated: 25 February 2019
Registered Office: 14 Ashhurst Way, Oxford, OX4 4RA
Major Shareholder: Charley Terri Dodson
Officers: Charley Terri Dodson [1993] Director/Bookmaker

The Top UK Soap and Detergent Manufacturers — dellam

Dijon Soaps Limited
Incorporated: 2 August 2016
Registered Office: Dijon Pless Road, Milford on Sea, Lymington, Hants, SO41 0NY
Major Shareholder: Annabelle Short
Officers: Annabelle Short [1959] Director/Medical Secretary

Dimex Limited
Incorporated: 20 October 1983
Net Worth: £332,260,992 *Total Assets:* £332,260,992
Registered Office: Yule Catto Building, Temple Fields, Harlow, Essex, CM20 2BH
Parent: Synthomer Holdings Limited
Officers: Richard Atkinson, Secretary; Richard Atkinson [1962] Director/Company Secretary; Stephen Guy Bennett [1964] Director

Dino-Mite Ltd
Incorporated: 13 October 2017
Registered Office: 5 Grange Court, High Road, Loughton, Essex, IG10 4QX
Major Shareholder: Jessica Ivy
Officers: Gowan Brindley [1991] Director; Jessica Ivy [1991] Managing Director

Diversey Holdings Limited
Incorporated: 30 October 2001
Net Worth: £72,696,000 *Total Assets:* £73,196,000
Registered Office: Weston Favell Centre, Northampton, NN3 8PD
Parent: BCPE Diamond UK Holdco Limited
Officers: Michael James Chapman, Secretary; Michael James Chapman [1961] Director/Solicitor; Colin Timothy Stubbs [1963] Director

Diversey Industrial Limited
Incorporated: 23 April 1985
Registered Office: Weston Favell Centre, Northampton, NN3 8PD
Parent: Diversey Limited
Officers: Colin Timothy Stubbs [1963] Director

Diversey Limited
Incorporated: 29 October 1997 *Employees:* 272
Net Worth: £43,086,000 *Total Assets:* £90,623,000
Registered Office: Weston Favell Centre, Northampton, NN3 8PD
Parent: Diversey Holdings Limited
Officers: Raymond Keith Partridge [1966] Sales Director; Patrick Garfield Redman [1967] Sales Director; Colin Timothy Stubbs [1963] Sales Director; John-Paul Surdo [1984] Director/General Manager [American]

Diversey UK Production Limited
Incorporated: 14 September 1981 *Employees:* 91
Net Worth: £12,839,000 *Total Assets:* £15,156,000
Registered Office: Weston Favell Centre, Northampton, NN3 8PD
Parent: Diversey Limited
Officers: Isobel Frances Cook [1971] Director/Quality Health and Safety and Environmental; David Charles White [1971] Director/Production Manager

Dizziak Ltd
Incorporated: 22 May 2017
Net Worth: £32,894 *Total Assets:* £44,072
Registered Office: 23 Exmouth Market, London, EC1R 4QL
Major Shareholder: Loretta de Feo
Officers: Loretta de Feo [1983] Director

Dogbreath Brewery Ltd
Incorporated: 29 June 2004 *Employees:* 3
Previous: Swampys Ltd
Net Worth Deficit: £47,252 *Total Assets:* £3,062
Registered Office: Portal House, 52 Hyde Lane, Kinver, Staffs, DY7 6AF
Officers: Elaine Woodley [1968] Director; Timothy Woodley [1964] Director

Dook Ltd
Incorporated: 9 January 2019
Registered Office: 17 Esplanade Terrace, Edinburgh, EH15 2ES
Major Shareholder: Helen Rosemary Atherton
Officers: Helen Rosemary Atherton [1980] Director/Manufacturer and Retailer

Dri-Pak Limited
Incorporated: 11 October 1961 *Employees:* 155
Net Worth: £6,890,068 *Total Assets:* £9,362,620
Registered Office: Furnace Road, Ilkeston, Derbys, DE7 5EP
Officers: Lynn Elizabeth Brett, Secretary; Bruce James Peter Maxwell [1969] Director; Carolyn Mary Maxwell [1944] Director; Jillian Maxwell [1971] Director/Administrator; Peter Stuart Maxwell [1943] Managing Director

Driftwood Shaper Ltd
Incorporated: 25 September 2017
Registered Office: Driftwood, Kirk Ireton, Ashbourne, Derbys, DE6 3JW
Shareholders: Robert Collington; Kelsey Collington
Officers: Kelsey Collington [1993] Director; Robert Collington [1962] Director

Droyt Products Limited
Incorporated: 8 January 1937 *Employees:* 12
Net Worth: £231,809 *Total Assets:* £413,473
Registered Office: Progress Mill, Progress Street, Chorley, Lancs, PR6 0RZ
Officers: Alistair Samuel David McCracken, Secretary; Christopher Michael Effendowicz [1959] Managing Director; Alistair Samuel David McCracken [1959] Sales Director

John Drury & Co. Limited
Incorporated: 23 July 1964 *Employees:* 37
Net Worth: £1,841,134 *Total Assets:* £2,252,378
Registered Office: The Soap Works, River Street, Brighouse, W Yorks, HD6 1LY
Parent: John Drury Holdings Limited
Officers: Martin Robert Drury, Secretary; Edward John Drury [1967] Director; Martin Robert Drury [1945] Director; Richard Arnold Drury [1939] Director

John Drury Holdings Limited
Incorporated: 15 June 1949
Net Worth: £1,307,410 *Total Assets:* £1,752,498
Registered Office: 28 River Street, Brighouse, W Yorks, HD6 1LY
Shareholder: Martin Robert Drury
Officers: Martin Robert Drury, Secretary; Edward John Drury [1967] Director; Martin Robert Drury [1945] Director; Richard Arnold Drury [1939] Director

Duchess Naturals Limited
Incorporated: 14 August 2018
Registered Office: 23 The Meadows, Heskin, Chorley, Lancs, PR7 5NR
Major Shareholder: Anita Jayne Parkinson
Officers: Anita Jayne Parkinson [1969] Director/Retailer

Durabond Chemicals Limited
Incorporated: 2 January 2019
Registered Office: Bentcliffe House, 15 Bentcliffe Court, Leeds, LS17 6SY
Major Shareholder: Robert (Elias) Wilson
Officers: Robert Wilson [1941] Director of Market Research

Dynamic Chemicals Limited
Incorporated: 12 December 1991
Net Worth: £10,191 *Total Assets:* £24,966
Registered Office: Units 1-3 Teiglum Road, Milton Industrial Estate, Lesmahagow, S Lanarks, ML11 0JN
Shareholder: Robert Alan Cardwell
Officers: Robert Alan Cardwell, Secretary; Linda Ann Cardwell [1957] Director/Bank Typist; Robert Alan Cardwell [1955] Director/Consultant

E-Sensual Oil Soap By Farah Ltd
Incorporated: 29 October 2018
Registered Office: 57 Westfield Way, Newport, NP20 6EW
Major Shareholder: Farzaneh Talai
Officers: Farzaneh Talai [1969] Director

Earth's Naturals Ltd
Incorporated: 7 November 2018
Registered Office: 44 Kingsway, Manchester, M19 2DD
Officers: Razna Bibi [1980] Director

Easy Newco Limited
Incorporated: 3 March 2017
Registered Office: Jeyes House, Brunel Way, Thetford, Norfolk, IP24 1HF
Major Shareholder: David James Pearce
Officers: Darren James Mosley [1966] Director/Chief Executive Officer; David James Pearce [1966] Director

Ebiox Limited
Incorporated: 13 March 1998
Net Worth Deficit: £44,796 *Total Assets:* £704
Registered Office: 2 Lords Court, Basildon, Essex, SS13 1SS
Parent: Medimark Scientific Ltd
Officers: Richard James Hayman [1968] Director

Eco Earth Limited
Incorporated: 8 February 2018
Registered Office: Eco-Earth, Chapel Street, Wellesbourne, Warwicks, CV35 9QU
Major Shareholder: Thomas Karl Rogers
Officers: Thomas Karl Rogers [1992] Director

Eco-Point Laboratories Limited
Incorporated: 6 December 2018
Registered Office: 68 Bilton Way, Enfield, Middlesex, EN3 7NH
Parent: Fisher Darville Holdings Limited
Officers: Anthony Clive Umfreville Fisher [1943] Director; Iwan Clive Umfreville Fisher [1969] Director

Ecolab Limited
Incorporated: 10 February 1960 *Employees:* 1,114
Net Worth: £79,304,000 *Total Assets:* £145,591,008
Registered Office: Winnington Avenue, Northwich, Cheshire, CW8 4DX
Parent: Ecolab (U.K.) Holdings Limited
Officers: Wendy Annette Joyce, Secretary; Paul Hey [1964] Director; Carl Richmond Lee [1963] Finance Director; Paul Rawding [1971] Director/General Manager

Ecosearch Limited
Incorporated: 8 November 1993
Net Worth: £192,686 *Total Assets:* £192,686
Registered Office: 68 Bilton Way, Enfield, Middlesex, EN3 7NH
Major Shareholder: Anthony Clive Umfreville Fisher
Officers: Valerie Margaret Elizabeth Darville, Secretary; Valerie Margaret Elizabeth Darville [1945] Director; Anthony Clive Umfreville Fisher [1943] Director/Chairman; Iwan Clive Umfreville Fisher [1969] Managing Director

Ed N' Grace Ltd
Incorporated: 11 February 2019
Registered Office: 84-86 Bravington Road, London, W9 3AL
Major Shareholder: Edman Relox Ocampo
Officers: Edman Relox Ocampo [1981] Director/Healthcare

Eden Classics Limited
Incorporated: 25 May 2006 *Employees:* 4
Net Worth: £87,562 *Total Assets:* £93,934
Registered Office: Unit 7 Bermer Place, Imperial Way, Watford, Herts, WD24 4AY
Shareholders: Dinesh Chhabildas; Jayshree Dinesh Shah
Officers: Mahendra Kanabar, Secretary; Dinesh Chhabildas Shah [1958] Director; Jayshree Dinesh Shah [1963] Director

The Edinburgh Natural Skincare Company (Retail Shops) Limited
Incorporated: 28 October 2010
Previous: The Edinburgh Natural Soap Company Ltd.
Net Worth: £1 *Total Assets:* £2,100
Registered Office: 126 Church Street, Tranent, E Lothian, EH33 1BL
Major Shareholder: Thomas James Crooks
Officers: Lynne Jo-Anne Grahame, Secretary; Thomas James Crooks [1963] Director/Saponifier

Edinburgh Soap Company Ltd
Incorporated: 1 November 2017
Registered Office: Hillhead Farm, Carberry, Musselburgh, E Lothian, EH21 8QE
Officers: Nita Ewart [1963] Director

Elegant Soap Co Ltd
Incorporated: 23 January 2018
Registered Office: 73 Deanscroft Avenue, London, NW9 8EP
Officers: Kawther Saik [1969] Director

Elimin8 Limited
Incorporated: 12 April 2010 *Employees:* 1
Net Worth Deficit: £1,417 *Total Assets:* £962
Registered Office: 4 Roman Ridge Road, Sheffield, S9 1GB
Shareholder: Michael James Crawford
Officers: Michael James Crawford [1955] Director/Engineer

Elinor-UK Ltd
Incorporated: 19 February 2018
Registered Office: 1st Floor, 2 Woodberry Grove, Finchley, London, N12 0DR
Major Shareholder: Vladislav Mihaylov Indzhov
Officers: Vladislav Mihaylov Indzhov, Secretary; Vladislav Mihaylov Indzhov [1986] Director [Bulgarian]

Elizabeth Vintage Soap Ltd
Incorporated: 9 May 2018
Registered Office: 5 Beech Close, Ross on Wye, Herefords, HR9 5RN
Shareholders: Glenda Harris; Chad Andrian Harris
Officers: Chad Harris, Secretary; Chad Andrian Harris [1962] Director; Glenda Harris [1967] Director

Eljay Group Ltd
Incorporated: 10 August 2018
Registered Office: Unit 44 Purfleet Industrial Park, Juliette Way, Purfleet, Essex, RM15 4YA
Shareholders: Ryan Saunders; Reece Saunders
Officers: Reece Saunders [1992] Director; Ryan Saunders [1996] Director

Emilia's Handmade Bath and Body Ltd
Incorporated: 18 June 2018
Registered Office: 41 Mountbatten Avenue, Romsey, Hants, SO51 8DX
Major Shareholder: Emilia Sophia Mary Primrose Head
Officers: Emilia Sophia Mary Primrose Head [1999] Director

Emily's Soap Shop Limited
Incorporated: 25 January 2019
Registered Office: 125 Simister Lane, Prestwich, Manchester, M25 2SA
Major Shareholder: Emily Lois Barratt
Officers: Emily Lois Barratt [1984] Director/Businesswoman

Emma Victoria Cosmetics Ltd
Incorporated: 7 January 2019
Registered Office: Emma Victoria Cosmetics, P O Box 1380, Cambridge, CB1 0HH
Shareholders: Wesley Timothy Sukdao; Emma Victoria Yates
Officers: Wesley Timothy Sukdao [1986] Director/Consultant [South African]; Dr Emma Victoria Yates [1988] Director/Chemist [British/American]

Emollience Ltd
Incorporated: 18 September 2017
Net Worth: £2,000 *Total Assets:* £2,000
Registered Office: 4 Braemore Road, Stewarton, Kilmarnock, E Ayrshire, KA3 3HB
Shareholder: Craig Malcolm Geddes
Officers: Craig Malcolm Geddes [1976] Director; David Williams Geddes [1974] Director/Software Developer

Enchanted Plants Ltd
Incorporated: 20 January 2003
Net Worth Deficit: £15,605 *Total Assets:* £3,442
Registered Office: 6 The Commons, Shaftesbury, Dorset, SP7 8JU
Major Shareholder: Jemma Ricketts
Officers: Jemma Ricketts, Secretary/Medical Herbalist; Jemma Ricketts [1979] Director/Medical Herbalist

Ennebee Ltd
Incorporated: 3 July 2013
Registered Office: 34 Tudor Road, Newton Abbot, Devon, TQ12 1HT
Officers: Niema Burns [1977] Director/HR Professional

ERH Propack Limited
Incorporated: 13 January 1947
Net Worth: £5,361,000 *Total Assets:* £5,522,000
Registered Office: 103-105 Bath Road, Slough, Berks, SL1 3UH
Parent: Reckitt Benckiser PLC
Officers: Christine Anne-Marie Logan, Secretary; Richard Mark Greensmith [1973] Group Tax Director; Jonathan Timmis [1975] Finance Director

Ersag UK Limited
Incorporated: 8 August 2017
Net Worth Deficit: £224,540
Registered Office: SME CofE Business Centre, Main Street, Ponteland, Northumberland, NE20 9NH
Major Shareholder: Mustafa Nejat Kilci
Officers: Mustafa Nejat Kilci [1966] Director

Essential Spirit Limited
Incorporated: 29 February 2000 *Employees:* 2
Net Worth Deficit: £2,574 *Total Assets:* £9,652
Registered Office: 123 Irish Street, Dumfries, DG1 2PE
Major Shareholder: Marina Emma Lucy Vundum
Officers: Des Watts, Secretary; Marina Emma Lucy Vundum [1961] Director/Soap Maker

Estela Dermocosmetics Ltd
Incorporated: 27 September 2018
Registered Office: 71-75 Shelton Street, Covent Garden, London, WC2H 9JQ
Major Shareholder: Ersin Akif Adil
Officers: Ersin Akif Adil [1982] Director [Bulgarian]

Ethicalsoap Limited
Incorporated: 26 May 2018
Registered Office: 7 Mitchison Road, London, N1 3NJ
Major Shareholder: Thomas Raymond William Doherty
Officers: Thomas Raymond William Doherty [1998] Director/Student [Irish]

Eucaderm Limited
Incorporated: 13 April 1992 *Employees:* 1
Net Worth: £25,661 *Total Assets:* £34,893
Registered Office: 18 Hyde Gardens, Eastbourne, E Sussex, BN21 4PT
Officers: Graham Walter White, Secretary/Director; David Christopher Satchell [1949] Director/Hair Consultant/Trichologist

Eurotank Limited
Incorporated: 2 March 2010
Registered Office: Parma House, Clarendon Road, London, N22 6UL
Major Shareholder: Martin Glauber
Officers: Martin Glauber [1958] Director/Merchant [Lithuanian]

Evans Vanodine International PLC
Incorporated: 10 April 1953 *Employees:* 151
Net Worth: £15,935,064 *Total Assets:* £20,189,306
Registered Office: Brierley Road, Walton Summit Centre, Bamber Bridge, Preston, Lancs, PR5 8AH
Shareholders: Peter David Evans; Anthony Ian Evans; Christopher John Evans
Officers: Christopher John Evans, Secretary; Anthony Ian Evans [1966] Systems Director; Christopher John Evans [1959] Operations Director; Derek Anthony Evans [1927] Director/Chairman; Peter David Evans [1955] Managing Director

Evbioo Ltd
Incorporated: 24 July 2018
Registered Office: Kemp House, 160 City Road, London, EC1V 2NX
Major Shareholder: Evbi O'Sullivan
Officers: Evbi O'Sullivan, Secretary; Evbi O'Sullivan [1972] Director/Consultant

Everfolk Limited
Incorporated: 2 May 2017
Net Worth Deficit: £2,591 *Total Assets:* £3,054
Registered Office: 150 Kingshill Road, Swindon, Wilts, SN1 4LN
Officers: Gloria Magali Torres Benitez [1983] Director [Paraguayan]

Evocativ Limited
Incorporated: 14 August 2017
Registered Office: 71-75 Shelton Street, Covent Garden, London, WC2H 9JQ
Shareholders: Thomas Bishop; Marta Blocka
Officers: Thomas Bishop, Secretary; Marta Bishop [1986] Director/Solicitor [Polish]; Thomas Bishop [1980] Director/Sales Executive

Evonik Goldschmidt UK Limited
Incorporated: 5 October 1972 *Employees:* 14
Net Worth: £19,500,316 *Total Assets:* £20,582,184
Registered Office: Tego House, Chippenham Drive, Kingston, Milton Keynes, Bucks, MK10 0AF
Parent: Evonik UK Holdings Limited
Officers: Geneva Angela Stapleton, Secretary; Clive Martin Gould [1956] Director/General Manager; Anh Luu [1979] Director/Legal Counsel

Exterin Ltd
Incorporated: 19 March 2018
Registered Office: Onllwyn, New Street, Lampeter, Ceredigion, SA48 7AJ
Officers: Peter Kundrak [1992] Director [Hungarian]

Fairy Treats Ltd
Incorporated: 19 October 2016
Registered Office: 6 Buick Drive, Arbroath, Angus, DD11 5LF
Major Shareholder: Rukhsana Dharmsee
Officers: Rukhsana Dharmsee [1981] Director/Crafter

Farasha-Cosmetics Ltd
Incorporated: 26 June 2018
Registered Office: 27 Old Gloucester Street, London, WC1N 3AX
Major Shareholder: Massimo Serra
Officers: Massimo Serra, Secretary; Massimo Serra [1965] Director/Self Employed [Italian]

Felicity Solutions Ltd
Incorporated: 5 April 2017
Registered Office: International House, 24 Holborn Viaduct, London, EC1A 2BN
Major Shareholder: Neha Vijay Sheth
Officers: Neha Vijay Sheth [1983] Director [Indian]

Fernandez Cosmetics Ltd
Incorporated: 18 January 2018
Registered Office: 2 Whinberry Drive, Kirkby, Merseyside, L32 9BA
Shareholder: Maria Del Carmen Fernandez
Officers: Maria Del Carmen Fernandez [1974] Director [Spanish]

Field International UK Limited
Incorporated: 3 September 2001
Net Worth: £17,229 *Total Assets:* £93,667
Registered Office: 2 Hickory Drive, Winchester, Hants, SO22 6NJ
Officers: Peter Alexander Naisbitt, Secretary; Jennifer Anne Hill [1959] Director; Peter Alexander Naisbitt [1957] Director Chemical Company

Fillcare Limited
Incorporated: 1 December 1981 *Employees:* 157
Net Worth: £10,460,000 *Total Assets:* £15,329,000
Registered Office: P O Box 66, Lanelay Road, Talbot Green, Pontyclun, Rhondda Cynon Taf, CF72 8YZ
Parent: Fareva UK Limited
Officers: Jean Pierre Fraisse [1959] Director [French]; Andrew John Mortimer [1959] Managing Director

Filthy Kids Ltd
Incorporated: 23 August 2018
Registered Office: Lanzerac Moorhill, Burley, Ringwood, Hants, BH24 4AH
Major Shareholder: Richard David Hale
Officers: Richard David Hale [1967] Director/Musician

Firecraft Ltd
Incorporated: 31 July 2018
Registered Office: 285 Camden High Street, London, NW1 7BX
Major Shareholder: Paschalina Arvanitopoulou
Officers: Paschalina Arvanitopoulou [1992] Director [Greek]

Fisher Research Ltd
Incorporated: 8 February 1988 *Employees:* 22
Net Worth: £2,718,162 *Total Assets:* £4,362,538
Registered Office: 68 Bilton Way, Enfield, Middlesex, EN3 7NH
Major Shareholder: Anthony Clive Umfreville Fisher
Officers: Valerie Margaret Elizabeth Darville, Secretary; Valerie Margaret Elizabeth Darville [1945] Director; Anthony Clive Umfreville Fisher [1943] Director/Chairman; Iwan Clive Umfreville Fisher [1969] Managing Director

Food Tech Hygiene Limited
Incorporated: 25 April 2008
Net Worth Deficit: £3,914
Registered Office: Carr Green Lane, Mapplewell, Barnsley, S Yorks, S75 6DY
Shareholder: John Stephen Lucas
Officers: John Stephen Lucas, Secretary; John Stephen Lucas [1956] Director/Chemical Manufacturer; Kevin Paul Lucas [1958] Director/Sales Assistant

Forward Chemicals Ltd
Incorporated: 18 October 2018
Registered Office: Kemp House, 160 City Road, London, EC1V 2NX
Officers: David Storf [1943] Director/Retired; Richard Charles Storf [1969] Director/Sales

Fragrance Tree Ltd
Incorporated: 19 November 2018
Registered Office: George Court, 17 George Street, Birmingham, B12 9RG
Major Shareholder: Mohammed Irfan
Officers: Mohammed Irfan [1971] Director

Fragrant Alchemy Ltd
Incorporated: 30 November 2018
Registered Office: 66 Gloucester Road, Bristol, BS7 8BH
Major Shareholder: Karen Gilbert
Officers: Karen Gilbert [1970] Director

Freestyle Beauty Products Limited
Incorporated: 29 July 1999
Net Worth: £598 *Total Assets:* £598
Registered Office: Unit 7 Bermer Place, Imperial Way, Watford, Herts, WD24 4AY
Shareholder: Dinesh Chhabildas Shah
Officers: Mahendra Kanabar, Secretary; Dinesh Chhabildas Shah [1958] Director; Jayshree Dinesh Shah [1963] Director; Karan Shah [1988] Director

Fresh from Nature Limited
Incorporated: 17 August 2017
Registered Office: The Garden Village, Bridgnorth Road, Wolverhampton, W Midlands, WV6 7EZ
Officers: Martin Holland [1962] Director; Dawn Webb [1960] Director

Freshorize Ltd
Incorporated: 26 March 2002 *Employees:* 11
Net Worth: £3,926,854 *Total Assets:* £4,209,926
Registered Office: University of East London, Royal Dock Business Centre, University Way, London, E16 2RD
Major Shareholder: Abdul Ebrahim Patel
Officers: Bilkis Master, Secretary; Abdul Ebrahim Patel, Secretary/Barrister; Abdul Ebrahim Patel [1963] Director

Friendly Soap Limited
Incorporated: 29 April 1996
Net Worth: £12,118 *Total Assets:* £85,586
Registered Office: Unit 6c Top Land Country Business Park, Hebden Bridge, W Yorks, HX7 5RW
Shareholders: Robin Costello; Geoffrey David Kerouac
Officers: Robin Costello, Secretary; Geoffrey David Kerouac, Secretary; Robin Costello [1968] Director/Warehouse Manager; Geoffrey David Kerouac [1969] Director

Funkydz Ltd
Incorporated: 30 June 2015 *Employees:* 2
Net Worth Deficit: £28,600 *Total Assets:* £3,812
Registered Office: 20-22 Wenlock Road, London, N1 7GU
Shareholders: Ashleigh Hamilton-Gillings; Juleigh Gail Hamilton-Gillings
Officers: Ashleigh Hamilton-Gillings, Secretary; Ashleigh Hamilton-Gillings [1979] Director [Irish]; Juleigh Gail Hamilton-Gillings [1977] Director/Interior Designer

Future Developments (Manufacturing) Limited
Incorporated: 8 August 1990 *Employees:* 12
Net Worth: £262,797 *Total Assets:* £638,869
Registered Office: Centurion House, Brunswick Industrial Estate, Davenport Street, Burslem, Stoke on Trent, Staffs, ST6 4HS
Shareholder: Paul Williams
Officers: Paul Williams, Secretary; Geoffrey Boulton [1958] Director; David Alfred Williams [1961] Director; Paul Williams [1955] Director and Secretary

Fysha Ltd
Incorporated: 8 June 2016
Net Worth Deficit: £7,123
Registered Office: 1 Charterhouse Mews, London, EC1M 6BB
Major Shareholder: Amina Papadopoulos
Officers: Amina Papadopoulos [1975] Director [Pakistani]

Fysifarm Limited
Incorporated: 16 January 2018
Registered Office: 27 Old Gloucester Street, London, WC1N 3AX
Major Shareholder: Nikolaos Chalvatzis
Officers: Panagiotis Laskaris [1966] Director [Greek]

Gard Chemicals Limited
Incorporated: 10 March 2003
Net Worth: £2 *Total Assets:* £2
Registered Office: Gard Chemicals Limited, Chapel Lane, Heckmondwike, W Yorks, WF16 9JP
Major Shareholder: James Christopher Knox
Officers: James Christopher Knox, Secretary; James Christopher Knox [1972] Director

GEA Farm Technologies (UK) Ltd
Incorporated: 8 January 1971 *Employees:* 54
Net Worth: £3,387,555 *Total Assets:* £10,718,982
Registered Office: Wylye Works, Watery Lane, Bishopstrow, Warminster, Wilts, BA12 9HT
Officers: Steven Murray Fifer, Secretary; Ilija Aprcovic [1966] Managing Director; Timothy John Donbavand [1967] Director; Tracey Ann O'Neill [1968] Director/Head of Human Resources UK

Gemini Cosmetics Ltd
Incorporated: 20 September 2017
Registered Office: The Coach House, The Square, Sawbridgeworth, Herts, CM21 9AE
Shareholders: Amanda Clare Cross; Nicholas Stephen Littlebury
Officers: Nicholas Stephen Littlebury [1985] Director

Genten Skincare Ltd
Incorporated: 31 December 2018
Registered Office: Flat 84, Ivor Court, Gloucester Place, London, NW1 6BP
Shareholders: Ayaka Fujiwara; Jie Yang
Officers: Ayaka Fujiwara [1988] Director/Investment Specialist [Japanese]

Gently Handcrafted Ltd
Incorporated: 20 July 2012
Net Worth Deficit: £7,756 *Total Assets:* £516
Registered Office: 1 The Claytons, Bridstow, Ross on Wye, Herefords, HR9 6QD
Shareholders: Martin Neicho; Monica Neicho
Officers: Martin Neicho [1958] Director/Manager; Monica Neicho [1968] Director/Designer Maker

Get The Scent Limited
Incorporated: 2 June 2017
Registered Office: 38 Grasmere Street, Carlisle, CA2 4AR
Major Shareholder: Craig Taylor
Officers: Craig Taylor [1963] Director/Lawyer

Ghastly Games Limited
Incorporated: 2 September 2016
Net Worth Deficit: £2,838 *Total Assets:* £3,647
Registered Office: 1 Avon Road, Henlow, Beds, SG16 6HF
Major Shareholder: Kedric Winks
Officers: Kedric Winks [1982] Director/Soldier

The Ginchiest Artisan Soap Company Ltd
Incorporated: 18 December 2018
Registered Office: 122 Main Road, Duston, Northampton, NN5 6RA
Major Shareholder: Charlotte Warrington
Officers: Charlotte Warrington [1986] Director/Supply Planner

Gio Natura Ltd
Incorporated: 8 May 2018
Registered Office: 153 Glenfield Road, Leicester, LE3 6DP
Major Shareholder: Joanna Tylko
Officers: Joanna Tylko [1972] Director/Cream Maker [Polish]

Glametuber Ltd
Incorporated: 22 July 2018
Registered Office: Ground Floor Office, 108 Fore Street, Hertford, SG14 1AB
Major Shareholder: Jodie McClelland
Officers: Michelle Dela Cruz [1973] Director [Filipino]

Glamour Natural Cosmetics Ltd
Incorporated: 17 February 2017
Net Worth Deficit: £8,969 *Total Assets:* £6
Registered Office: Unit 15 Cavendish Centre, Winnall Close, Winchester, Hants, SO23 0LB
Shareholder: Tamas V.David
Officers: Krisztin V.David [1969] Director [Hungarian]; Tamas V.David [1965] Director [Hungarian]

Globemeth Limited
Incorporated: 20 December 2011
Net Worth: £63,000 *Total Assets:* £66,000
Registered Office: Unit R, Birch House Business Centre, Birch Walk, off Fraser Road, Erith, Kent, DA8 1QX
Major Shareholder: Raymond Atughwe
Officers: Raymond Atughwe [1971] Director/Chemical and Software Engineer [Nigerian]

GM Globalhealth Ltd
Incorporated: 4 February 2019
Registered Office: 27 Old Gloucester Street, London, WC1N 3AX
Major Shareholder: Ghazi Abbass Mohammed Ali Hussein
Officers: Dr Ghazi Abbass Mohammed Ali Hussein, Secretary; Dr Mohamed Ahmed Fadlallah Elsheikh [1980] Director/Veterinary Surgeon [Sudanese]; Dr Ghazi Abbass Mohammed Ali Hussein [1981] Director/Veterinarian

The Goat Soap Company Ltd
Incorporated: 29 January 2019
Registered Office: Hill Top Cottage, Star Road, Oakamoor, Cheadle, Staffs, ST10 3BN
Major Shareholder: Jennifer Ann Bedford
Officers: Jennifer Ann Bedford [1972] Commercial Director

Goatally Soaps Ltd
Incorporated: 31 January 2018
Registered Office: 37 St Margaret's Street, Canterbury, Kent, CT1 2TU
Shareholders: David James Wilcock; Chloe Wilcock
Officers: Chloe Wilcock [1990] Director; David James Wilcock [1992] Director

Goats on the Coast Ltd
Incorporated: 10 August 2017
Registered Office: Lakeside Paddocks, Lincombe, Lee, Ilfracombe, Devon, EX34 8LL
Shareholders: Deborah Jane Radley; Stuart James Radley
Officers: Deborah Jane Radley [1973] Director; Stuart James Radley [1974] Director

Golden Soaps Ltd
Incorporated: 8 December 2006
Net Worth: £5,885 *Total Assets:* £5,885
Registered Office: Barnfield Farm, Pleshey, Essex, CM3 1HU
Major Shareholder: Kirsty Emma Anderson-Taylor
Officers: Dr Gordon Anderson-Taylor, Secretary; Kirsty Emma Anderson-Taylor [1971] Director/Housewife

Gondar Soaps Ltd
Incorporated: 7 September 2017
Registered Office: 28 Portland Street, St Albans, Herts, AL3 4RB
Officers: Robert Michael Stone [1987] Director; Aleksandra Wozniak [1985] Director [Polish]

Jared Gonzalez Ltd
Incorporated: 4 January 2019
Registered Office: 240a North Street, Bedminster, Bristol, BS3 1JD
Major Shareholder: Jared Gonzalez Exposito
Officers: Jared Gonzalez Exposito [1991] Director/Chef [Spanish]

The Good Soap Company Ltd
Incorporated: 5 February 2019
Registered Office: Ground Floor, 2 Woodberry Grove, London, N12 0DR
Major Shareholder: Greg Torres-Hernandez
Officers: Sally Hoy [1955] Director; Greg Torres-Hernandez [1954] Director/Soap Maker [Spanish]

GoodNaturedSkincare Ltd
Incorporated: 23 November 2017
Registered Office: 20-22 Wenlock Road, London, N1 7GU
Major Shareholder: Mazel Caryl John
Officers: Mazel Caryl John [1984] Director/Owner

Daisy Gordon Limited
Incorporated: 25 October 2016
Net Worth: £3 *Total Assets:* £3
Registered Office: Room 316, 3-9 Hyde Road, Manchester, M12 6BQ
Officers: Qindong Zhou [1982] Director [Chinese]

Gosling Soap Ltd
Incorporated: 28 February 2019
Registered Office: 22A Manor Road, Chichester, W Sussex, PO20 0SD
Major Shareholder: Sarah Lawrence
Officers: Sarah Lawrence [1965] Director/International Social Programme

Grassroots Health Ltd
Incorporated: 2 September 2016
Net Worth Deficit: £12,019 *Total Assets:* £20,254
Registered Office: 2-7 Links Place, Edinburgh, EH6 7EZ
Officers: Joanne Patricia Thomas [1972] Director; Dean Thomas William Tillbrook [1974] Director

Greatest of All Time Soapworks Ltd
Incorporated: 23 August 2017
Registered Office: Booley House, Booley, Stanton upon Hine Heath, Shrewsbury, Salop, SY4 4LY
Shareholders: Adam Jarvis; Sarah Jarvis
Officers: Adam Jarvis [1981] Director; Sarah Jarvis [1987] Director

The Green Housekeeper Ltd
Incorporated: 5 October 2016
Registered Office: The Barns, High Yewdale, Coniston, Cumbria, LA21 8DF
Shareholders: Philippa Van Heeswijk; Alice Van Heeswijk; Gillian Humphreys
Officers: Gillian Humphreys [1969] Director/Caterer; Alice Van Heeswijk [1998] Director; Philippa Van Heeswijk [1996] Director

Green Spa Therapy Ltd
Incorporated: 3 September 2018
Registered Office: 37 Second Avenue, Bolton, Lancs, BL1 4LW
Major Shareholder: Patricia Cotovio
Officers: Patricia Cotovio [1988] Director/Commercial Traveller [Portuguese]

The Greener Good Ltd
Incorporated: 29 September 2018
Registered Office: Chapel Grange, Chapel Lane, East Chiltington, Lewes, E Sussex, BN7 3BA
Major Shareholder: Helen Louise Munier
Officers: Helen Louise Munier, Secretary; Helen Louise Munier [1974] Director/Graphic Designer; Marc Andrew James Munier [1978] Director/Sales Manager

Greener Solutions Ltd
Incorporated: 10 August 2010 *Employees:* 5
Net Worth: £241,554 *Total Assets:* £596,972
Registered Office: Unit 10 West Point Business Park, Aylesford, Kent, ME20 6XJ
Major Shareholder: Angela Dilloway
Officers: Angela Dilloway [1967] Director

Ian Greenwood Engineering Limited
Incorporated: 21 May 1985 *Employees:* 1
Net Worth: £3,949 *Total Assets:* £13,617
Registered Office: 17 Linehouse Lane, Lickey Rock, Bromsgrove, Worcs, B60 1HR
Officers: Bridget Greenwood, Secretary; Ian Greenwood [1938] Director/Engineer

The Top UK Soap and Detergent Manufacturers

Grumpy Gorilla Ltd
Incorporated: 3 January 2019
Registered Office: 2 Lower Rock Street, New Mills, High Peak, Derbys, SK22 4DA
Major Shareholder: Jason John Turner
Officers: Jason John Turner [1976] Director

Halritt Ltd
Incorporated: 13 August 2018
Registered Office: 85 Aldykes, Hatfield, Herts, AL10 8EB
Shareholders: Derrick William Halsey; Kelly Louise Barritt
Officers: Kelly Louise Barritt [1981] Director/Entrepreneur; Derrick William Halsey [1969] Director/Entrepreneur

Handmade Naturals Ltd
Incorporated: 22 October 2009 *Employees:* 3
Net Worth: £8,299 *Total Assets:* £88,006
Registered Office: 66 Sandbach Road South, Alsager, Stoke on Trent, Staffs, ST7 2LP
Shareholder: Alan Cartlidge
Officers: Alan Cartlidge [1963] Director; Rossitza Vassileva Roudeva Cartlidge [1971] Director

The Happy Bee Company Ltd
Incorporated: 26 October 2012 *Employees:* 1
Net Worth Deficit: £5,384 *Total Assets:* £3,859
Registered Office: 2 Ridge Way, Edenbridge, Kent, TN8 6AR
Major Shareholder: Tracy Jane Johnson
Officers: Tracy Jane Johnson [1965] Director

Harmonious Brown Limited
Incorporated: 12 June 2017
Registered Office: Suite 115, Challenge House Business Centre, 616 Mitcham Road, Croydon, Surrey, CR0 3AA
Major Shareholder: Chantelle Brown
Officers: Chantelle Brown [1987] Creative Director

Harmony Bodycare Limited
Incorporated: 9 May 2018
Registered Office: 226 Hillside Road, St George, Bristol, BS5 7PS
Major Shareholder: Maureen Marie Campbell
Officers: Maureen Marie Campbell [1965] Director/Employee Relations Consultant

Haromatic Ltd
Incorporated: 22 August 2018
Registered Office: 3 Bray Lane, Telford, Salop, TF3 5HH
Shareholders: Richard Molli Boulock; Sonia Molli Boulock
Officers: Sonia Molli Boulock, Secretary; Richard Molli Boulock [1981] Director/Teacher [Cameroonian]

Heavenly Fragrance (UK) Limited
Incorporated: 12 August 2010
Registered Office: Dalton House, 60 Windsor Avenue, London, SW19 2RR
Major Shareholder: Titty Pappachen Thomas
Officers: Titty Pappachen Thomas [1974] Director/Engineer [Indian]

Hebridean Soap Company Ltd
Incorporated: 12 June 1997
Net Worth: £121,192 *Total Assets:* £180,689
Registered Office: 1325a Stratford Road, Hall Green, Birmingham, B28 9HL
Major Shareholder: Linda Gail Sutherland
Officers: Linda Gail Sutherland [1959] Director

Hempia Limited
Incorporated: 24 October 2018
Registered Office: 3 Milfort Green, Banbridge, Co Down, BT32 4NX
Major Shareholder: Ilja Matvejevs
Officers: Ilja Matvejevs, Secretary; Ilja Matvejevs [1986] Director/Compliance Identification Officer [Latvian]

HGH Trading Ltd
Incorporated: 13 June 2018
Registered Office: 6 Huntly Gardens, Glasgow, G12 9AS
Major Shareholder: Helen Grainne Hamilton
Officers: Helen Grainne Hamilton [1975] Director

The Highland Soap Co. Limited
Incorporated: 17 July 2006 *Employees:* 23
Net Worth: £205,939 *Total Assets:* £294,882
Registered Office: The Highland Soap Co Ltd, Spean Bridge, Highland, PH34 4EP
Major Shareholder: Archibald Sven MacDonald
Officers: Angus Francis MacDonald [1962] Director; Archibald Sven MacDonald [1990] Director; Emma Parton [1973] Director

Hitchin Soap Company Ltd
Incorporated: 11 January 2019
Registered Office: 135 Coleridge Close, Hitchin, Herts, SG4 0QY
Major Shareholder: Dominic Neil Wainwright
Officers: Dominic Neil Wainwright [1976] Director/Salesman

Hocktester Ltd
Incorporated: 20 August 2018
Registered Office: 11 Pengwern Grove, Liverpool, L15 1HJ
Major Shareholder: Lee McClennan
Officers: Lee McClennan [1982] Director/Consultant

The Holchem Group Limited
Incorporated: 10 April 2006 *Employees:* 236
Net Worth: £16,430,000 *Total Assets:* £37,337,000
Registered Office: Gateway House, Pilsworth Road, Pilsworth Industrial Estate, Bury, Lancs, BL9 8RD
Officers: Samantha Jayne Hardman, Secretary/Administration Director; Stephen Charles Bagshaw [1954] Marketing Director; Simon Lee Bell [1972] Managing Director; Nicholas Quentin Edwards [1959] Sales Director; Katherine Emma Hallows [1968] Director; Samantha Jayne Hardman [1966] Administration Director; Dr John Trevor Holah [1958] Director/Microbiologist; Stuart Middleton [1959] Finance Director

Holchem Laboratories Limited
Incorporated: 14 December 1982 *Employees:* 199
Net Worth: £21,501,000 *Total Assets:* £28,292,000
Registered Office: Gateway House, Pilsworth Road, Pilsworth Industrial Estate, Bury, Lancs, BL9 8RD
Parent: The Holchem Group Ltd
Officers: Samantha Jayne Hardman, Secretary; Stephen Charles Bagshaw [1954] Director; Simon Lee Bell [1972] Managing Director; Nicholas Quentin Edwards [1959] Sales Director; Samantha Jayne Hardman [1966] Administration Director; Dr John Trevor Holah [1958] Director/Microbiologist; Stuart Middleton [1959] Director/Chartered Accountant

Holistic Plant Technologies Ltd
Incorporated: 5 November 2015
Net Worth Deficit: £18,970 *Total Assets:* £35,000
Registered Office: Office 228, The Legacy Business Centre, 2a Ruckholt Road, London, E10 5NP
Major Shareholder: Tomasz Kwiecinski
Officers: Tomasz Kwiecinski [1985] Director/Coach [Polish]

Holt Lloyd International Limited
Incorporated: 25 November 1975 *Employees:* 125
Net Worth: £5,490,000 *Total Assets:* £37,460,000
Registered Office: Holt Lloyd International Ltd, Unit 100 Barton Dock Road, Stretford, Manchester, M32 0YQ
Parent: Holt Lloyd Group Limited
Officers: Steven Patrick Clancy [1962] Director [American]; Bruce Edward Ellis [1975] Director; Michael Christopher Meehan [1954] Director

The Home of The Green Gobblin Ltd
Incorporated: 13 September 2017
Registered Office: 5 The Avenue, Bessacarr, Doncaster, S Yorks, DN4 5JU
Shareholder: Delvyn Bradley Firth
Officers: Simon Howard Davies [1959] Director/Head Chemist; Delvyn Bradley Firth [1959] Director; Carolyn Patricia Kimble [1962] Director/Legal Advisor [South African]

Humble Bee Botanica Ltd.
Incorporated: 25 May 2017
Net Worth Deficit: £2,032 *Total Assets:* £4,624
Registered Office: 18 Fowler Street, Taunton, Somerset, TA2 6JB
Shareholder: Mathias Deman
Officers: Mathias Deman [1989] Director [Belgian]; Eline Snoekx [1993] Director [Belgian]

Hunam Limited
Incorporated: 8 November 2016
Registered Office: Flat 1, 55C Molly Huggins Close, London, SW12 0LZ
Major Shareholder: Anna Imoru
Officers: Anna Imoru [1964] Director/Skincare Formulator

Hunca Munka Limited
Incorporated: 5 April 2017
Net Worth Deficit: £4,212 *Total Assets:* £6,125
Registered Office: 1 West Towers Mews, Marple, Cheshire, SK6 7GR
Shareholders: Sarah Jane Healey; Stephen Healey
Officers: Sarah Jane Healey [1972] Director

Hutrade Ltd.
Incorporated: 17 June 2013
Previous: Une Limited
Net Worth: £871 *Total Assets:* £871
Registered Office: 71 Edmonds Road, Oldbury, W Midlands, B68 9AT
Major Shareholder: Anne Stephanie Rita Huckert
Officers: Anne Stephanie Rita Huckert [1972] Director/Providing and Selling Goods and Services [French]

Hydrophilic Ltd
Incorporated: 7 March 2017
Net Worth Deficit: £850 *Total Assets:* £3,800
Registered Office: 27 Culvert Lane, Uxbridge, Middlesex, UB8 2XB
Major Shareholder: Simon Driscoll
Officers: Simon Driscoll [1972] Director/Manager

Hygenol Cleaning Supplies Ltd
Incorporated: 31 August 2000 *Employees:* 12
Net Worth: £94,757 *Total Assets:* £460,982
Registered Office: Chester House, Lloyd Drive, Cheshire Oaks Business Park, Ellesmere Port, Cheshire, CH65 9HQ
Shareholder: June Ann Yearsley
Officers: Robert William Yearsley [1948] Director

Icilda's Ltd
Incorporated: 22 October 2018
Registered Office: 71-75 Shelton Street, London, WC2H 9JQ
Major Shareholder: Diane Hutchinson
Officers: Diane Hutchinson, Secretary; Diane Hutchinson [1972] Director

ICP Direct Limited
Incorporated: 18 June 2014 *Employees:* 2
Net Worth: £28,807 *Total Assets:* £111,235
Registered Office: Unit 3 Barnfield Way, Altham, Accrington, Lancs, BB5 5WJ
Shareholders: Gary Chapman; Assist FM Ltd
Officers: Gary Chapman [1956] Director; Ian Guest [1955] Director

Ideal Manufacturing Limited
Incorporated: 24 June 1980 *Employees:* 33
Net Worth: £925,826 *Total Assets:* £2,007,665
Registered Office: Atlas House, Burton Road, Finedon, Wellingborough, Northants, NN9 5HX
Shareholders: Michael Kalli; Philip Kalli
Officers: Darren Lee Booker [1968] Operations Director; David Goodger [1951] Director/Production Manager; Michael Kalli [1942] Director/Chemist; Phillip Kalli [1978] Director

Ideation Solutions Limited
Incorporated: 6 June 2013
Registered Office: 1 Gartons Close, Enfield, Middlesex, EN3 4BZ
Officers: Cherry Elizabeth Pedler [1962] Director/Manager

Industrial Chemical Experts Limited
Incorporated: 16 June 2017 *Employees:* 7
Net Worth: £30,710 *Total Assets:* £71,166
Registered Office: 86-90 Paul Street, London, EC2A 4NE
Officers: Rory Scarffe [1973] Director

Industrial Chemicals Limited
Incorporated: 30 November 1999 *Employees:* 495
Net Worth: £17,625,142 *Total Assets:* £48,816,096
Registered Office: Titan Works, Titan Industrial Estate, Hogg Lane, Grays, Essex, RM17 5DU
Shareholders: John William Carver; Allen Rodney Carver; Charles Daryl Carver
Officers: Benjamin James Lowthian, Secretary; Allen Rodney Carver [1947] Director; Charles Daryl Carver [1964] Director; John William Carver [1945] Director; Edwin John Strang [1958] Finance Director

Innoscent Ltd
Incorporated: 11 October 2018
Registered Office: 38 Sandlands Road, Walton on the Hill, Tadworth, Surrey, KT20 7XA
Major Shareholder: Lisa St Claire Davison
Officers: Lisa St Claire Davison [1974] Director

Insensed Ltd
Incorporated: 31 December 2018
Registered Office: 8 Cwmdraw Court, Pontllanfraith, Blackwood, Monmouthshire, NP12 2GH
Major Shareholder: Sasha King
Officers: Sasha King [1972] Director/Manufacturer

Inter Bio Chemicals Ltd
Incorporated: 17 September 2016
Net Worth: £1,693 *Total Assets:* £10,581
Registered Office: 15 Hatch Lane, Chingford, London, E4 6LP
Major Shareholder: David Brian McMillan
Officers: David Brian McMillan [1977] Director

International Maintenance Chemicals Ltd
Incorporated: 18 April 1986
Net Worth: £8,515 *Total Assets:* £26,341
Registered Office: 21 Kilwinning Drive, Monkston, Milton Keynes, Bucks, MK10 9BW
Major Shareholder: Gavin John Girling
Officers: Gavin John Girling [1952] Director

Irae Limited
Incorporated: 4 September 2017
Registered Office: Unit 20 Pedmore Road Industrial Estate, Brierley Hill, W Midlands, DY5 1TJ
Shareholders: Hannah Griffiths; Mark Griffiths
Officers: Hannah Griffiths, Secretary; Hannah Griffiths [1996] Director/UK Manager; Mark Griffiths [1963] Director

Sarah Ireland Perfumes Ltd
Incorporated: 4 April 2018
Registered Office: Crown House, 27 Old Gloucester Street, London, WC1N 3AX
Major Shareholder: Sarah Louise Ireland
Officers: Sarah Louise Ireland [1981] Director/Perfumer

Island Soapery Ltd
Incorporated: 1 November 2017
Registered Office: 44 Hudson Way, Abbey Meads, Swindon, Wilts, SN25 4WJ
Major Shareholder: Amanda Jane Sim-Morbey
Officers: Amanda Jane Sim-Morbey [1975] Director

Itaconix (U.K.) Limited
Incorporated: 27 October 2005 *Employees:* 27
Previous: Revolymer (U.K.) Limited
Net Worth Deficit: £20,604,000 *Total Assets:* £3,310,000
Registered Office: Fieldfisher, Riverbank House, 2 Swan Lane, London, EC4R 3TT
Parent: Revolymer PLC
Officers: Michael John Norris, Secretary; Laura Elizabeth Denner [1983] Director [American]; John Roger Shaw [1959] Director [American]

The Italist Skincare Ltd
Incorporated: 23 February 2018
Registered Office: Flat 44 Calais Gate, Cormont Road, London, SE5 9RQ
Major Shareholder: Shemaraiah Bloomfield-Johnson
Officers: Shemaraiah Bloomfield-Johnson [1993] Director/Bank Advisor/Teller; Suneil Mowatt [1986] Director/Student

Jackanoryjones Limited
Incorporated: 4 January 2016
Registered Office: 48 Springhill Road, Grendon Underwood, Aylesbury, Bucks, HP18 0TE
Shareholders: Steven Karl Moore; Nicola Jane Moore
Officers: Nicola Jane Moore [1976] Director; Steven Karl Moore [1972] Director

Java Coffee Company Limited
Incorporated: 13 March 2018
Registered Office: Ripley Drive, Normanton Industrial Estate, Normanton, W Yorks, WF6 1QT
Parent: Proton Holdings Limited
Officers: Murray Angus [1955] Managing Director; David Shaw [1952] Finance Director

KA Shere-Khan Limited
Incorporated: 6 March 2018
Registered Office: 28 Orchard Road, Southminster, Essex, CM7 0DQ
Shareholders: Susan Angelico; Jeffrey Beverley
Officers: Jeffrey Beverley, Secretary; Susan Angelico [1965] Director/Craftsman; Jeffrey Beverley [1962] Director/Craftsman

Kalabash Limited
Incorporated: 4 January 2018
Registered Office: First Floor, 85 Great Portland Street, London, W1W 7LT
Major Shareholder: Sharron Jenkins
Officers: Sharron Jenkins [1963] Director/Business Owner

Kallisti Ltd
Incorporated: 28 April 2017
Net Worth Deficit: £1,041 *Total Assets:* £2,959
Registered Office: 3 High Street, Islip, Kettering, Northants, NN14 3JS
Major Shareholder: Leigh Hatfull
Officers: Leigh Hatfull [1974] Director

Kalula Cosmetics Ltd
Incorporated: 30 January 2019
Registered Office: Suite A, 82 James Carter Road, Mildenhall, Bury St Edmunds, Suffolk, IP28 7DE
Major Shareholder: Justice Marie Bynoe
Officers: Justice Marie Bynoe [1994] Director/Recruitment Consultant

Kindness Collective Limited
Incorporated: 11 July 2017
Registered Office: Flat J, 51 Elm Park Gardens, London, SW10 9PA
Shareholders: Natalia Bulgakova; Irina Fedorenko
Officers: Irina Fedorenko, Secretary; Natalia Bulgakova [1981] Director

Kirkwood Chemicals Ltd
Incorporated: 5 May 2017 *Employees:* 1
Net Worth: £5,577 *Total Assets:* £57,281
Registered Office: 8 Kirkwood Park, Saintfield, Ballynahinch, Co Down, BT24 7DP
Major Shareholder: Samuel David Andrew Thompson
Officers: Samuel David Andrew Thompson [1966] Director/Business Proprietor

Kitchenmaster (N.I.) Limited
Incorporated: 29 March 1985
Net Worth: £2,065,005 *Total Assets:* £2,497,036
Registered Office: 11 Comber Road, Carryduff, Co Down, BT8 8AN
Parent: Carn Consultants Limited
Officers: Brian O'Kane, Secretary; Michael Hamilton Irvine [1974] Director/Chartered Accountant; David Michael McCloy [1973] Director/Corporate Financier; Brian A O'Kane [1960] Director [Irish]; Colin John Stanley [1973] Managing Director [Irish]; Jacqualine Walsh [1966] Sales Director

Klenzan Direct Limited
Incorporated: 2 August 1990
Registered Office: 2 Cameron Court, Winwick Quay, Warrington, Cheshire, WA2 8RE
Officers: Nicholas James Garthwaite [1957] Director

Kleos Naturals Ltd
Incorporated: 10 July 2018
Registered Office: 20-22 Wenlock Road, London, N1 7GU
Major Shareholder: Enitan Adebola Femi-Obasan
Officers: Enitan Adebola Femi-Obasan [1980] Director [Nigerian]

Ko. Essentials Ltd.
Incorporated: 26 February 2018
Registered Office: 161 Tinshill Lane, Leeds, LS16 6EE
Major Shareholder: Megan Landreth-Smith
Officers: Christine Gilland Robinson [1984] Director/Entrepreneur; Joseph Landreth-Smith [1990] Director/Entrepreneur; Megan Landreth-Smith [1991] Director/Entrepreneur; Naomi Joy Partridge [1984] Director/Entrepreneur; Thomas Michael Partridge [1981] Director/Entrepreneur

Kokoa UK Limited
Incorporated: 13 June 2017
Registered Office: 13 The Downs, Altrincham, Cheshire, WA14 2QD
Major Shareholder: Catherine Akobeng
Officers: Catherine Akobeng [1993] Director/Chief Executive Officer (CEO) & Founder

Koorax Ltd
Incorporated: 29 September 2016
Registered Office: 7 Camerton Grove, Hull, HU9 3PS
Shareholder: Ndoh Akpan Okoji
Officers: Ndoh Akpan Okoji [1976] Director/Cosmetics Sales

KrUde Cosmetics Ltd
Incorporated: 15 January 2019
Registered Office: Flat 3, 14 Wharton Square, Edinburgh, EH3 9FH
Major Shareholder: Doris Dimitrova
Officers: Doris Dimitrova [1993] Director [Bulgarian]

Kush Moma Limited
Incorporated: 13 January 2009
Registered Office: 113 Holcroft Court, Clipstone Street, London, W1W 5DF
Major Shareholder: Darren Brown
Officers: Darren Brown [1966] Director/Teacher

La Boulle Ltd
Incorporated: 19 November 2018
Registered Office: 1b Gombards, St Albans, Herts, AL3 5NW
Shareholders: Rozsika Ilea; Dorin Epureanu
Officers: Dorin Epureanu [1971] Director [Romanian]

Lady Smidgeton's Apothecary Ltd
Incorporated: 13 March 2018
Registered Office: 3 Galway House, Radnor Street, London, EC1V 3SL
Major Shareholder: Kirsty Patricia Fisher McRoberts
Officers: Kirsty Patricia Fisher McRoberts [1993] Director

Lamella Structures Limited
Incorporated: 13 August 2002
Net Worth: £6,637 *Total Assets:* £58,162
Registered Office: Cedar House, Hazell Drive, Newport, NP10 8FY
Shareholders: Anthony Stuart Goss; Richard Neil Thomas
Officers: Anthony Stuart Goss, Secretary/Director; Anthony Stuart Goss [1968] Director; Richard Neil Thomas [1945] Director/Industrial Chemist

Lamina Animal Limited
Incorporated: 12 November 2018
Registered Office: 62 Lower Road, London, SE16 2TU
Major Shareholder: Charlotte Elsie Rose Collier-Hunter
Officers: Charlotte Elsie Rose Collier-Hunter [1976] Director

Lana-Rae Ltd Ltd
Incorporated: 23 June 2014
Previous: Lana-Rae Ltd
Registered Office: 3rd Floor, 207 Regent Street, London, W1B 3HH
Officers: Raechel Muhammad, Secretary; Raechel Muhammad [1989] Director/Student

Langhedge Limited
Incorporated: 14 October 2008
Net Worth Deficit: £15,428 *Total Assets:* £347
Registered Office: 68 Bilton Way, Enfield, Middlesex, EN3 7NH
Major Shareholder: Anthony Clive Umfreville Fisher
Officers: Valerie Margaret Elizabeth Darville, Secretary; Valerie Margaret Elizabeth Darville [1945] Director/Administrator; Anthony Clive Umfreville Fisher [1943] Director/Scientist; Iwan Clive Umfreville Fisher [1969] Director/Scientist

Lankem Ltd.
Incorporated: 20 September 1999 *Employees:* 23
Net Worth: £791,759 *Total Assets:* £2,130,363
Registered Office: Charles Street, Dukinfield, Cheshire, SK16 4SD
Shareholders: Sean Graham Hodgkinson; Andrea Marie Hodgkinson
Officers: Andrea Marie Hodgkinson, Secretary; Andrea Marie Hodgkinson [1973] Director/Personnel Manager; Sean Graham Hodgkinson [1968] Director/Sales Manager

Larragard Limited
Incorporated: 28 September 1977 *Employees:* 7
Net Worth: £593,565 *Total Assets:* £755,636
Registered Office: Chapel Lane, Heckmondwike, W Yorks, WF16 9JP
Major Shareholder: James Christopher Knox
Officers: James Christopher Knox, Secretary; James Christopher Knox [1972] Director; Sarah Kate Knox [1969] Director

Lather Cute Soap Limited
Incorporated: 5 March 2018
Registered Office: 71-75 Shelton Street, London, WC2H 9JQ
Major Shareholder: Charlene Kenny
Officers: Charlene Kenny [1989] Director/Accountant

Lathersmith Ltd
Incorporated: 31 January 2013
Net Worth: £929 *Total Assets:* £929
Registered Office: 129 Dairsie Road, London, SE9 1XL
Officers: Aiste Kekiene [1982] Director/Cosmetics [Lithuanian]

James Law (Chemicals) Limited
Incorporated: 9 April 1937 *Employees:* 6
Net Worth: £66,291 *Total Assets:* £220,872
Registered Office: Crossley Street Works, Crossley Street, Smallbridge, Rochdale, Lancs, OL16 2QA
Parent: James Law (Holdings) Limited
Officers: Toby Marcus Jefferson [1969] Director; Sean Wilkinson [1971] Director

Lemon Spring Ltd
Incorporated: 4 September 2015
Net Worth Deficit: £1,947 *Total Assets:* £2,444
Registered Office: 40 Saville Street, Emley, Huddersfield, W Yorks, HD8 9RX
Officers: Mary Schofield [1967] Director/Buyer

Let It Bee Ltd
Incorporated: 2 July 2018
Registered Office: 88 Northfield Road, Kings Norton, Birmingham, B30 1JG
Shareholders: Jane Elvere Nimmo; Gillian Elizabeth Davies
Officers: Gillian Elizabeth Davies [1963] Director/Manager; Jane Elvere Nimmo [1964] Director/Manager

The Top UK Soap and Detergent Manufacturers

Letlalo Ltd
Incorporated: 26 May 2018
Registered Office: 15 Tidebrook Gardens, Eastbourne, E Sussex, BN23 7AH
Major Shareholder: Ryan James Malet
Officers: Ryan James Malet [1990] Director

Leum Skin Care Ltd
Incorporated: 7 April 2014
Net Worth Deficit: £114 *Total Assets:* £35
Registered Office: 20-22 Wenlock Road, London, N1 7GU
Major Shareholder: Ieva Dos Santos Rita de Jesus
Officers: Ieva Dos Santos Rita de Jesus [1975] Director [Latvian]

Levant Soap Limited
Incorporated: 1 April 2016
Net Worth Deficit: £15,915 *Total Assets:* £11,064
Registered Office: Premier Business Centre, 47-49 Park Royal Road, London, NW10 7LQ
Officers: Hasan Alkassem [1987] Director [Syrian]

Libra Speciality Chemicals Limited
Incorporated: 27 April 1971 *Employees:* 57
Net Worth: £8,203,749 *Total Assets:* £13,247,113
Registered Office: 5 Acorn Business Park, Woodseats Close, Sheffield, S8 0TB
Officers: David Thomas Kearns, Secretary; Philip Mathew Carson [1981] Supply Chain Director; Dr Graham Cox [1960] Operations Director; Lorraine Forshaw [1963] Finance Director; David Thomas Kearns [1968] Director; Richard Antony David Lock [1982] Sales & Marketing Director; Graham Royle [1959] Director

Lick Labs Limited
Incorporated: 2 October 2018
Registered Office: 45 Mount Ambrose, Redruth, Cornwall, TR15 1NX
Shareholders: Ross Anthony Rosewarne; Levi Ripley
Officers: Levi Ripley [1987] Founder/Director; Ross Anthony Rosewarne [1986] Managing Director

The Little Goat Soap Company Limited
Incorporated: 18 April 2013 *Employees:* 1
Net Worth: £4,976 *Total Assets:* £41,716
Registered Office: Park Farm, Littleworth, Faringdon, Oxon, SN7 8ED
Shareholders: Joanne King; Andrew King
Officers: Andrew King [1965] Director/Woodturner; Joanne King [1969] Director/Soap Manufacturer

Little Green Beehive Ltd
Incorporated: 23 April 2018
Registered Office: 7 Potts Close, Kenilworth, Warwicks, CV8 2SD
Shareholders: Josephine Cassell; Nikki Lee
Officers: Dr Josephine Cassell [1987] Director/Co-Founder; Dr Nikki Lee [1989] Director/Co-Founder [Canadian]

Little Lodge Bees Ltd
Incorporated: 14 January 2019
Registered Office: The Lodge, Whitchurch, Tavistock, Devon, PL19 9EQ
Shareholders: William Stuart Mills; Stephanie Rachel Anne Mills
Officers: Dr Stephanie Rachel Anne Mills [1987] Managing Director; William Stuart Mills [1988] Managing Director

Little Soap Company Limited
Incorporated: 20 October 2008 *Employees:* 4
Net Worth: £360,586 *Total Assets:* £569,896
Registered Office: 99 Upper High Street, Broadway, Worcs, WR12 7AL
Major Shareholder: Emma Julie Heathcote-James
Officers: Steven Trevor Heathcote, Secretary; Steven Trevor Heathcote [1948] Director/Accountant; Emma Julie Heathcote James [1977] Director/Media Researcher

The Little Wax Workshop Limited
Incorporated: 17 April 2018
Registered Office: 16 Quern Road, Deal, Kent, CT14 9EQ
Officers: Maxine Sharon White [1969] Director

LJSP Ltd
Incorporated: 23 August 2016
Net Worth: £1,000 *Total Assets:* £1,000
Registered Office: First Floor, 85 Great Portland Street, London, W1W 7LT
Major Shareholder: Mark Boulos
Officers: Mark Boulos [1980] Director; Jonathan Sumner [1980] Director; Robert Bird Sumner [1982] Director

Locks in Goodness Ltd
Incorporated: 21 December 2018
Registered Office: 20 Sefton Avenue, London, NW7 3QD
Shareholders: Victoria Aviva Ashton; Graham Alexander Ashton
Officers: Graham Alexander Ashton [1980] Director/Chartered Accountant; Victoria Aviva Ashton [1982] Director

Lofty Gardens Ltd
Incorporated: 9 October 2018
Registered Office: 1st Floor, Block C, The Wharf, Manchester Road, Burnley, Lancs, BB11 1JG
Major Shareholder: Muhammad Mohsin Khan
Officers: Muhammad Mohsin Khan [1989] Director [Pakistani]

London Cosmetics (UK) Limited
Incorporated: 20 July 2011
Registered Office: 185 The Sycamores, Milton, Cambridge, CB24 6ZH
Major Shareholder: Mirza Yousaf Baig
Officers: Mirza Yousaf Baig [1970] Director/IT Engineer

London Soap and Chemical Co. Limited
Incorporated: 19 June 1987 *Employees:* 10
Net Worth: £248,285 *Total Assets:* £329,151
Registered Office: LSC House, Murray Road, Orpington, Kent, BR5 3QY
Parent: Totem Properties Limited
Officers: Susan Anne Moon, Secretary; Susan Anne Moon [1959] Director/Chartered Accountant

London Soap Company Ltd
Incorporated: 5 September 2018
Registered Office: Flat 6, Minton Court, 105 Fairfield Road, London, E3 2ZB
Major Shareholder: Simon Christopher Blowes
Officers: Simon Christopher Blowes [1984] Director

Love To B Skincare Ltd
Incorporated: 17 May 2012
Previous: Chilly B Soap Company Limited
Net Worth Deficit: £32,752 *Total Assets:* £44,064
Registered Office: 898-902 Wimborne Road, Moordown, Bournemouth, BH9 2DW
Major Shareholder: Julia Maria Astley Weston
Officers: Richard John Astley Weston, Secretary; Julie Maria Astley Weston [1963] Director

Loveve. Ltd
Incorporated: 11 December 2018
Registered Office: 1 Topsfield Close, Crouch End, London, N8 8DW
Major Shareholder: Evelyn Isabel Blackman
Officers: Evelyn Isabel Blackman [1974] Director/Manufacturer

Lower Swell Chemicals Limited
Incorporated: 5 February 1979
Net Worth: £5,471 *Total Assets:* £60,366
Registered Office: 3-5 Hazel Court, Bourton Industrial Park, Bourton on the Water, Glos, GL54 2HQ
Shareholders: William George Davies; Jayne Elizabeth Davies
Officers: Jayne Elizabeth Davies, Secretary; William George Davies [1947] Director

LU Aromatherapy Ltd
Incorporated: 20 February 2018
Registered Office: 2 Whinberry Drive, Kirkby, Merseyside, L32 9BA
Officers: Lucrecia Silvana Bianchi [1976] Director [Italian]; Eliseo Bustamante [1996] Director [Italian]

Luvly Bubbly Limited
Incorporated: 12 July 2011 *Employees:* 1
Net Worth Deficit: £330 *Total Assets:* £1,149
Registered Office: 374 Ley Street, Ilford, Essex, IG1 4AE
Major Shareholder: Beverley Jane Bispham
Officers: Beverley Bispham [1970] Director/Businesswoman

M.A. Industries Limited
Incorporated: 16 June 2017
Registered Office: 5 Alder Mews, Batley, W Yorks, WF17 7JD
Major Shareholder: Mohamad Abdallah
Officers: Mohamad Abdallah [1990] Director

Macob Online Shopping Ltd.
Incorporated: 8 November 2016
Net Worth: £2,764 *Total Assets:* £2,764
Registered Office: Clarence Centre for Entreprise & Innovation, 6 St Georges Circus, London, SE1 6FE
Major Shareholder: Sandrine Galbert
Officers: Sandrine Galbert [1974] Director/Website Designer [French]

Madalyn and Rose Ltd
Incorporated: 13 July 2015
Net Worth Deficit: £3,713 *Total Assets:* £599
Registered Office: 21 Dowanhill Road, London, SE6 1SU
Major Shareholder: Natalee Nelson
Officers: Natalee Nelson [1991] Director

Madcow Brand Limited
Incorporated: 15 February 2018
Registered Office: 39 Tower Street, Peterborough, Cambs, PE2 9AE
Officers: Thomas Allen [1984] Director/Self Employed

Magpie's Ocean Ltd
Incorporated: 19 September 2018
Registered Office: 34 Wain Street, Stoke on Trent, Staffs, ST6 4ES
Shareholders: Samantha Ophelia Chinnery; Eleanor Lunaria Hetherington
Officers: Samantha Ophelia Chinnery [1980] Director/Manufacturer; Eleanor Lunaria Hetherington [1992] Director/Manufacturer

Main Chemical Co Limited
Incorporated: 4 June 1982 *Employees:* 5
Net Worth: £125,940 *Total Assets:* £228,986
Registered Office: Chapel Lane, Heckmondwike, W Yorks, WF16 9JP
Officers: James Christopher Knox, Secretary; James Christopher Knox [1972] Director; Sarah Kate Knox [1969] Director

Makin' Scents Ltd
Incorporated: 28 December 2017
Registered Office: 26 Main Street, Kircubbin, Co Down, BT22 2SP
Major Shareholder: Nicola Lynn Anderson
Officers: Nicola Lynn Anderson [1981] Managing Director

Making Scents Ltd
Incorporated: 21 August 2017
Registered Office: Thirtleby House, High Street, Eastrington, Goole, E Yorks, DN14 7PH
Officers: Joanne Winters [1973] Director

Tony Maleedy Hair Ltd.
Incorporated: 27 October 2015
Net Worth Deficit: £26,734 *Total Assets:* £27,412
Registered Office: Keld Cottage, Main Street, Kirkby Overblow, Harrogate, N Yorks, HG3 1HD
Shareholders: Anthony Thomas Maleedy; Jonathan Frederick Lawson-Brown
Officers: Jonathan Frederick Lawson-Brown [1975] Managing Director; Anthony Thomas Maleedy [1952] Founding Director

Malibu Health Products Limited
Incorporated: 13 April 1999
Net Worth: £1,099,033 *Total Assets:* £7,536,565
Registered Office: 23 Dennis Lane, Stanmore, Middlesex, HA7 4JS
Officers: Stuart Anthony Spurling [1965] Director

Mama Bee Soaps Ltd
Incorporated: 2 May 2018
Registered Office: 17 Jackson Road, London, N7 6ES
Officers: Beata Vasilkovaite [1984] Director/Clerical Officer [Lithuanian]

Mano Pack Limited
Incorporated: 3 January 2017
Registered Office: 17 Hunters Way, Sawtry, Cambs, PE28 5SJ
Major Shareholder: Benjamin Martin
Officers: Benjamin Martin [1975] Director

Marble Hill Soaps Limited
Incorporated: 2 June 2005
Net Worth Deficit: £95,474 *Total Assets:* £46,854
Registered Office: 7 Colby Avenue, Derry, BT48 8PP
Major Shareholder: Maria Teresa McGee
Officers: Ciaran McGee, Secretary; Dr Maria Teresa McGee [1956] Director/Craftsperson [Irish]

Maribella London Limited
Incorporated: 31 October 2017
Registered Office: 11 Gateway, Walworth Road, London, SE17 3HQ
Major Shareholder: Godman Usman
Officers: Godman Usman [1986] Director/Banker

The Top UK Soap and Detergent Manufacturers   dellam

Marsh Valley Ltd
Incorporated: 16 January 2018
Registered Office: 501 Loxley Road, Loxley, Sheffield, S6 6RR
Shareholders: Samuel Kyle Marshall; Jessica Louise Cutler
Officers: Jessica Louise Cutler [1993] Director/Manager; Samuel Kyle Marshall [1992] Director/Manager

Elizabeth Martin Creative Studio Ltd
Incorporated: 17 January 2019
Registered Office: 2 Heol-Y-Nant, Heol-Y-Cyw, Bridgend, Mid Glamorgan, CF35 6HT
Major Shareholder: Elizabeth Martin
Officers: Elizabeth Martin [1972] Director

Mauchit Ltd
Incorporated: 28 March 2018
Registered Office: 15 Monks Walk, Grange, Errol, Perthshire, PH2 7AU
Major Shareholder: Sandra McCourt
Officers: Sandra McCourt [1962] Director/Manager

Christina May Limited
Incorporated: 29 September 2000 *Employees:* 31
Net Worth: £364,412 *Total Assets:* £964,391
Registered Office: Rotherdale, Fir Toll Road, Mayfield, E Sussex, TN20 6NB
Parent: Stompee Holdings Limited
Officers: Christina Juliet Butts, Secretary; Christina Juliet Butts [1949] Director/Company Secretary; Courtenay Arthur Robert Butts [1951] Director; Oliver Courtenay Richard Butts [1985] Director

Mayde Essence Ltd
Incorporated: 7 November 2016
Registered Office: 101 Aldershaw Road, Birmingham, B26 1HL
Major Shareholder: Charlotte Andrews
Officers: Charlotte Andrews [1987] Director

Mazu Seaweed Limited
Incorporated: 17 April 2014
Net Worth Deficit: £1,187 *Total Assets:* £184
Registered Office: 456 Gower Road, Killay, Swansea, SA2 7AL
Shareholders: Justin Ovens; Hayley Ovens
Officers: Hayley Ovens [1974] Director; Justin Ovens [1965] Director

Mbikudi Ltd
Incorporated: 29 March 2016
Net Worth: £6,515 *Total Assets:* £9,015
Registered Office: 272 Bath Street, Glasgow, G2 4JR
Officers: Hermine Makangu, Secretary; Natalie Cita [1980] Director/Administrator; Sara Ntumba Kalukenda [1991] Director/Manager [Congolese]; Hermine Makangu [1989] Director

Robert McBride Ltd
Incorporated: 9 March 1927 *Employees:* 1,169
Net Worth: £12,255,000 *Total Assets:* £158,680,000
Registered Office: Middleton Way, Middleton, Manchester, M24 4DP
Shareholders: McBride PLC; McBride Holdings Limited
Officers: Carol Williams, Secretary; David Thomas Rattigan [1969] Director/Accountant; Christopher Ian Charles Smith [1964] Director/Accountant; Rik Jean Pierre Dora Albert de Vos [1960] Director [Belgian]

Paul McCaffrey Systems Ltd
Incorporated: 19 October 1989
Net Worth: £53,915 *Total Assets:* £275,418
Registered Office: South East Lodge, Rede Road, Whepstead, Bury St Edmunds, Suffolk, IP29 4ST
Major Shareholder: Paul McCaffrey
Officers: Josephine McCaffrey, Secretary; Josephine Anne McCaffrey [1965] Company Secretary/Director; Paul David McCaffrey [1959] Director

McIntyre Group Ltd.
Incorporated: 23 April 1998
Registered Office: 34 Clarendon Road, Watford, Herts, WD17 1JJ
Parent: Rhodia Holdings Limited
Officers: Alison Murphy, Secretary/Financial Controller; Tom Dutton [1964] Director/Health, Safety & Environment Manager; Alison Murphy [1965] Director/Financial Controller

MDCO Ltd
Incorporated: 12 February 2013 *Employees:* 2
Net Worth: £97,772 *Total Assets:* £145,720
Registered Office: Kenant Chambers, 2 Bath Avenue, Wolverhampton, W Midlands, WV1 4EQ
Major Shareholder: Martin Simon Doran
Officers: Martin Simon Doran [1961] Managing Director; Susan Doran [1967] Director

Meadow Farm Friends Ltd
Incorporated: 14 July 2014
Registered Office: Meadow Cottage, 23 Church Road, Sparkford, Somerset, BA22 7JN
Major Shareholder: Verity Kate Bracher
Officers: Verity Kate Bracher [1975] Director

Meaningful Earth Soap Company Limited
Incorporated: 14 February 2017
Registered Office: 4 The Quay, Ilfracombe, Devon, EX34 9EQ
Shareholder: Ana Paula Alves Dos Reis Fielder
Officers: Ana Paula Alves Dos Reis Fielder [1976] Director/Soap Artisan [British/Brazilian]; Benjamin Douglas Fielder [1981] Director

Medichem Manufacturing Ltd
Incorporated: 14 December 2015 *Employees:* 87
Net Worth: £3,065,575 *Total Assets:* £5,051,155
Registered Office: Stalham Business Park, Rushenden Road, Queenborough, Kent, ME11 5HE
Major Shareholder: Thomas Donald Allsworth
Officers: Thomas Donald Allsworth [1965] Director; Clive Andrew Morris [1970] Director

Melpass Limited
Incorporated: 3 September 1980 *Employees:* 48
Net Worth: £826,838 *Total Assets:* £2,312,102
Registered Office: Unit A, 1-6 Farrington Close, Burnley, Lancs, BB11 5SH
Parent: VIL Holdings Limited
Officers: Philip William Richardson, Secretary; Harold Collier [1952] Technical Director; Ian Whillas Harrison [1959] Director; Philip William Richardson [1982] Director; Andrew Wray Wallen [1947] Director; James Wray Wallen [1987] Director; Richard Wray Wallen [1974] Director

Merlin Chemicals Limited
Incorporated: 5 June 1991 *Employees:* 36
Net Worth: £1,461,601 *Total Assets:* £2,378,341
Registered Office: Gateway House, Pilsworth Road, Pilsworth Industrial Estate, Bury, Lancs, BL9 8RD
Parent: The Holchem Group Limited
Officers: Simon Bell [1972] Director; Stuart Middleton [1959] Director

Midland Chemicals Limited
Incorporated: 14 March 1991 Employees: 8
Net Worth: £542,075 Total Assets: £702,480
Registered Office: Midlands House, 13a Brindley Close, Abeles Way, Holly Lane Industrial Estate, Atherstone, Warwicks, CV9 2QZ
Major Shareholder: Sunil Pathak
Officers: Sunil Pathak, Secretary; Nina Pathak [1961] Sales Director; Sunil Pathak [1956] Managing Director; Jeffrey Schofield [1943] Director

Mild + Wild Ltd
Incorporated: 15 August 2018
Registered Office: 2 Canning Close, Hindley, Wigan, Lancs, WN2 3NQ
Shareholders: Natalie Sarah Richards; Zoe Nalini Cook
Officers: Zoe Nalini Cook [1979] Director/Businesswoman; Natalie Sarah Richards [1979] Director/Businesswoman

Millchem (UK) Limited
Incorporated: 27 April 1990
Net Worth: £1,254,640 Total Assets: £1,423,789
Registered Office: 23 Lovers Lane, Grasscroft, Oldham, Lancs, OL4 4DT
Shareholders: Jevan Maurice Lees; Sheila Lees
Officers: Sheila Lees, Secretary; Jane Lees [1980] Director; Jevan Maurice Lees [1952] Director; Sheila Lees [1951] Director

Mitcheldean Soap Ltd
Incorporated: 12 May 2008
Net Worth Deficit: £29,757 Total Assets: £611
Registered Office: 41 The Crescent, Mitcheldean, Glos, GL17 0SB
Shareholders: George Christopher Gates; Sara Jayne Gates
Officers: Sara Jayne Gates, Secretary; George Christopher Gates [1972] Director; Sara Jayne Gates [1973] Director

Ian Mitchell Distribution Limited
Incorporated: 18 May 1995 Employees: 5
Net Worth: £150,808 Total Assets: £241,511
Registered Office: Unit 14 Summerlands Industrial Estate, Endmoor, Kendal, Cumbria, LA8 0FB
Shareholder: Ian James Mitchell
Officers: Janice Mitchell, Secretary; Ian James Mitchell [1957] Director/Chemical Distributor

MOL Soap Ltd.
Incorporated: 3 January 2017
Registered Office: 4 Borodin Court, Old Farm Park, Milton Keynes, Bucks, MK7 8PH
Major Shareholder: Shaista Hina Imran
Officers: Shaista Hina Imran [1983] Managing Director

Molecula Ltd
Incorporated: 5 December 2017
Registered Office: 20-22 Wenlock Road, London, N1 7GU
Major Shareholder: Martina Dragicevic
Officers: Danijel Palic, Secretary; Martina Dragicevic [1975] Director [Croatian]

Molton Brown Limited
Incorporated: 21 August 1989 Employees: 737
Net Worth: £33,251,000 Total Assets: £55,077,000
Registered Office: 130 Shaftesbury Avenue, London, W1D 5EU
Parent: Kao Corporation
Officers: Graham John Edgerton, Secretary; Eric Anthonius Brockhus [1964] Director/President Consumer Products [Dutch]; Graham John Edgerton [1961] Finance Director; Mark Johnson [1973] Director/President [American]; Yoshihiro Murakami [1963] Director/Chairman [Japanese]

Momar Limited
Incorporated: 29 October 2002
Registered Office: 23 Dyott Road, Moseley, Birmingham, B13 9QZ
Shareholder: Suraj Naik
Officers: Kalpana Rajesh Naik, Secretary; Suraj Naik [1984] Director/Marketing

Montague Lloyd Limited
Incorporated: 23 November 2006
Registered Office: North Main Street, Carronshore, Falkirk, FK2 8HT
Parent: Alexander Ross Management Services Limited
Officers: Derek Blair Ross [1942] Director; Robert Columbine Ross [1971] Director; Thomas Agnew Hamilton Slater [1956] Director/Accountant; William Brown Wilson [1961] Director

Mrs Whelan Ltd
Incorporated: 27 February 2019
Registered Office: 28 South Luton Place, Cardiff, CF24 0EX
Major Shareholder: Claire Margaret Whelan
Officers: Claire Margaret Whelan [1967] Director/Administrator

MSH Chemical Manufacturing Limited
Incorporated: 24 March 1995
Net Worth: £355,594 Total Assets: £1,121,021
Registered Office: Unit 1-6 Shaw Road, Dudley, W Midlands, DY2 8TP
Shareholder: Rajesh S Naik
Officers: Kalpana Rajesh Naik, Secretary; Kalpana Rajesh Naik [1960] Director; Rajesh S Naik [1956] Director

MSL Limited
Incorporated: 7 February 1980 Employees: 16
Net Worth: £152,364 Total Assets: £355,537
Registered Office: 101 Smithycroft Road, Riddrie, Glasgow, G33 2RH
Shareholders: Barbara Lang; Gillies Lang
Officers: Barbara Lang, Secretary; Barbara Lang [1954] Director; Gillies Lang [1948] Director; Bryce McCaig [1960] Sales Director

Murray-Smith Consulting Limited
Incorporated: 10 April 2015 Employees: 2
Net Worth: £61,110 Total Assets: £71,401
Registered Office: 119 Adams Drive, Willesborough, Ashford, Kent, TN24 0FX
Major Shareholder: Ivan Leo Murray-Smith
Officers: Ivan Leo Murray-Smith, Secretary; Elizabeth Louise Odam [1991] Director

MWK Cosmetics (UK) Ltd
Incorporated: 31 December 2018
Registered Office: 2/2, 37 Morar Drive, Paisley, Renfrewshire, PA2 9BG
Major Shareholder: Francis Nderitu Gatongi
Officers: Francis Nderitu Gatongi [1965] Managing Director

Naked Cosmetics Ltd
Incorporated: 13 June 2018
Registered Office: North Cottage, 11 Ryecroft Lane, Storrington, Pulborough, W Sussex, RH20 4PA
Officers: Tara Isabel Josephine Dewey [1999] Director

Nana's Studio Ltd
Incorporated: 19 July 2018
Registered Office: 76 Flaxwell Court, Northampton, NN3 9DF
Major Shareholder: Haja Salifu
Officers: Haja Salifu [1977] Director [German]

The Top UK Soap and Detergent Manufacturers

Narauli Ltd
Incorporated: 23 April 2018
Registered Office: 2 Maidenhall Farm Cottages, St Boswells, Melrose, Roxburghshire, TD6 0EF
Major Shareholder: Helena Alice Lucy Anderson
Officers: Helena Alice Lucy Anderson [1996] Director

Natural British Limited
Incorporated: 15 September 2017
Net Worth Deficit: £51,736 *Total Assets:* £23,236
Registered Office: Unit 4 Premier Court, Kings Mill Way, Mansfield, Notts, NG18 5ER
Major Shareholder: Mark Ryan
Officers: Mark Ryan [1965] Director

Natural By Nature Limited
Incorporated: 8 May 2018
Registered Office: 82 Reeves Avenue, Cross Heath, Newcastle-under-Lyme, Staffs, ST5 9LA
Officers: Richard Edward Cooke [1983] Director/Analyst; Daniel Willatt [1992] Director/General Manager

Natural Jem Limited
Incorporated: 30 January 2018
Registered Office: Lower Ground Floor, 40 Bloomsbury Way, London, WC1A 2SE
Shareholders: Awulatu Enitan Salawu; Alfred Ekpenyong
Officers: Alfred Ekpenyong [1985] Director/Operations Manager; Awulatu Enitan Salawu [1983] Director/Social Worker

The Natural Soap Company Limited
Incorporated: 4 October 2000
Net Worth Deficit: £164 *Total Assets:* £30,984
Registered Office: 2d Maryland, Wells-Next-The-Sea, Norfolk, NR23 1LY
Major Shareholder: Sara Elizabeth Phillips
Officers: Sara Phillips, Secretary; Max Phillips [1963] Director/Consultant; Sara Phillips [1959] Director/Designer

Naturali360 Limited
Incorporated: 3 February 2017
Net Worth: £1 *Total Assets:* £1
Registered Office: 88 Sherborne Court, London, SW5 0SU
Officers: Katia Bongermino [1981] Director [Italian]

Naturally Nourishing Ltd
Incorporated: 4 October 2018
Registered Office: 10 Hawkshead Avenue, Dronfield Woodhouse, Dronfield, Derbys, S18 8NB
Major Shareholder: Christopher Kirby
Officers: Christopher Kirby [1991] Director/Civil Servant

Nature B Limited
Incorporated: 11 October 2017
Registered Office: Kemp House, 160 City Road, London, EC1V 2NX
Officers: Bruno Martin-Gilmore [1957] Director/Entrepreneur

Nature Native Limited
Incorporated: 18 May 2017
Net Worth: £1 *Total Assets:* £1
Registered Office: 110 Wellcroft Road, Welwyn Garden City, Herts, AL7 3JU
Major Shareholder: Simone Edwards
Officers: Simone Edwards [1964] Director/Soap Maker

Nature Reflects Limited
Incorporated: 3 July 2017
Registered Office: 78 Maiden Erlegh Avenue, Bexley, Kent, DA5 3PE
Major Shareholder: Deborah Ann Colton
Officers: Deborah Ann Colton [1982] Managing Director

NCH (UK) Limited
Incorporated: 18 August 1964 *Employees:* 195
Net Worth: £8,439,000 *Total Assets:* £30,053,000
Registered Office: NCH House, Springvale Avenue, Bilston, W Midlands, WV14 0QL
Officers: Martyn Jeffrey Ruscoe, Secretary; John Leslie Currie [1955] Director/Business Executive [American]; John Irvin Levy [1961] Director [American]; Russell Lawrence Price [1965] Director/Lawyer [American]

Newry Chemicals Ltd
Incorporated: 29 March 2007
Net Worth: £217 *Total Assets:* £72,562
Registered Office: 82 Seavers Road, Newry, Co Down, BT35 8LD
Major Shareholder: Margaret Rice
Officers: Margaret Rice, Secretary; James Rice [1949] Director [Irish]; Margaret Rice [1953] Director [Irish]

Newton Formulations Limited
Incorporated: 1 March 2007
Net Worth: £1,000 *Total Assets:* £1,000
Registered Office: Unicorn House, 141 Mowbray Drive, Blackpool, Lancs, FY3 7UN
Parent: Ave Limited
Officers: Alan William Reilly, Secretary; Timothy Fraser Kilpatrick [1967] Director

Nimble Babies Limited
Incorporated: 25 February 2014 *Employees:* 1
Net Worth Deficit: £50,714 *Total Assets:* £87,912
Registered Office: c/o Joom Accounting Ltd, Beauchamp House, 1 Kenilworth Road, Leamington Spa, Warwicks, CV32 5TG
Major Shareholder: von Ryan Chua Sy
Officers: Rajinder Kumar Sharma [1968] Director; Von Ryan Chua Sy [1981] Director; Yinghui Wang [1970] Director/Consultant [Chinese]

Nomad Soapery Limited
Incorporated: 4 June 2018
Registered Office: Orwell House, All Saints Lane, Sutton Courtenay, Abingdon, Oxon, OX14 4AG
Shareholders: Frederic Alexander Broughton Pilkington; Sharlene Suyin Boey
Officers: Sharlene Suyin Boey [1990] Director/Researcher [Malaysian]; Frederic Alexander Broughton Pilkington [1992] Director/Researcher

Northumbrian Botanicals Limited
Incorporated: 23 May 2018
Registered Office: Unit 2 Legion House, Alnwick Road, Hexham, Northumberland, NE46 4TU
Major Shareholder: Janice Wilson
Officers: Janice Wilson [1957] Director

NS Industries Ltd
Incorporated: 10 August 2016
Net Worth Deficit: £582 *Total Assets:* £389
Registered Office: 21 Parkview Industrial Estate, Hartlepool, Cleveland, TS25 1UD
Major Shareholder: Andrew Korkus
Officers: Andrew Korkus [1963] Director [Lithuanian]

Nu-E55ence Ltd
Incorporated: 8 January 2019
Registered Office: 20-22 Wenlock Road, London, N1 7GU
Officers: Charmaine Cameron [1983] Director

Nuts About Soap Limited
Incorporated: 16 November 2010
Net Worth Deficit: £21,900 *Total Assets:* £255
Registered Office: c/o Very Ard Times Limited, Tower 42, 25 Old Broad Street, London, EC2N 1HQ
Officers: Tony Collins [1960] Director; Isabelle Dupire [1957] Director [French]; Lee Francis [1965] Director; George Cinadu Nnochiri [1961] Director

OC Transformation Limited
Incorporated: 27 November 2008
Net Worth Deficit: £48,137 *Total Assets:* £49,471
Registered Office: The Bell House, 57 West Street, Dorking, Surrey, RH4 1BS
Major Shareholder: Rachael Ogario
Officers: Norris Ogario [1950] Technical Director; Rachael Ogario [1970] Director/Consultancy

OCD Finish Limited
Incorporated: 29 January 2018
Registered Office: Clock House Farm, Bittell Farm Road, Barnt Green, Birmingham, B45 8BP
Major Shareholder: Neil Trew
Officers: Neil Trew [1981] Director/Owner

Ochil Skincare Company Ltd
Incorporated: 26 January 2015
Net Worth: £8,324 *Total Assets:* £24,315
Registered Office: Unit 1 Carsebridge Court, Whins Road, Alloa, Clackmannanshire, FK10 3LQ
Shareholder: Fiona Ritchie
Officers: Fiona Ritchie [1971] Director

Ohana CBD Limited
Incorporated: 1 October 2016
Registered Office: 37 Brune House, Bell Lane, London, E1 7NW
Shareholders: Stefan Joshua Greer; Jasmin Thomas
Officers: Stefan Joshua Greer [1990] Director; Jasmin Thomas [1991] Director

Ohana Soaps and More Limited
Incorporated: 17 April 2018
Registered Office: 21 Liberty Lane, Addlestone, Surrey, KT15 1LU
Major Shareholder: Jackie Smith
Officers: Jackie Smith [1964] Director

Old Park Farm Estate Limited
Incorporated: 20 July 2005
Net Worth Deficit: £28,688 *Total Assets:* £707
Registered Office: Third Floor, 20 Old Bailey, London, EC4M 7AN
Major Shareholder: Susan Jane Wells
Officers: Susan Jane Wells [1959] Director/Project Manager

Oleonix Solutions Limited
Incorporated: 13 August 2012
Registered Office: 5 Redgrave Business Centre, Gallows Hill, Redgrave, Diss, Norfolk, IP22 1RZ
Shareholder: Emma Victoria Edwards
Officers: Emma Victoria Edwards [1963] Director/Holistic Massage Therapist; Richard Mark Edwards [1953] Director/Cleaning Chemical Consultant

Omnova Performance Chemicals Limited
Incorporated: 17 March 1999 *Employees:* 4
Net Worth: £1,069,000 *Total Assets:* £1,761,000
Registered Office: 14-18 City Road, Cardiff, CF24 3DL
Parent: Omnova UK Holding Limited
Officers: Andrew Higgin, Secretary; Andrew Higgin [1963] Director Business Operations; James Lemay [1956] Director/Legal Counsel Omnova Solutions [American]; Anne Patricia Noonan [1963] Director/President and CEO, Omnova Solutions Inc [American]

Oooh Skincare Ltd
Incorporated: 11 October 2011
Net Worth Deficit: £1,728 *Total Assets:* £3,680
Registered Office: 15 Melverley Grove, Birmingham, B44 8LA
Officers: Desmond Henry, Secretary; Sonia Barnett [1967] Director/Accountant; Desmond De'oliver Henry [1963] Director/Designer

Ora-Heal Ltd
Incorporated: 12 January 2007
Net Worth Deficit: £11,255 *Total Assets:* £2,508
Registered Office: 210 Hillcross Avenue, Morden, Surrey, SM4 4ET
Shareholder: Anna Akkuratova
Officers: Anna Akkuratova, Secretary/Economist [Belarusian]; Anna Akkuratova [1982] Director/Economist; Dr Errol Pastoll [1959] Director/Dental Surgeon

Origin Pet Products Limited
Incorporated: 13 January 2010
Net Worth: £35,439 *Total Assets:* £37,711
Registered Office: Dalton House, 60 Windsor Avenue, London, SW19 2RR
Officers: David Finlay [1967] Director

The Original Soapchair Company Ltd
Incorporated: 9 July 2018
Registered Office: Northview, Nympsfield Road, Nailsworth, Stroud, Glos, GL6 0EL
Shareholders: Douglas Fullarton Gilmour; Elisa Rosa Marije Carolus
Officers: Elisa Rosa Marije Carolus [1982] Director/Cartoonist [Dutch]; Douglas Fullarton Gilmour [1963] Director/Project Manager

Orikii Naturals Ltd
Incorporated: 7 January 2019
Registered Office: 28 Felipe Road, Chafford Hundred, Grays, Essex, RM16 6NE
Major Shareholder: Olubunmi Oyetoun Johnson
Officers: Olubunmi Oyetoun Johnson [1968] Director

Oryza Naturale Limited
Incorporated: 4 June 2018
Registered Office: 27 Old Gloucester Street, London, WC1N 3AX
Major Shareholder: Thitima Alabi
Officers: Thitima Alabi [1980] Director/Marketing Executive [Thai]

Ottimo Supplies Limited
Incorporated: 7 January 1980
Net Worth: £3,112 *Total Assets:* £248,284
Registered Office: 7 Livingstone Mills, Howard Street, Batley, W Yorks, WF17 6JH
Shareholders: Reginald Frank Harwood; Harry Edward Wilson
Officers: Harry Edward Wilson, Secretary; Zakir Hussain Chopdat [1984] Director; Reginald Frank Harwood [1956] Director; Dorothy Wilson [1943] Director; Harry Edward Wilson [1943] Director

P & H Natural Skincare Ltd
Incorporated: 25 January 2019
Registered Office: The Long Lodge, 265-269 Kingston Road, Wimbledon, London, SW19 3NW
Shareholder: Pavla Humpulova
Officers: Jiri Humpula [1978] Director [Czech]; Pavla Humpulova [1981] Director [Czech]

The Paisley Soap Company Ltd
Incorporated: 2 August 2018
Registered Office: 18 Kirkton Road, Neilston, Glasgow, G78 3HN
Major Shareholder: Marie Margaret Ballesteros
Officers: Marie Margaret Ballesteros [1964] Director/Businesswoman

Pampered Me Ltd
Incorporated: 22 November 2017
Registered Office: 71 Brantwood Road, London, N17 0DT
Shareholders: Natasha Ngozi Abani; Philomena Agnes Abani
Officers: Edip Can Binatli, Secretary; Natasha Ngozi Abani [1992] Director; Philomena Agnes Abani [1963] Director

Pangaea Laboratories Limited
Incorporated: 7 June 1999 *Employees:* 76
Net Worth: £6,909,211 *Total Assets:* £8,474,315
Registered Office: Berg Kaprow Lewis, 35 Ballards Lane, Finchley, London, N3 1XW
Major Shareholder: Elliot James Isaacs
Officers: Elliot James Isaacs [1971] Director; Owen Richard Lewis [1979] Director; Dean Pearson [1979] Director

Paragon PE Ltd
Incorporated: 18 August 2004 *Employees:* 17
Net Worth: £197,852 *Total Assets:* £467,082
Registered Office: 6-8 Botanic Road, Churchtown, Southport, Merseyside, PR9 7NG
Major Shareholder: Paul Ward
Officers: Paul Ward, Secretary/Chemicals Packing; John Lyndon James [1949] Director; Paul Ward [1968] Director/Chemicals Packing

Paragon Technical PE Services Limited
Incorporated: 20 May 2017
Registered Office: Unit 4-5 Block C Oldgate, St Michaels Industrial Estate, Widnes, Cheshire, WA8 8TL
Major Shareholder: Paul Ward
Officers: Paul Ward [1968] Director

Paramount Chemicals Limited
Incorporated: 20 December 1982
Net Worth: £13,630 *Total Assets:* £69,467
Registered Office: Lydney Industrial Estate, Harbour Road, Lydney, Glos, GL15 4EJ
Major Shareholder: Stephen Paul Greenway
Officers: Jane Greenway, Secretary; Stephen Paul Greenway [1958] Director/General Manager

Paws and Unwind Limited
Incorporated: 25 February 2019
Registered Office: 13 St James Avenue, Bury, Lancs, BL8 1TD
Shareholders: Natasha Klymczuk; Rachel Field
Officers: Rachel Field [1981] Director/Marketing Manager; Natasha Klymczuk [1992] Director/Recruitment Consultant

The Peaceful Potager Limited
Incorporated: 30 January 2019
Registered Office: 39 Victoria Road, Mortimer Common, Reading, Berks, RG7 3SH
Major Shareholder: Elise Anne Fraser
Officers: Dr Elise Anne Fraser [1983] Director/Archaeologist

Peak Soap Ltd
Incorporated: 19 November 2018
Registered Office: 31 Vale Mills, Boyer Street, Derby, DE22 3TE
Major Shareholder: Michael Holloway
Officers: Michael Holloway [1976] Director

Pebble Soap Ltd
Incorporated: 30 November 2017
Registered Office: 37 Highfield Avenue, Grimsby, N E Lincs, DN32 0JG
Shareholders: Talon Patience; Natalia Kalomoiri
Officers: Natalia Kalomoiri [1988] Director [Greek]; Talon Patience [1986] Director

Pembrokeshire Seaweeds Ltd
Incorporated: 12 September 2017
Net Worth: £100 *Total Assets:* £100
Registered Office: 33 Goat Street, St Davids, Haverfordwest, Pembrokeshire, SA62 6RF
Shareholder: John Phares Mansfield
Officers: John Phares Mansfield, Secretary; Julia Horton-Mansfield [1949] Director/Business Owner; John Phares Mansfield [1944] Director/Company Secretary

Perboscolo Ltd
Incorporated: 14 August 2018
Registered Office: 86 Honey Hall Road, Liverpool, L26 1TQ
Major Shareholder: Ian Jones
Officers: Ian Jones [1985] Director/Consultant

PH Direct Limited
Incorporated: 27 July 1998
Net Worth: £141,105 *Total Assets:* £176,810
Registered Office: 25 Breach Road, Denby Village, Derbys, DE5 8PS
Major Shareholder: David John Gribben
Officers: Janet Mary Gribbin, Secretary; David John Gribbin [1948] Director

Piesse and Kinney Limited
Incorporated: 20 October 2011 *Employees:* 2
Net Worth Deficit: £46,653 *Total Assets:* £33,715
Registered Office: The Copper Room, Deva Centre, Trinity Way, Manchester, M3 7BG
Shareholders: Christopher Plant; Francis Henry Shrigley-Feigl
Officers: Christopher Plant [1974] Director; Francis Henry Shrigley-Feigl [1976] Director/Property Management

Pilling Trading Limited
Incorporated: 21 March 2007 *Employees:* 25
Net Worth: £4,314,439 *Total Assets:* £6,115,209
Registered Office: Mallison Street, Bolton, Lancs, BL1 8PP
Officers: Nigel Drinkwater, Secretary; Brandon Pilling [1962] Director; Elizabeth Pilling [1962] Director/HR Manager

Mimi Pisano Limited
Incorporated: 26 April 2005
Registered Office: 64 Green Lane, Imperial Road, Windsor, Berks, SL4 3SA
Officers: Dr Anthony Pisano [1963] Director/Scientist [Italian]

Pluswipes Limited
Incorporated: 12 November 2002 *Employees:* 76
Net Worth: £4,584,373 *Total Assets:* £7,709,593
Registered Office: Pywell Road, Willowbrook East Industrial Estate, Corby, Northants, NN17 5XJ
Parent: Professional Disposables International Ltd
Officers: David Cowell, Secretary; David Cowell [1964] Director/Accountant; Andrew James Culkin [1963] Director; Andrew Thomas Lockley [1968] Sales Director; Michael Alexander Staton [1947] Director; Marten Llewellyn Teasdale Brown [1960] Director

Polka Lab Limited
Incorporated: 5 September 2018
Registered Office: Flat 8a, Bridge Street, Denbigh, LL16 3TF
Major Shareholder: Michalina Elzbieta Piekarska
Officers: Michalina Elzbieta Piekarska [1991] Director/Chemist [Polish]

Poppy Products Limited
Incorporated: 27 February 2018
Registered Office: 495 Kings Road, London, SW10 0TU
Officers: Monika Nouri [1991] Director [Swedish]

Portland Janitorial Products Limited
Incorporated: 10 December 1990
Net Worth: £302,778 *Total Assets:* £567,171
Registered Office: York House, 14 York Street, Ayr, KA8 8AN
Shareholders: Johann Mitchell Kenmuir; Neil Shannon Baird Kenmuir
Officers: Grace Brown Kenmuir, Secretary; Grace Brown Kenmuir [1947] Director; Neil Shannon Baird Kenmuir [1946] Director/Proprietor; Paul Baird Kenmuir [1975] Director

Powerclean Chemicals Limited
Incorporated: 10 March 1988 *Employees:* 10
Net Worth: £707,296 *Total Assets:* £962,367
Registered Office: Eastlands Road Industrial Estate, Leiston, Suffolk, IP16 4LL
Shareholder: Stephen Allan Coulter
Officers: Carole Victoria Anne Phillips, Secretary; Anthony James Matthew Coulter [1980] Director; Daren Russell Stephen Coulter [1971] Director/Sales Coordinator; Graham Leslie Nigel Coulter [1974] Director/Sales Coordinator; Stephen Allan Coulter [1947] Director/Chemical Engineer

The Pretty Little Treat Company (Yorkshire) Ltd
Incorporated: 10 July 2017
Registered Office: 2 Western Street, Barnsley, S Yorks, S70 2BP
Major Shareholder: Victoria Helen Woodger
Officers: Victoria Helen Woodger [1976] Director

Prime Industries Ltd
Incorporated: 15 October 2004 *Employees:* 16
Net Worth: £81,777 *Total Assets:* £1,798,181
Registered Office: 24 St Andrews Place, Llandudno, Conwy, LL30 2YR
Major Shareholder: Roy Longshaw
Officers: Roy Longshaw, Secretary; Stephen Paul Leigh [1967] Operations Director; Roy Longshaw [1967] Director/Wholesaler

Procter & Gamble Product Supply (U.K.) Limited
Incorporated: 27 June 1995 *Employees:* 839
Net Worth: £290,435,008 *Total Assets:* £432,592,992
Registered Office: The Heights, Brooklands, Weybridge, Surrey, KT13 0XP
Parent: Procter & Gamble (Health & Beauty Care) Limited
Officers: Anthony Joseph Appleton, Secretary; Anthony Joseph Appleton [1962] Director/Solicitor; Gianluca Branda [1970] Director/Product Supply Leader [Italian]; Alexander George Buckthorp [1973] Finance Director; Adina Pascu [1971] Director/Plant Manager [Romanian]; Vijay Indroo Sitlani [1975] Finance Director [Singaporean]; Gary Kenneth Wightman [1971] Director/Plant Manager; Christopher John Young [1974] HR Director

Proskin Europe Ltd
Incorporated: 25 February 2016
Net Worth: £29,250 *Total Assets:* £59,762
Registered Office: 2nd Floor, Block H, 286c Chase Road, Southgate Office Village, London, N14 6HF
Shareholder: Rafal Tomasz Krajewski
Officers: Ilona Anna Krajewska [1976] Director [Polish]; Rafal Tomasz Krajewski [1975] Director [Polish]

The Proton Group Limited
Incorporated: 28 January 1971 *Employees:* 23
Net Worth: £1,631,352 *Total Assets:* £2,773,480
Registered Office: Beckbridge Industrial Estate, Normanton, Wakefield, W Yorks, WF6 1QT
Parent: Proton Holdings Ltd
Officers: David Shaw, Secretary; Murray Angus [1955] Managing Director; David Shaw [1952] Finance Director

PRSS Solutions (UK) Limited
Incorporated: 16 June 2004 *Employees:* 8
Net Worth: £84,905 *Total Assets:* £234,443
Registered Office: 10 Lyon Road Industrial Estate, Kearsley, Bolton, Lancs, BL4 8NB
Shareholders: Ashok Chauhan; Elaxi Chauhan; Dhanesh Chauhan
Officers: Ashok Chauhan, Secretary; Elaxi Chauhan [1960] Director

Puddlemud Ltd.
Incorporated: 20 December 2016
Registered Office: 30 Goodwood Mansions, Stockwell Road, London, SW9 0XZ
Major Shareholder: Phillip Ellington
Officers: Phillip Ellington [1955] Director

Pur Natural Soaps Ltd
Incorporated: 12 February 2019
Registered Office: Ty Madog, 32 Queens Road, Aberystwyth, Ceredigion, SY23 2HN
Major Shareholder: Pamela Anne Gray
Officers: Pamela Anne Gray [1963] Director

Purdie's of Argyll Ltd
Incorporated: 31 January 2017
Net Worth: £100 *Total Assets:* £60,500
Registered Office: 6b Main Street West, Inveraray, Argyll & Bute, PA32 8TU
Shareholder: Gavin Ernest Purdie
Officers: Gavin Ernest Purdie [1962] Director

Pure Purpose Cosmetics Ltd
Incorporated: 25 May 2017
Registered Office: 31 Queen Street, Ramsgate, Kent, CT11 9DZ
Major Shareholder: Magdalena Dabrowska
Officers: Magdalena Dabrowska [1974] Director/Owner [Polish]

The Top UK Soap and Detergent Manufacturers

Pure Solve UK Limited
Incorporated: 18 December 1996 *Employees:* 24
Net Worth: £2,767,000 *Total Assets:* £3,395,000
Registered Office: NCH House, Springvale Avenue, Bilston, W Midlands, WV14 0QL
Parent: CPS Industries Limited
Officers: Martyn Jeffrey Ruscoe, Secretary; Richard Bastable [1973] Director/Operations Manager; John Leslie Currie [1955] Director/VP Finance & Global Controller [American]

Purealba Limited
Incorporated: 21 February 2019
Registered Office: No 1 Dressertland Cottages, Closeburn, Thornhill, Dumfries & Galloway, DG3 5HG
Major Shareholder: Tracy Barber
Officers: Stuart Barber [1971] Director

Quill International Chemicals Limited
Incorporated: 6 October 2000 *Employees:* 16
Net Worth: £191,447 *Total Assets:* £719,551
Registered Office: Unit 9 Melbourne Industrial Estate, Castle Lane, Melbourne, Derbys, DE73 8JB
Major Shareholder: Nicholas David James Dore
Officers: Nicholas David James Dore [1974] Director/Production Manager

Quill International Group Limited
Incorporated: 5 October 1976 *Employees:* 24
Net Worth: £1,060,436 *Total Assets:* £1,970,767
Registered Office: Unit 1 Castle Lane, Melbourne, Derbys, DE73 8JB
Major Shareholder: David James Dore
Officers: Susan Yvonne Dore, Secretary; David James Dore [1946] Managing Director; Susan Yvonne Dore [1947] Director/Lecturer

The Quint Essence Lab Ltd
Incorporated: 13 February 2019
Registered Office: Hova House, 1 Hova Villas, Hove, E Sussex, BN3 3DH
Shareholders: Agnes Renata Majoros; Attila Varro
Officers: Agnes Renata Majoros [1978] Director [Hungarian]; Attila Varro [1959] Director [Hungarian]

R & T Natural Cosmetics Limited
Incorporated: 31 December 2018
Registered Office: Kemp House, 160 City Road, London, EC1V 2NX
Major Shareholder: Rose Etim-Ibom
Officers: Rose Etim-Ibom, Secretary; Rose Etim-Ibom [1973] Director/Teacher; Tracy Ibom [2002] Director/Student

R-MC Power Recovery Limited
Incorporated: 23 November 2001 *Employees:* 5
Net Worth: £416,596 *Total Assets:* £544,903
Registered Office: 6 Stamford Business Park, Ryhall Road, Stamford, Lincs, PE9 1XT
Major Shareholder: Jonathon Michael O'Donnell
Officers: Jonathon Micheal O'Donnell, Secretary/Chief Executive [Irish]; Paul Lambart [1962] Managing Director; Jonathon Micheal O'Donnell [1967] Director/Chief Executive [Irish]

Rapid Washrooms Limited
Incorporated: 19 May 2016 *Employees:* 4
Net Worth: £81,662 *Total Assets:* £142,476
Registered Office: 2 Relay Road, Waterlooville, Hants, PO7 7XA
Officers: Ian Mark Gregory [1971] Director; Edward George Lymn [1980] Design Director

RBL Laboratories Ltd
Incorporated: 6 October 2015
Net Worth Deficit: £29,422 *Total Assets:* £38,309
Registered Office: 54 Bootham, York, YO30 7XZ
Shareholders: Paul Leon Handy; Chris Handy
Officers: Christopher Handy [1966] Director; Paul Leon Handy [1960] Director/Bricklayer/Builder

Red Cottage Industries Ltd
Incorporated: 12 June 2018
Registered Office: 1 Clay Lane, South Nutfield, Redhill, Surrey, RH1 4EG
Major Shareholder: Hannelore Hartmann
Officers: Hannelore Hartmann [1977] Director/Soap Maker

Reesoaps.co.uk Ltd
Incorporated: 18 December 2018
Registered Office: 13a Heath Gap Road, Cannock, Staffs, WS11 6DY
Major Shareholder: Marie Ann Williams
Officers: Marie Ann Williams [1968] Director and Company Secretary

Refresh Tea & Soap Co. Ltd.
Incorporated: 19 June 2018
Registered Office: P O Box 49, 78 Golders Green Road, London, NW11 8LN
Major Shareholder: Ashley Joan Fleischer
Officers: Ashley Joan Fleischer [1980] Director [Canadian]

Relax Candle and Bath Company Limited
Incorporated: 21 February 2018
Registered Office: Usher Spiby & Co, Manchester Road, Denton, Manchester, M34 3PS
Major Shareholder: Jacqueline Ann Gilluley
Officers: Jacqueline Ann Gilluley [1966] Director

Renbow Haircare Limited
Incorporated: 27 May 2009
Registered Office: Unit 3 Newmains Avenue, Inchinnan Business Park, Renfrew, PA4 9RR
Officers: Brian Aitken, Secretary; Stephen James MacDonogh [1962] Director

Residual Barrier Technology Limited
Incorporated: 3 September 2009 *Employees:* 8
Net Worth: £674,653 *Total Assets:* £841,910
Registered Office: The Die Pat Centre, Broad March, Daventry, Northants, NN11 4HE
Shareholder: Christine Linda Brander
Officers: Christine Linda Brander [1957] Director; Stuart John Gleghorn [1952] Director/Engineer; David Dennis McIntosh [1963] Director; Nicholas Alistair Swan [1960] Director

Respect Soaps Limited
Incorporated: 5 November 2018
Registered Office: 28 Bentinck Road, Fairfield, Stockton on Tees, Cleveland, TS19 7QB
Shareholders: Sandra Richardson; Geoffrey Leslie Hall
Officers: Sandra Richardson [1965] Director

Revert Limited
Incorporated: 16 January 2002 *Employees:* 14
Net Worth: £356,718 *Total Assets:* £669,704
Registered Office: Unit 1 Rhodes Court, South Nelson Road Industrial Estate, Cramlington, Northumberland, NE23 1WF
Officers: Joseph Mark Hugill, Secretary; Joseph Mark Hugill [1973] Director; Kieron Patrick Knight [1970] Director/Engineer

The Rite Solution Limited
Incorporated: 15 April 1994
Registered Office: Hillside, Sewell, Dunstable, Beds, LU6 1RP
Shareholders: Luke Michael Burton; Andrea Burton; Ian Anthony Burton
Officers: Andrea Burton, Secretary; Andrea Burton [1950] Director/Insight & Research Consultant; Ian Anthony Burton [1948] Managing Director; Luke Michael Burton [1990] Director/Chemical Development & Production Manager

Roots & Paradise Ltd
Incorporated: 29 June 2018
Registered Office: 84a Sandringham Road, London, E8 2LL
Major Shareholder: Keisha Chanel Destang
Officers: Keisha Chanel Destang [1995] Director

Rowanhays Ltd
Incorporated: 27 May 2014
Registered Office: 29 Station Road, Budleigh Salterton, Devon, EX9 6RW
Officers: Daphne Veronica Williams [1949] Director/Cottage Industry

Royal Sanders (UK) Limited
Incorporated: 19 September 2008 *Employees:* 119
Net Worth: £3,750,000 *Total Assets:* £10,738,000
Registered Office: Unit A4, Red Scar Industrial Estate, Longridge Road, Ribbleton, Preston, Lancs, PR2 5NA
Parent: UKPC B.V.
Officers: Mark Christiaan de Lange [1967] Finance Director [Dutch]; Bart Otger Hullegie [1971] Director [Dutch]; Gavin Patrick McNally [1962] Managing Director

Rural Skills Centre Limited
Incorporated: 4 January 2018
Registered Office: New Park Farm, Penylan Road, Castleton, Cardiff, CF3 2UR
Shareholders: Gillian Lavinia Jones; Kate Harriet Jones
Officers: Dr Gillian Lavinia Jones [1955] Director; Kate Harriet Jones [1980] Director

Rustic Blends Limited
Incorporated: 19 June 2017
Registered Office: 27 Old Gloucester Street, London, WC1N 3AX
Shareholder: Remecae Gordon
Officers: Remecae Gordon [1982] Director/Entrepreneur

Rutherford Bambury Ltd
Incorporated: 12 June 2018
Registered Office: Coachwerks, 19 Hollingdean Terrace, Brighton, BN1 7HB
Officers: Jasmine Bambury [1988] Director/Brand Owner/Manager/Manufacturer/Care Worker

Rutpen Limited
Incorporated: 6 October 1993 *Employees:* 40
Net Worth: £4,628,269 *Total Assets:* £5,982,748
Registered Office: Membury Airfield, Lambourn, Berks, RG17 7TJ
Parent: Rutpen Holdings Limited
Officers: Kevin David Whittle, Secretary; Stuart Emmett [1977] Director/Works Manager; David Thomas Roberts [1966] Director/Technical; Richard Terence Tripp [1955] Director/Chemical Manufacturer; David George Wheeler [1961] Sales Director; Kevin David Whittle [1959] Director

Saanro International Limited
Incorporated: 2 September 1997
Net Worth: £124,869 *Total Assets:* £243,597
Registered Office: Unit 3 Taylor Court, Carrs Industrial Estate, Haslingden, Rossendale, Lancs, BB4 5LA
Shareholder: Lee Daryl Murray
Officers: Deborah Michelle Murray, Secretary; Lee Daryl Murray [1966] Managing Director

Safe Solutions (Safe4) Limited
Incorporated: 18 March 2004 *Employees:* 10
Net Worth: £398,754 *Total Assets:* £864,871
Registered Office: Wharton Green, Bostock Road, Winsford, Cheshire, CW7 3BD
Officers: Allan David Stockwin, Secretary/Director; Alan Robert Dudley [1960] Director; John Rochford [1959] Director; Allan David Stockwin [1947] Director

Safeway Wood Care Limited
Incorporated: 26 January 2018
Registered Office: 71-75 Shelton Street, Covent Garden, London, WC2H 9JQ
Major Shareholder: Alexander Levy
Officers: Alexander Levy, Secretary; Alexander Levy [1985] Director/Production Manager

Salopian Ltd
Incorporated: 10 July 2017
Registered Office: 15 Harlescott Barns, Harlescott Lane, Shrewsbury, Salop, SY1 3SZ
Shareholders: Jorg Alexander Richard Muschner; Jenny Muschner
Officers: Jenny Muschner [1966] Director; Jorg Alexander Richard Muschner [1962] Director

Saltaire Soap Ltd
Incorporated: 25 May 2017
Registered Office: Q20 Theatre, Creative Arts Hub, Dockfield Road, Shipley, W Yorks, BD17 7AD
Officers: Fiona Smith [1981] Director/Soap Maker

Samola Industries Limited
Incorporated: 8 May 2017
Registered Office: 103 Harts Lane, 51 Colne Colne, Barking, Essex, IG11 8LT
Major Shareholder: Adeyinka Samuel Oladejo
Officers: Adeyinka Samuel Oladejo [1976] Director/Procurement Administrator

Sani Professional Limited
Incorporated: 15 February 2017
Registered Office: Pywell Road, Willowbrook East Industrial Estate, Corby, Northants, NN17 5XJ
Parent: Pluswipes Limited
Officers: Andrew Thomas Lockley [1968] Director; Marten Llewellyn Teasdale-Brown [1960] Director

Sankofa Heritage Ltd
Incorporated: 3 October 2017
Registered Office: 24 Anderson Heights, 1260 London Road, Norbury, London, SW16 4EH
Major Shareholder: Rebecca Bonsu-Stewart
Officers: Rebecca Bonsu-Stewart [1973] Director/Teacher [Ghanaian]

Sanofi International Biotech Company Ltd.
Incorporated: 8 May 2017
Registered Office: 3/3, 4 Firpark Close, Glasgow, G31 2HQ
Officers: Zhanhong HE [1992] Director/Manager [Chinese]

The Top UK Soap and Detergent Manufacturers

SAS Environmental Services Ltd
Incorporated: 28 November 2002 *Employees:* 3
Previous: Aboleo Ltd.
Net Worth: £13,722 *Total Assets:* £65,918
Registered Office: 9 Caputhall Road, Deans Industrial Estate, Deans, Livingston, W Lothian, EH54 8AS
Shareholders: Mark Zwinderman; John Wyndham Fowler Harrison
Officers: Mark Zwinderman, Secretary/Environmental Scientist; John Wyndham Fowler Harrison [1972] Director/Scientist; Mark Zwinderman [1973] Director/Engineer

Savage Alchemy Limited
Incorporated: 3 January 2018
Net Worth Deficit: £7,462 *Total Assets:* £2,436
Registered Office: Ossington Chambers, 6-8 Castle Gate, Newark, Notts, NG24 1AX
Major Shareholder: Adam Watson
Officers: Adam Watson, Secretary; Adam Watson [1990] Director/Self Employed

Savon de V Ltd
Incorporated: 6 November 2017
Registered Office: Meriton Foundry, Meriton Street, Bristol, BS2 0SZ
Major Shareholder: Veronika Korytakova
Officers: Veronika Korytakova [1981] Director [Czech]

Savon Paradis Ltd
Incorporated: 4 December 2015
Registered Office: 70 Admiralty Street, Keyham, Plymouth, PL2 2BS
Major Shareholder: Lee Richard Duke
Officers: Lee Richard Duke [1972] Director/Teacher

SC Johnson Professional Limited
Incorporated: 2 January 1941 *Employees:* 197
Previous: Deb Limited
Net Worth: £33,252,000 *Total Assets:* £62,328,000
Registered Office: Denby Hall Way, Denby, Ripley, Derbys, DE5 8JZ
Parent: Deb Holdings Limited
Officers: Nadia Patricia Estrada [1976] Director/Chief Financial Officer [American]; Nicholas Noel Hardwick Matterson [1963] Director/Lawyer

SC567361 Ltd.
Incorporated: 31 May 2017
Registered Office: 22-6, 2 Taylor Place, Glasgow, G4 0PA
Major Shareholder: Meiling Chen
Officers: Meiling Chen [1994] Director/Manager [Chinese]

Scent By Hand Ltd
Incorporated: 6 October 2017
Registered Office: Unit 98 Cariocca Business Park, 2 Hellidon Close, Ardwick, Manchester, M12 4AH
Major Shareholder: Christine Bradley
Officers: Christine Bradley [1978] Director/Artisan Soap Manufacturer

Scinn Limited
Incorporated: 1 November 2017
Registered Office: 2a Rowborn Drive, Oughtibridge, Sheffield, S35 0JR
Major Shareholder: Sarah Kay Middleton
Officers: Sarah Kay Middleton [1966] Director/Retired

Scorcher Idea Limited
Incorporated: 27 November 2002
Previous: Newmarket Technologies Limited
Net Worth Deficit: £437,000 *Total Assets:* £419,000
Registered Office: Unit 1b Lynx Business Park, Fordham Road, Snailwell, Newmarket, Cambs, CB8 7NY
Parent: Tristel PLC
Officers: Elizabeth Amanda Dixon [1970] Director; Paul Christopher Swinney [1957] Director

Scottish Fine Soaps Limited
Incorporated: 28 September 1960 *Employees:* 47
Net Worth: £1,900,832 *Total Assets:* £3,429,628
Registered Office: 5th Floor, Condor House, 10 St Paul's Churchyard, London, EC4M 8AL
Parent: Alexander Ross Management Services Limited
Officers: Derek Blair Ross [1942] Chairman and Director; Robert Collumbine Ross [1971] Director; Thomas Agnew Hamilton Slater [1956] Director/ACMA; William Brown Wilson [1961] Director

SE & SA Limited
Incorporated: 5 April 2017
Registered Office: 245 Sherrard Road, London, E12 6UG
Shareholders: Fulya Salur; Gizem Ezgi Senturk
Officers: Fulya Salur [1983] Director/Sales [Turkish]; Gizem Ezgi Senturk [1985] Director/Finance [Turkish]

Seadpearl Ltd
Incorporated: 20 August 2018
Registered Office: Suite 4, 43 Hagley Road, Stourbridge, W Midlands, DY8 1QR
Major Shareholder: Paula Rowe
Officers: Brenda Balendres [1980] Director [Filipino]

Season Clean Ltd
Incorporated: 17 September 2018
Registered Office: 18 Haygrove Close, Warminster, Wilts, BA12 8SL
Major Shareholder: Rebecca Jane Stadward
Officers: Rebecca Jane Stadward [1985] Director/Chief Executive Officer

Sechelle Manufacturing Limited
Incorporated: 27 November 1997 *Employees:* 16
Net Worth: £541,546 *Total Assets:* £1,929,081
Registered Office: Unit 18 Uplands Business Park, Blackhorse Lane, London, E17 5QJ
Shareholders: Kevin Halesworth; Stephen Roger Taylor; Sechelle Investments Limited; Sechelle Investments Limited
Officers: Deborah Taylor, Secretary; Kevin Halesworth [1966] Director Manager; Stephen Roger Taylor [1968] Director

Seilich Limited
Incorporated: 12 November 2018
Registered Office: 7 Tyneholm Cottages, Pencaitland, Tranent, E Lothian, EH34 5AD
Major Shareholder: Sally Gouldstone
Officers: Dr Sally Gouldstone [1980] Director/Botanist

Selden Research Limited
Incorporated: 10 July 1970 *Employees:* 203
Net Worth: £12,177,326 *Total Assets:* £19,214,784
Registered Office: Staden Business Park, Staden Lane, Buxton, Derbys, SK17 9RZ
Shareholders: Sandra Buchanan Woodhead; Denis Edwin Woodhead
Officers: Sandra Buchanan Woodhead, Secretary; David Alexander Woodhead [1967] Works Director; Denis Edwin Woodhead [1937] Director Industrial Chemist; Mark Andrew Woodhead [1963] Sales Director; Peter Philip Woodhead [1975] Technical Director; Sandra Buchanan Woodhead [1942] Director Secretary

Serchem Limited
Incorporated: 30 March 1981 *Employees:* 17
Net Worth: £1,570,259 *Total Assets:* £1,953,030
Registered Office: Arleston, Alleston Village, Wellington, Telford, Salop, TF1 2LY
Shareholders: Alison June Arnold; Andrew John Arnold
Officers: Alison Jane Arnold, Secretary; Andrew John Arnold, Secretary; Andrew John Arnold [1958] Director/Production Manager; Elizabeth Amelia Arnold [1930] Director; Paul David Arnold [1966] Director/Sales Manager

Seren Soaps Limited
Incorporated: 18 October 2016
Net Worth Deficit: £1,042 *Total Assets:* £4,721
Registered Office: 27 Park Place, Brynmill, Swansea, SA2 0DJ
Shareholders: Gareth David Llewellyn Williams; Jillian Llewellyn Williams
Officers: Dr Jillian Llewellyn Williams, Secretary; Gareth David Llewellyn Williams [1953] Director/Retired; Dr Jillian Llewellyn Williams [1955] Director/University Lecturer

Sevin London Limited
Incorporated: 19 January 2016
Net Worth Deficit: £45,225 *Total Assets:* £29,075
Registered Office: 58 Alexandra Road, London, SW19 7LB
Major Shareholder: Sevin Ersin
Officers: Sevin Ersin [1978] Director/Fashion Consultant

SGHP Ltd
Incorporated: 30 October 2017
Registered Office: Kemp House, 152-160 City Road, London, EC1V 2NX
Major Shareholder: Sabrina Sonia Hernandez Guaitolini
Officers: Sabrina Sonia Hernandez Guaitolini [1986] Director [Spanish]

Shea Life Limited
Incorporated: 11 May 2012
Registered Office: 111 Hopton Road, Lambeth, London, SW16 2EL
Major Shareholder: Nana Yaw Djin
Officers: Nana Djin [1971] Director

Sheabynature Ltd
Incorporated: 14 March 2017
Net Worth Deficit: £7,000 *Total Assets:* £4,000
Registered Office: 4 Victorian Crescent, Doncaster, S Yorks, DN2 5BW
Major Shareholder: Chinwe Mercy Russell
Officers: Chinwe Mercy Russell [1970] Director

Sheer Bliss Retail Ltd
Incorporated: 30 October 2018
Registered Office: 38 Benbow Road, Clydebank, W Dunbartonshire, G81 4DP
Officers: Alan Campbell [1993] Director/Administrator; Mark Alexander Tait [1990] Director

Shifting London Ltd
Incorporated: 15 November 2018
Registered Office: 22 Queen Street, Gravesend, Kent, DA12 2EE
Major Shareholder: Angelo Mancuso
Officers: Angelo Mancuso [1961] Director [Italian]

Shinerite Solutions Limited
Incorporated: 12 March 2018
Registered Office: 19 Greenhill Road, Ardmore, Brookeborough, Co Fermanagh, BT94 4EF
Shareholders: Darren Johnston McCormick; George Robert Coulter
Officers: Darren Johnston McCormick, Secretary; George Robert Coulter [1996] Director; Darren Johnston McCormick [1978] Director

Shorrock Trichem Limited
Incorporated: 14 March 2001 *Employees:* 277
Net Worth: £9,309,733 *Total Assets:* £16,001,280
Registered Office: Chanters Industrial Estate, Atherton, Manchester, M46 9SD
Shareholder: Keith Entwistle Shorrock
Officers: Joel Howard Lewis, Secretary; David Paul Allison [1964] Technical Director; Caron Michelle Darlington [1966] Director; Malcolm Denning [1939] Director; Ian James Eckersley [1959] Managing Director; Duncan Fishwick [1966] Sales Director; Joel Howard Lewis [1941] Managing Director; David Lee Oliver [1976] Finance Director; Keith Entwistle Shorrock [1936] Director

The Shrieking Soap Shack Limited
Incorporated: 13 November 2017
Registered Office: 208 High Street, Upton, Northampton, NN5 4FQ
Major Shareholder: Aimee Sarah Barker
Officers: Aimee Sarah Barker [1983] Director

Sikania Ltd
Incorporated: 26 January 2017
Net Worth: £357 *Total Assets:* £1,447
Registered Office: 50 Mayfield Road, Gosport, Hants, PO12 1RA
Major Shareholder: Consolazione Ranno
Officers: Consolazione Ranno [1979] Director/Chemist [Italian]

Silk Detergent Limited
Incorporated: 12 December 2016
Net Worth Deficit: £39,296 *Total Assets:* £500,256
Registered Office: Asco House, 3-4 Helions Bumpstead Road, Haverhill, Suffolk, CB9 7AA
Officers: Kemal Ipek [1977] Director; Rustem Ozdemir [1977] Director

Simply Ewe Limited
Incorporated: 10 April 2017
Net Worth Deficit: £331 *Total Assets:* £69
Registered Office: 5 Targetts Mead, Tisbury, Salisbury, Wilts, SP3 6SR
Major Shareholder: Clare Brunton
Officers: Clare Brunton [1983] Director

Sisi Cosmetics Ltd
Incorporated: 7 August 2017
Registered Office: 6/2 Wardlaw Place, Edinburgh, EH11 1UB
Major Shareholder: Stellah Linda Chonzi
Officers: Stellah Linda Chonzi [1994] Director/Entrepreneur

SKC Resources Ltd
Incorporated: 26 September 2012
Registered Office: 13 Great Gates Close, Rochdale, Lancs, OL11 2HW
Shareholder: Saima Chowdhary
Officers: Parveen Chowdhary, Secretary; Saima Chowdhary [1984] Director

Smartic Truckwash Ltd
Incorporated: 9 September 1998
Registered Office: Ricketts Close, Firs Industrial Estate, Kidderminster, Worcs, DY11 7QN
Major Shareholder: Neil William Munro
Officers: Neil William Munro, Secretary; Neil William Munro [1971] Director/Chemical Engineer; William Donald Munro [1939] Director

Smellifiscent Ltd
Incorporated: 19 September 2017
Registered Office: 29 Kings Close, Lazenby Village, Middlesbrough, Cleveland, TS6 8FA
Major Shareholder: Lisa Swithenbank
Officers: Lisa Swithenbank [1983] Director/Owner

Smelliz Ltd
Incorporated: 15 February 2019
Registered Office: 2 Factory Way, Chorley, Lancs, PR7 3FH
Shareholders: Sarah Christina Stewart; Emma Jayne Lewis
Officers: Emma Jayne Lewis [1998] Managing Director; Sarah Christina Stewart [1987] Managing Director

So.Soap Company Limited
Incorporated: 5 October 2015
Net Worth Deficit: £5,571 *Total Assets:* £720
Registered Office: 18 Boscombe Avenue, Heysham, Morecambe, Lancs, LA3 1LW
Shareholders: Patricia Ann Spence; Ian Dale Benham Spence
Officers: Patricia Ann Spence, Secretary; Ian Dale Benham Spence [1959] Director/Information Security Consultant; Patricia Ann Spence [1951] Director/Therapist

Soap & Soak Limited
Incorporated: 22 December 2014
Registered Office: Suite 11050, Chynoweth House, Trevissome Park, Truro, Cornwall, TR4 8UN
Officers: Sojia Khatun, Secretary; Dean Alvin Hubbins [1979] Director/Video Editor; Luke Hubbins [1991] Director/Electrician; Sojia Khatun [1981] Director/Carer; Kerry Stokes [1993] Director/Entrepreneur

The Soap Arcade Limited
Incorporated: 13 May 2013
Registered Office: Basford House, 29 Augusta Street, Llandudno, Conwy, LL30 2AE
Major Shareholder: Beatrice Emma Williams
Officers: Beatrice Emma Williams [1959] Director/Soap Maker

The Soap Cellar Limited
Incorporated: 11 July 2016
Registered Office: 9 South Town, Dartmouth, Devon, TQ6 9BX
Major Shareholder: Daniel Khoo
Officers: Daniel Khoo, Secretary; Daniel Khoo [1980] Director [Malaysian]

The Soap Collection Limited
Incorporated: 26 February 2019
Registered Office: 68 Pensfield Park, Bristol, BS10 6LD
Officers: Victoria Coleman [1977] Director/WW Wellness Coach; Kate Wilde [1981] Director/Administration

The Soap Foundry Limited
Incorporated: 5 February 2019
Registered Office: 19 Florence Street, Lincoln, LN2 5LR
Major Shareholder: Benjamin Charles Lewis Mills
Officers: Benjamin Charles Lewis Mills [1987] Director/Soap Maker

Soap Lab Limited
Incorporated: 29 November 2017
Registered Office: 25 East Cliff, Folkestone, Kent, CT19 6BU
Officers: Timea Tothova [1983] Director/Nanny [Slovak]

The Soap Legacy Ltd
Incorporated: 15 May 2018
Registered Office: 40c Preston New Road, Blackburn, BB2 6AH
Shareholders: Muhammad Mobeen-Ul-Anwar Ismail; Husnabanu Patel
Officers: Muhammad Mobeen-Ul-Anwar Ismail [1987] Director; Husnabanu Patel [1982] Director

The Soap People Ltd
Incorporated: 2 October 2018
Registered Office: Chapel Grange, Chapel Lane, East Chiltington, Lewes, E Sussex, BN7 3BA
Major Shareholder: Helen Louise Munier
Officers: Helen Louise Munier, Secretary; Helen Louise Munier [1974] Director/Graphic Designer

Soap School Ltd
Incorporated: 22 February 2013
Net Worth: £32,533 *Total Assets:* £40,194
Registered Office: 20 The Grove, Fartown, Huddersfield, W Yorks, HD2 1BL
Officers: Shawn Dritz [1969] Director/Soap Maker [American]; Sarah Jane Janes [1965] Director/Soap Maker

Soap Sensations Ltd
Incorporated: 15 October 2018
Registered Office: 10 New Road, Blackwater, Camberley, Surrey, GU17 9AY
Major Shareholder: Rachel Isabella Sinclair
Officers: Rachel Isabella Sinclair [1966] Director

The Soap Shop Ltd
Incorporated: 13 September 2013 *Employees:* 3
Net Worth: £93,505 *Total Assets:* £123,931
Registered Office: 960 Capability Green, Luton, Beds, LU1 3PE
Major Shareholder: Faye Rogerson
Officers: Faye Rogerson [1984] Managing Director

The Soap Souk Ltd
Incorporated: 23 August 2017
Net Worth Deficit: £602 *Total Assets:* £370
Registered Office: 41 Quinton Road, Coventry, Warwicks, CV3 5FE
Major Shareholder: Marria Jeena
Officers: Marria Jeena [1992] Director/Accountant

The Soap Story Limited
Incorporated: 14 February 2017
Net Worth: £20,307 *Total Assets:* £108,590
Registered Office: Number One, Lanyon Quay, Belfast, BT1 3LG
Shareholders: William Banks Waring; Simon Banks Waring
Officers: William Banks Waring, Secretary; Simon Banks Waring [1975] Director; William Banks Waring [1950] Director

Soapaffection Ltd
Incorporated: 19 July 2018
Registered Office: 28 Snowman House, Abbey Road, London, NW6 4DN
Major Shareholder: Cecilia Monika Jenny Lindberg
Officers: Cecilia Monika Jenny Lindberg [1965] Director/Soap Manufacturer [Swedish]

Soapberries Ltd
Incorporated: 25 April 2018
Registered Office: 20-22 Wenlock Road, London, N1 7GU
Shareholders: Valerie Anne Humphrey; Sophie Louise Humphrey
Officers: Sophie Louise Humphrey [1996] Marketing Director; Valerie Anne Humphrey [1963] Director

Soapnsoak Limited
Incorporated: 22 December 2014
Registered Office: Suite 11050, Chynoweth House, Trevissome Park, Truro, Cornwall, TR4 8UN
Officers: Sojia Khatun, Secretary; Dean Alvin Hubbins [1979] Director/Video Editor; Sojia Khatun [1981] Director/Carer

Soaps By Stacey Limited
Incorporated: 5 November 2018
Registered Office: 103 Harcourt Way, Northampton, NN4 8JR
Officers: Stacey Jamie Palmer [1988] Director

Soapsmith Limited
Incorporated: 28 September 2010 *Employees:* 4
Net Worth Deficit: £66,144 *Total Assets:* £25,275
Registered Office: Unit 2 Clockworks, 656 Forest Road, London, E17 3ED
Major Shareholder: Samantha Miranda Jameson
Officers: Samantha Miranda Jameson [1976] Director

Soapworks Limited
Incorporated: 5 November 2010 *Employees:* 88
Net Worth: £443,957 *Total Assets:* £3,110,872
Registered Office: Soapworks Ltd, Units 2-11, Block 8, Coltness Street, Glasgow, G33 4JD
Officers: Manuel Julian Davila [1964] Director [Colombian]; Jeroen Douglas [1964] Director [Dutch]; Astrid Duque [1970] Director; Stuart Seddon [1975] Finance Director

The Soapy Goat Ltd
Incorporated: 16 August 2017
Registered Office: Elegance Natural Skin Care, Greenbank Business Park, Bradeley Green, Whitchurch, Salop, SY13 4HD
Officers: Hazel Margaret Beddows [1964] Director; Gemma Rita McCrystal Edge [1986] Director

Soapy Skin Limited
Incorporated: 18 April 2013
Net Worth Deficit: £22,049 *Total Assets:* £13,866
Registered Office: 1 Springwater Close, Bolton, Lancs, BL2 4NT
Shareholders: David Gordon Shorrocks; Janet Marie Shorrocks
Officers: Janet Shorrocks, Secretary; Janet Marie Shorrocks [1968] Director

Soul of Ayurveda Ltd
Incorporated: 10 September 2018
Registered Office: 40 Hay Close, London, E15 4HN
Major Shareholder: Shahishtaanjum Irfan Shaikh
Officers: Shahishtaanjum Irfan Shaikh [1986] Director

Spa Mommy Limited
Incorporated: 27 December 2018
Registered Office: 75 Stanley Street, Bedford, MK41 7RX
Major Shareholder: Natasha Botha
Officers: Natasha Botha [1984] Director

Spartisan Ltd
Incorporated: 30 April 2012
Net Worth Deficit: £6,395 *Total Assets:* £2,853
Registered Office: Hineswood Farm, Dane in Shaw, Congleton, Cheshire, CW12 3PJ
Major Shareholder: Anna Vyacheslavovna Birtles
Officers: Anna Vyacheslavovna Birtles [1972] Director

Specialised Aerosols Company Limited
Incorporated: 31 May 1977 *Employees:* 9
Net Worth: £664,577 *Total Assets:* £837,709
Registered Office: Carr Green Lane, Mapplewell, Barnsley, S Yorks, S75 6DY
Major Shareholder: Noel Heeley Lucas
Officers: Marene Lucas, Secretary; John Stephen Lucas [1956] Director/Chemical Manufacturer; Kevin Paul Lucas [1958] Director/Sales Assistant; Marene Lucas [1936] Director/Secretary; Noel Heeley Lucas [1935] Director/Chemical Manufacturer

Spectrum Industrial Limited
Incorporated: 11 June 1976 *Employees:* 11
Net Worth: £1,082,197 *Total Assets:* £1,240,598
Registered Office: 19-24 Bedesway, Bede Industrial Estate, Jarrow, Tyne & Wear, NE32 3EG
Shareholder: Wayne Evan Carr
Officers: Margaret Rose Carr, Secretary; Dean Alexander Carr [1961] Director/Print Manager; Harry James Carr [1936] Director; Margaret Rose Carr [1939] Director; Wayne Evan Carr [1968] Director/Works Manager

Spirit of The Isle Ltd.
Incorporated: 26 February 2013
Net Worth Deficit: £14,488 *Total Assets:* £14,584
Registered Office: Penrhiw Bach, Bryngwran, Holyhead, Anglesey, LL65 3RD
Officers: Nia Jones [1967] Director/Housewife; Tony Wyn Jones [1962] Director/Local Government Officer

Spiritual Cleanse Ltd
Incorporated: 28 June 2018
Registered Office: Flat 12, 147 Cromwell Road, London, SW7 4DW
Major Shareholder: Mica Grace Lillian Hamilton
Officers: Mica Grace Lillian Hamilton [1990] Director/Community Worker

Splosh Limited
Incorporated: 23 January 2009 *Employees:* 1
Net Worth Deficit: £581,640 *Total Assets:* £89,054
Registered Office: Pavement House, The Pavement, Hay on Wye, Hereford, HR3 5BU
Major Shareholder: Angus Robert Grahame
Officers: Corisande Albert, Secretary; Angus Robert Grahame [1965] Director

Springdawn Bolton Limited
Incorporated: 3 April 2007 *Employees:* 54
Net Worth: £2,204,736 *Total Assets:* £3,214,154
Registered Office: Mallison Street, Bolton, Lancs, BL1 8PP
Shareholders: Heinrich Gerhard Kurt Beckmann; Johann Gerhard Krauss
Officers: Nigel Drinkwater, Secretary; Heiner Kurt Beckmann [1947] Director/General Manager [German]; Nils Beckmann [1983] Director/Managing Partner [German]; Gareth William James Edwards [1958] Managing Director; Johann Gerhard Krauss [1961] Director/General Manager [German]; Brandon Pilling [1962] Director

The Top UK Soap and Detergent Manufacturers

The Springer Soap Company Ltd
Incorporated: 27 March 2018
Registered Office: 87 Mirabelle Way, Harworth, Doncaster, S Yorks, DN11 8SQ
Major Shareholder: Olga Day
Officers: Olga Day [1985] Managing Director [Latvian]

St Andrews Soap Co Ltd
Incorporated: 25 January 2019
Registered Office: Unit 3 Queensway Business Units, 28 Flemington Road, Glenrothes, Fife, KY7 5QF
Shareholders: Barbara Ann Robertson; Brian Scott Robertson
Officers: Barbara Ann Robertson [1973] Director

Star Brands (Holdings) Limited
Incorporated: 17 June 2004 *Employees:* 107
Net Worth: £2,458,500 *Total Assets:* £10,583,399
Registered Office: Unit E, Millshaw Business Living, Global Avenue, Leeds, LS11 8PR
Shareholders: Andrew Micklethwaite; Timothy Robertshaw
Officers: Diane Margaret Siddall, Secretary/Manufacturer of Cleaning Products; Andrew Micklethwaite [1959] Director; Philip Graham Siddall [1966] Director/Manufacturer of Cleaning Products

Star Brands Limited
Incorporated: 19 March 2001 *Employees:* 96
Net Worth: £2,247,359 *Total Assets:* £10,309,552
Registered Office: Unit E, Millshaw Living, Global Avenue, Leeds, LS11 8PR
Parent: Star Brands Holdings Ltd
Officers: Diane Margaret Siddall, Secretary/Manufacturer of Cleaning Products; Philip Graham Siddall [1966] Director/Manufacturer of Cleaning Products

Stepan UK Limited
Incorporated: 17 October 1996 *Employees:* 116
Net Worth: £26,791,000 *Total Assets:* £51,685,000
Registered Office: Bridge House, Bridge Street, Stalybridge, Cheshire, SK15 1PH
Parent: Stepan Europe S.A
Officers: Stephen David Smales, Secretary; Wojciech Mazurek [1966] Director [Polish]; Didier Ray [1962] Commercial Director [French]; Stephen David Smales [1974] Director/Accountant

Stephenson Group Ltd
Incorporated: 21 December 1900 *Employees:* 84
Net Worth: £2,225,355 *Total Assets:* £9,778,523
Registered Office: Brookfoot House, Low Lane, Horsforth, Leeds, LS18 5PU
Parent: Thos. Bentley & Son Limited
Officers: Thomas James MacAulay Bentley [1971] Director; Thomas Richard Bentley [1943] Director/Chairman; Robert Leo Carr [1973] Operations Director; James Aaron Clews [1988] Sales & Marketing Director; Lisa Flannery [1965] Finance Director; John Michael Story [1963] Managing Director

Steri-7 Brazil Limited
Incorporated: 9 April 2014
Registered Office: 34 Baron Grove, Mitcham, Surrey, CR4 4EH
Major Shareholder: James Thomas Fraser
Officers: James Thomas Fraser [1954] Director

Steri-7 Worldwide Limited
Incorporated: 19 September 2006
Net Worth: £400,000 *Total Assets:* £400,000
Registered Office: 34 Baron Grove, Mitcham, Surrey, CR4 4EH
Major Shareholder: James Thomas Fraser
Officers: Mark Raymond Dyer, Secretary; James Thomas Fraser [1954] Director

Stockcare Limited
Incorporated: 26 May 1983 *Employees:* 15
Net Worth: £442,258 *Total Assets:* £590,150
Registered Office: 83 West Street, Leven, Hull, HU17 5LR
Officers: Amanda Jayne Good [1965] Director

Strathpeffer Spa Soap Company Limited
Incorporated: 3 March 2004
Registered Office: Woodside, Heights of Inchvannie, Strathpeffer, Ross & Cromarty, IV14 9AE
Shareholders: John Thomas Fulton; Elizabeth Brock Kendall
Officers: Elizabeth Brock Kendall, Secretary/Teacher [American]; John Thomas Fulton [1952] Director/Technician; Elizabeth Brock Kendall [1957] Director/Teacher [American]

Suds & Salve Ltd
Incorporated: 16 July 2018
Registered Office: 43 Beighton Road, Acle, Norwich, NR13 3DD
Major Shareholder: Jamie Andrew Roe
Officers: Jamie Andrew Roe [1990] Director

Superfine Manufacturing Limited
Incorporated: 9 January 1963 *Employees:* 20
Net Worth: £3,607,568 *Total Assets:* £4,200,140
Registered Office: Orchard Bank, Glamis Road, Forfar, Angus, DD8 1TD
Major Shareholder: Nigel John Archer
Officers: Julie Patricia Philip, Secretary; Gemma Louise Archer [1984] Director; Lyn Archer [1981] Director; Maureen Archer [1956] Director; Nigel John Archer [1956] Managing Director

Supreme Wax Limited
Incorporated: 24 May 2017
Registered Office: 6 Broomhouse Path, Broomhouse, Edinburgh, EH11 3UL
Officers: Sief Addeen Mujahed Ibrahim Abuqasem [1995] Director/Manufacturing Car Care Products [Jordanian]

Sustain Global Limited
Incorporated: 18 September 2018
Registered Office: 99 High Street, Broadway, Worcs, WR12 7AL
Shareholder: Emma Julie Heathcote-James
Officers: Emma Julie Heathcote-James [1977] Director; Dr Sharon Redrobe [1969] Director/Veterinary Surgeon

Swan Lake Candle Ltd
Incorporated: 18 June 2018
Registered Office: 5 Davis Field, New Milton, Hants, BH25 6SS
Major Shareholder: Daniel William Hall
Officers: Daniel William Hall [1992] Director

Sweet Orange Soapery Ltd
Incorporated: 24 October 2017
Registered Office: 2 Pightle Close, Mulbarton, Norfolk, NR14 8GJ
Shareholder: Laurel White
Officers: Mark White, Secretary; Laurel White [1966] Director/Soap Maker [American]

Sycamore (UK) Limited
Incorporated: 25 November 1997 *Employees:* 10
Net Worth: £192,214 *Total Assets:* £1,805,902
Registered Office: The Cleaning Centre, Bath Road, Littlewick Green, Maidenhead, Berks, SL6 3QR
Shareholders: Uziel Pfeffer; Nigel Fraser Dibbo
Officers: Nicola Dibbo, Secretary/General Manager; Nigel Fraser Dibbo [1962] Director; Uziel Pfeffer [1952] Managing Director [Israeli]

Syntec Manufacturing Limited
Incorporated: 9 March 1984 *Employees:* 14
Net Worth: £183,538 *Total Assets:* £491,538
Registered Office: Mid Road Blairlinn Industrial Estate, Cumbernauld, N Lanarks, G67 2TT
Shareholders: Paul Richard Booth; Kenneth William Campbell
Officers: Kenneth William Campbell, Secretary; Paul Richard Booth [1954] Sales Director; Kenneth William Campbell [1956] Managing Director; Karen Kirk [1966] Commercial Director; John Naysmith [1953] Director/Sales Manager; James Provan Winning [1952] Director

T. & Toff Ltd
Incorporated: 22 November 2017
Registered Office: 31 Lodge Road, Coventry, Warwicks, CV3 1FU
Officers: Georgina Daniel [1991] Director

TAC Perfumes & Cosmetics (UK) Ltd
Incorporated: 12 February 2018
Registered Office: Kemp House, 160 City Road, London, EC1V 2NX
Shareholders: Khandoker Choudhury; Tasbirul Ahmed Choudhury
Officers: Khandoker Choudhury, Secretary; Tasbirul Choudhury, Secretary; Khandoker Choudhury [1976] Director [Bangladeshi]; Tasbirul Ahmed Choudhury [1966] Managing Director [Bangladeshi]

Team Titan Performance Ltd
Incorporated: 6 August 2018
Registered Office: 168 Somerset, Southampton, SO18 5FT
Shareholders: Chandler Conner Robson; Courteney Ellen Baxter
Officers: Chandler Conner Robson [1998] Director/Founder

Techtron Limited
Incorporated: 9 June 1980 *Employees:* 26
Net Worth: £164,105 *Total Assets:* £1,696,945
Registered Office: Suite 1.02, Grosvenor House, Hollinswood Road, Central Park, Telford, Salop, TF2 9TW
Parent: Rubery Owen Holdings Limited
Officers: Elaine Eaton, Secretary; Richard Mark Jenkins [1967] Director; Kevin Generald McGuigan [1976] Director/Chartered Accountant

Tersus Niteo Limited
Incorporated: 16 January 2014
Net Worth: £3,257 *Total Assets:* £42,793
Registered Office: 21 Tanners Drive, Blakelands, Milton Keynes, Bucks, MK14 5BU
Major Shareholder: Gary John Cronnolley
Officers: Gary John Cronnolley [1975] Director

Texatherm Systems Limited
Incorporated: 12 September 1996 *Employees:* 5
Previous: Textile Cleaning Solutions Limited
Net Worth: £7,497 *Total Assets:* £253,807
Registered Office: Centre House, Coker Road, Worle Industrial Estate, Weston-Super-Mare, Somerset, BS22 6BX
Shareholders: Mark Gary Mullane; Patricia Ann Mullane
Officers: Mark Gary Mullane, Secretary; Mark Gary Mullane [1963] Director; Patricia Ann Mullane [1959] Director

Thebubblebar Ltd
Incorporated: 11 February 2019
Registered Office: 62 Ullswater Avenue, Nuneaton, Warwicks, CV11 6HS
Major Shareholder: Anissa Boumecid-Thompson
Officers: Anissa Boumecid-Thompson [1995] Director [British/Algerian]

The Therapy Factory Ltd
Incorporated: 23 April 2018
Registered Office: 27 Old Gloucester Street, London, WC1N 3AX
Major Shareholder: Emma Adjei
Officers: Emma Adjei, Secretary; Emma Adjei [1981] Director/Therapist

Thistle & Berry Ltd
Incorporated: 3 January 2019
Registered Office: 272 Bath Street, Glasgow, G2 4JR
Major Shareholder: Anish Prabhakar Deshpande
Officers: Anish Prabhakar Deshpande [1990] Director/Actuarial Professional

Thornton Baron Ltd
Incorporated: 22 October 2018
Registered Office: Cotswold, Estcourt Road, Darrington, Pontefract, W Yorks, WF8 3AJ
Major Shareholder: Geoff Thomas Glenn Thornton
Officers: Geoff Thomas Glenn Thornton [1980] Director

Tiger Lily Soapery Ltd
Incorporated: 27 September 2017
Registered Office: 8 Westhorpe Close, King's Lynn, Norfolk, PE30 3WB
Major Shareholder: Michele Leagh Beard
Officers: Michele Leagh Beard [1974] Director/Tiger Lily Soapery [American]

Kathryn Tilly Limited
Incorporated: 14 December 2017
Registered Office: 87 South Parade, Northallerton, N Yorks, DL7 8SJ
Shareholders: Kathryn Sophie Atkins; Charles David Atkins
Officers: Charles David Atkins [1986] Director; Kathryn Sophie Atkins [1987] Director

Times Capital Industry Limited
Incorporated: 10 December 2018
Registered Office: Kemp House, 152-160 City Road, London, EC1V 2NX
Officers: Joseph Chukwubuike Ezeakunne [1975] Director/Manufacturer [Nigerian]

Toilet Safe UK Limited
Incorporated: 4 September 2018
Registered Office: 29a Stratford Office Village, Walker Avenue, Wolverton Mill, Milton Keynes, Bucks, MK12 5TW
Major Shareholder: Shabbir Merali
Officers: Shabbir Merali [1971] Director

Total Liquid Solutions Ltd
Incorporated: 31 January 2017 *Employees:* 5
Net Worth: £53,391 *Total Assets:* £417,052
Registered Office: 19 Warren Park Way, Enderby, Leicester, LE19 4SA
Officers: Martin Cameron Roberts, Secretary; Martin Cameron Roberts [1967] Director/Chemist

Totem Properties Limited
Incorporated: 18 June 1987 *Employees:* 2
Net Worth: £2,270,058 *Total Assets:* £3,717,022
Registered Office: 29 Robyns Way, Sevenoaks, Kent, TN13 3EB
Major Shareholder: Helen Doris Moon
Officers: John Andrew Moon [1950] Production Director; Susan Anne Moon [1959] Director/Chartered Accountant

Touch of Nature Limited
Incorporated: 24 September 2018
Registered Office: 27 Old Gloucester Street, London, WC1N 3AX
Major Shareholder: Ahmad Abid
Officers: Ahmad Abid [1978] Director/MSc Student

Touch Soap Ltd
Incorporated: 7 November 2018
Registered Office: 44 Kingsway, Manchester, M19 2DD
Officers: Razna Bibi [1980] Director

Travik Chemicals (UK) Limited
Incorporated: 8 November 2010   *Employees:* 10
Net Worth: £300,620   *Total Assets:* £380,966
Registered Office: Unit 24-26 Maitland Road, Lion Barn Business Park, Needham Market, Suffolk, IP6 8NS
Shareholders: Carl John Climpson; Kim Joy Climpson
Officers: Carl John Climpson [1963] Director; Kim Joy Climpson [1961] Director; Laura Climpson [1988] Director; Robert James Climpson [1990] Director

Trichem Scotland Limited
Incorporated: 24 December 1996   *Employees:* 12
Net Worth: £116,783   *Total Assets:* £526,209
Registered Office: 36e Inchmuir Road, Whitehill Industrial Estate, Bathgate, W Lothian, EH48 2EP
Shareholders: Mairi Drummond; Malcolm Robert Drummond
Officers: Mairi Drummond, Secretary/Director; Mairi Drummond [1960] Director; Malcolm Robert Drummond [1958] Director

TRU Products Limited
Incorporated: 19 March 2015
Registered Office: Swallowfield House, Station Road, Wellington, Somerset, TA21 8NL
Parent: Swallowfield PLC
Officers: Jane Fletcher [1967] Director/Sales and Marketing; Matthew Gazzard [1971] Group Financial Director; Timothy James Perman [1962] Director

TWA Production Ltd.
Incorporated: 10 January 2018
Registered Office: 8 Langlodge Road, Coventry, Warwicks, CV6 4EG
Major Shareholder: Mihaly Babics
Officers: Mihaly Babics [1978] Director [Hungarian]

UK Better Cleaner Industry Co., Limited
Incorporated: 22 June 2018
Registered Office: Unit G25, Waterfront Studios, 1 Dock Road, London, E16 1AH
Major Shareholder: Shizhong Huang
Officers: Shizhong Huang [1967] Director [Chinese]

UK Nuduun Personal-Care Supply Co., Limited
Incorporated: 21 June 2018
Registered Office: Unit G25, Waterfront Studios, 1 Dock Road, London, E16 1AH
Major Shareholder: Qiaoyin Ye
Officers: Qiaoyin Ye [1957] Director [Chinese]

UK Pandora Fairy Skin Beautiyfying Co., Ltd
Incorporated: 11 December 2018
Registered Office: 9 Pantygraigwen Road, Pontypridd, Mid Glamorgan, CF37 2RR
Major Shareholder: Qingye Ruan
Officers: Qingye Ruan [1979] Director [Chinese]

Ultima Direct Limited
Incorporated: 1 May 2018
Registered Office: 12 Dyke Street, Brymbo, Wrexham, Clwyd, LL11 5AH
Shareholders: Kieran Dean Owens; Fraser William Gorden
Officers: Fraser William Gorden [1987] Director; Kieran Dean Owens [1992] Director

Ultimate Car Care Ltd
Incorporated: 17 July 2014
Net Worth Deficit: £401   *Total Assets:* £6,151
Registered Office: 166 Sandbed Lane, Belper, Derbys, DE56 0SN
Major Shareholder: Adam Graham Beard
Officers: Adam Graham Beard [1991] Director/Professional Car Valeter

Ultra Bien Limited
Incorporated: 12 June 2018
Registered Office: Hedingham House, Seven Kings Way, Kingston upon Thames, Surrey, KT2 5AE
Shareholders: Nathan Antonio; Leah Mitchell
Officers: Nathan Antonio [1996] Director/Engineering; Leah Mitchell [1997] Director/Events Manager

Unilever UK Limited
Incorporated: 9 December 1937   *Employees:* 2,976
Net Worth: £1,239,565,952   *Total Assets:* £1,671,614,976
Registered Office: Unilever House, Springfield Drive, Leatherhead, Surrey, KT22 7GR
Parent: Unilever UK Group Limited
Officers: James Oliver Earley, Secretary; Richard Clive Hazell, Secretary; Hazel Karen Detsiny [1972] Managing Director FMCG; Paul William Fenwick [1970] Director/Accountant; Placid Oriol Jover Goma [1981] Director/VP HR UK & Ireland [Spanish]; Sebastian John Munden [1968] Director/EVP & GM Unilever UK & Ireland; Jonathan David Strachan [1964] Director/Manager; Marc John Woodward [1974] Director/VP Customer Development

United Company Specialty Chemicals & Mineral Oils Ltd.
Incorporated: 19 April 2018
Registered Office: 120 High Road, East Finchley, London, N2 9ED
Officers: Lotfy Mahmoud Abdelaliem Rashwan [1982] Director/General Manager [Egyptian]; Nader Mahmoud Abdelalim Elzawily [1980] Sales and Marketing Director [Egyptian]

Unitor Limited
Incorporated: 7 September 1994
Net Worth: £4,875   *Total Assets:* £24,044
Registered Office: 44 Marmion Road, Hove, E Sussex, BN3 5FT
Officers: John Dudley D'Urben Pearson, Secretary/Manufacturer; Cynthia Jean Pearson [1948] Director/Secretary; John Dudley D'Urben Pearson [1948] Director/Manufacturer

Universal Chemicals Limited
Incorporated: 24 February 1986   *Employees:* 4
Net Worth: £3,348   *Total Assets:* £29,102
Registered Office: Radnor House, Greenwood Close, Cardiff Gate Business Park, Pontprennau, Cardiff, CF23 8AA
Shareholders: Malcolm David Shepherd; Ryan David Shepherd
Officers: Brenda Jean Shepherd, Secretary; Daryl Paxton Shepherd [1974] Director; Malcolm David Shepherd [1948] Managing Director; Ryan David Shepherd [1978] Director

Universal Toiletries Corporation Limited
Incorporated: 27 October 1999 *Employees:* 7
Net Worth: £779,298 *Total Assets:* £1,933,357
Registered Office: Unit 7 Bermer Place, Imperial Way, Watford, Herts, WD24 4AY
Major Shareholder: Dinesh Shah
Officers: Mahendra Kanabar, Secretary; Dinesh Chhabildas Shah [1958] Director; Jayshree Dinesh Shah [1963] Director; Karan Shah [1988] Director

Vanillin Limited
Incorporated: 29 August 2014
Registered Office: 44 Desford Road, Aigburth, Liverpool, L19 3RD
Officers: Giles Pinnington [1984] Director/Import Services

The Vegan Soap Company Ltd
Incorporated: 28 February 2019
Registered Office: 17 Horsley Close, Epsom, Surrey, KT19 8HB
Major Shareholder: Claudia Elizabeth Hedger
Officers: Claudia Elizabeth Hedger [1999] Director/Student

Vehicle Cleaning Products Limited
Incorporated: 7 January 2009
Registered Office: 1 Derby Road, Eastwood, Nottingham, NG16 3PA
Shareholders: Sharon Davis; Andrew Charles Davis
Officers: Andrew Charles Davis [1962] Director; Sharon Davis [1962] Director

Very Good Vegan Company Limited
Incorporated: 9 August 2018
Registered Office: 114 Cambrian Way, Basingstoke, Hants, RG22 5AL
Shareholders: Ash Paul Dobrock; Hannah Faye Dobrock
Officers: Ash Paul Dobrock [1983] Director/Civil Servant; Hannah Faye Dobrock [1986] Director/Manager

Vienne Luca Limited
Incorporated: 2 November 2016
Registered Office: 31 Portland Road, Milcombe, Banbury, Oxon, OX15 4RL
Major Shareholder: Marie Perring
Officers: Marie Perring [1981] Director/Natural Soap and Skincare Manufacturer

Von Bons Bath Bombs Limited
Incorporated: 11 December 2017
Registered Office: Dafforda Cottage, Rumble Street, Monkswood, Usk, Monmouthshire, NP15 1QG
Major Shareholder: Yvonne Taylor-Dix
Officers: Yvonne Taylor-Dix [1961] Director/Candle Maker

Vuitton Group Ltd
Incorporated: 26 November 2018
Registered Office: 20-22 Wenlock Road, London, N1 7GU
Major Shareholder: Simon Kayode Ogunlesi
Officers: Simon Kayode Ogunlesi [1977] Director

W & J Global Ltd.
Incorporated: 8 June 2011
Registered Office: 219a Stanwell Road, Ashford, Surrey, TW15 3QY
Major Shareholder: Huangjia Cai
Officers: Weijia John Chen, Secretary; Huangjia William Cai [1980] Director/Sales [Chinese]

Wagonwash Limited
Incorporated: 7 April 2010
Net Worth Deficit: £75 *Total Assets:* £8,970
Registered Office: Unicorn House, 141 Mowbray Drive, Blackpool, Lancs, FY3 7UN
Major Shareholder: Alan William Reilly
Officers: Alan William Reilly, Secretary; Alan William Reilly [1959] Director

Wash Bomb Ltd
Incorporated: 27 November 2017
Registered Office: 68 Old Wareham Road, Poole, Dorset, BH12 4QR
Major Shareholder: Michael Jarmey
Officers: Michael Jarmey [1970] Director

Washworks Bodycare Limited
Incorporated: 11 April 2013
Net Worth Deficit: £125,821 *Total Assets:* £51,509
Registered Office: 207 Regent Street, London, W1B 3HH
Shareholder: Alexandra Louise Turner
Officers: Tejal Ajay Ramnathkar [1981] Director/Entrepreneur [Indian]; Alexandra Louise Turner [1975] Director/Entrepreneur

The Waterside Soap Company Limited
Incorporated: 27 October 2016
Net Worth Deficit: £3,255 *Total Assets:* £3,135
Registered Office: 3 Gordon Brown Place, Mallaig, Highland, PH41 4RL
Major Shareholder: Ami-Jayne Hall
Officers: Ami-Jayne Hall [1991] Director

Welsh Valley Soapery Ltd
Incorporated: 11 February 2019
Registered Office: Tal Y Bryn, Balaclava Road, Dowlais, Merthyr Tydfil, Mid Glamorgan, CF48 3BS
Shareholders: Abigail Juliet Hanks; Emma Louise Hanks
Officers: Abigail Juliet Hanks [1979] Director; Emma Louise Hanks [1976] Director

West Trading Ltd
Incorporated: 9 November 2011
Registered Office: Office 2093, 1 Fore Street, London, EC2Y 5EJ
Major Shareholder: Carlo Alberto Spina
Officers: Lady Lidia Tarlev, Secretary; Carlo Alberto Spina [1971] Director [Japanese]

Deloris White Limited
Incorporated: 26 February 2019
Registered Office: 5 Overton Close, St Raphael, London, NW10 0QB
Major Shareholder: Deloris Elaine White
Officers: Deloris Elaine White [1972] Director [Jamaican]

Wholesome Toiletries Ltd
Incorporated: 22 December 2017
Registered Office: International House, 12 Constance Street, London, E16 2DQ
Shareholders: Sophaia Mamoloko Farmer-Moruthoane; Joseph Peart-Johnson
Officers: Sophaia Mamoloko Farmer-Moruthoane [1998] Director; Joseph Peart-Johnson [1997] Director

Wild Planet Products Ltd
Incorporated: 24 June 2010
Net Worth: £221 *Total Assets:* £16,763
Registered Office: Workshop 1, The Quadrangle, Shoreham Rodd, opp Fackenden Road, Shoreham, Sevenoaks, Kent, TN14 7RP
Shareholder: Eileen Clare Holford
Officers: David John Holford [1962] Director/IT Consultant; Eileen Clare Holford [1964] Director/Soap Maker

Wild Stem Soaps Limited
Incorporated: 27 September 2018
Registered Office: Kemp House, 160 City Road, London, EC1V 2NX
Officers: Zeena Luchowa [1987] Director

Wildcraft Ltd
Incorporated: 4 May 2018
Registered Office: 353 Holton Road, Barry, Vale of Glamorgan, CF63 4HX
Major Shareholder: Isamba Tausi Thomas
Officers: Isamba Tausi Thomas [1980] Director/Financier

Willis Doyle Limited
Incorporated: 4 April 2017
Registered Office: Bluebell Cottage, 10 Saxbys Lane, Lingfield, Surrey, RH7 6DN
Major Shareholder: Nicola Healy
Officers: Darrel Willis, Secretary; Nicola Healy [1976] Director/Artisan Soap Maker [Irish]

Winchester Soap Company Limited
Incorporated: 28 February 2018
Registered Office: 5 Kingsway Gardens, Chandler's Ford, Eastleigh, Hants, SO53 1FF
Major Shareholder: Joanne Brinton
Officers: Joanne Brinton, Secretary; Joanne Brinton [1969] Director/Entrepreneur

Windy Mill Ltd
Incorporated: 8 August 2014
Net Worth: £232 *Total Assets:* £1,627
Registered Office: 27 Fidlers Walk, Wargrave, Reading, Berks, RG10 8BA
Major Shareholder: Melanie Quinn
Officers: Melanie Gail Campbell Quinn [1966] Director/Bookkeeper

Wizard Soap Company Ltd
Incorporated: 29 October 2018
Registered Office: Office 4, Somerset House, 30 Wynnstay Road, Colwyn Bay, Conwy, LL29 8NB
Major Shareholder: Robert Anthony Kelly
Officers: Robert Anthony Kelly [1962] Director

Wordsworth Handcrafted Soap Co. Ltd.
Incorporated: 18 September 2017
Net Worth: £500 *Total Assets:* £500
Registered Office: 43 Wright Drive, Dudley, Cramlington, Northumberland, NE23 7BS
Major Shareholder: Gillian Margaret Wordsworth-Goodram
Officers: Gillian Margaret Wordsworth-Goodram [1983] Director/Business Owner

Wren and Willow Limited
Incorporated: 16 May 2017
Registered Office: 5 Speller Way, Little Canfield, Dunmow, Essex, CM6 1GX
Major Shareholder: Hannah Stevens
Officers: Hannah Stevens, Secretary; Hannah Stevens [1976] Director

The Wrinkly Elephant Company Limited
Incorporated: 18 May 2017
Net Worth Deficit: £3,169
Registered Office: 16 St Andrews Way, Bromsgrove, Worcs, B61 7NR
Shareholders: Lisa Turner; Stuart Paul Turner
Officers: Lisa Turner [1969] Director/Artisan Soap Manufacturer; Stuart Paul Turner [1961] Director/Artisan Soap Manufacturer

X.R.O. Chemical Services Limited
Incorporated: 4 November 1991 *Employees:* 13
Net Worth: £64,076 *Total Assets:* £607,515
Registered Office: Unit 1 The Cedars, Moor Farm Road, Airfield Industrial Estate, Ashbourne, Derbys, DE6 1HD
Major Shareholder: Philip Roger Cox
Officers: Wendy Elaine Greatorex, Secretary; Philip Roger Cox [1946] Director/Industrial Chemist; Wendy Elaine Greatorex [1967] Director

Yeardeal Limited
Incorporated: 22 March 1993
Net Worth: £580 *Total Assets:* £6,881
Registered Office: Suite E, 1-3 Canfield Place, London, NW6 3BT
Shareholder: Hugh Alan Buck
Officers: Esther Woodward, Secretary; Dr Hugh Alan Buck [1944] Director

Yess Essentials Limited
Incorporated: 17 January 2001
Net Worth: £22,355 *Total Assets:* £22,355
Registered Office: 82 Felixstowe Road, London, SE2 9QH
Shareholders: Oluyemisi Olabisi Shode; Olufemi Olukayode Shode
Officers: Babatunde Oladipo Obisesan, Secretary; Dr. Olufemi Olukayode Shode [1953] Director/Chemist; Dr Oluyemisi Olabisi Shode [1954] Director/Chemist

Yogi Fresh Limited
Incorporated: 21 February 2018
Registered Office: The View, 20 Palace Street, Westminster, London, SW1E 5BB
Officers: Sarah Jayne Murphy [1990] Director

The Yorkshire Dales Soap Company Limited
Incorporated: 26 June 2017
Registered Office: 11 Little Studley Road, Ripon, N Yorks, HG4 1HD
Major Shareholder: Jonathan Scott Forsyth
Officers: Jonathan Scott Forsyth, Secretary; Jonathan Scott Forsyth [1962] Director/Pilot

You're Gorgeous Handmade Soap Limited
Incorporated: 27 April 2010
Net Worth: £29,564 *Total Assets:* £69,323
Registered Office: Basford House, 29 Augusta Street, Llandudno, Conwy, LL30 2AE
Major Shareholder: Beatrice Emma Williams
Officers: Beatrice Emma Williams [1959] Director

Zamo Household Products Limited
Incorporated: 6 September 1995
Net Worth: £128,124 *Total Assets:* £208,480
Registered Office: 85 Park Drive, Winchmore Hill, London, N21 2LT
Major Shareholder: Terence Richard Rhodes
Officers: Terence Richard Rhodes [1945] Director/Household Chemical Manufacturer

Zenith Hygiene Group Limited
Incorporated: 25 September 2008 *Employees:* 504
Previous: Zenith Hygiene Group PLC
Net Worth: £13,743,000 *Total Assets:* £47,140,000
Registered Office: Zenith House, A1(M) Business, Dixons Hill Road, Welham Green, Herts, AL9 7JE
Parent: BCPE Diamond UK Holdco Limited
Officers: Alison Pettitt, Secretary; Simon Peter Bower [1964] Director/Accountant; Michael James Chapman [1961] Director; Ringo Daisley Francis [1955] Director; Alexander Arthur MacDonald [1953] Director; Alison Jane Pettitt [1967] Finance Director; John-Paul Surdo [1984] Director [American]

Zenith Hygiene Systems Limited
Incorporated: 15 May 1996 *Employees:* 502
Net Worth: £749,000 *Total Assets:* £32,489,000
Registered Office: Zenith House, A1(M) Business Centre, Dixons Hill Road, Welham Green, Herts, AL9 7JE
Parent: Zenith Hygiene Food and Beverage Limited
Officers: Tony Clough [1964] Technical Director; Warren Edmondson [1982] Sales and Marketing Director; Colin Kenneth Fogarty [1958] Director; Ringo Daisley Francis [1955] Director/Chief Executive Officer; Bakhtiar Hanan [1971] Group Purchasing Director; James Duncan Hannaway [1976] Operations Director; Jennifer James [1960] HR Director; Derek John Lafbery [1968] Director; Rakesh Patel [1971] IT Director; Alison Jane Pettitt [1967] Finance Director

Zenken Limited
Incorporated: 23 April 2018
Registered Office: 4 Kingston Road, Nailsea, Bristol, BS48 4RD
Officers: Zoltan Gottlieb [1976] Director [Hungarian]; Szonja Fruzsina Marosi [1979] Director [Hungarian]

Zep UK Limited
Incorporated: 12 June 1979 *Employees:* 43
Net Worth: £5,600,584 *Total Assets:* £9,409,107
Registered Office: P O Box 12, Tanhouse Lane, Widnes, Cheshire, WA8 0RD
Parent: Hale Group (Widnes) Limited
Officers: Rob Novo [1957] Director [American]; Paolo Polegri [1965] Finance Director [Italian]; Peter Reilly [1964] Director [American]

Zok Group Limited
Incorporated: 30 July 1998
Registered Office: Airworthy House, Elsted, Midhurst, W Sussex, GU29 0JT
Major Shareholder: Keith Gordon Cartwright

ZOK International Group Limited
Incorporated: 1 May 1996 *Employees:* 10
Net Worth: £996,680 *Total Assets:* £1,239,409
Registered Office: Airworthy House, Elsted, Midhurst, W Sussex, GU29 0JT
Officers: Ruth Horton [1955] Director

Zomi Ltd
Incorporated: 3 July 2018
Registered Office: Flat 26, Plamer Court, 34 Charcot Road, London, NW9 5US
Major Shareholder: Efrat Shemesh Idelson
Officers: Avi Idelson, Secretary; Efrat Shemesh Idelson [1974] Director/Lawyer [Canadian/Israeli]

Zyzven Naturals Cosmetics Ltd
Incorporated: 7 January 2019
Registered Office: 12 Mayday Road, Thornton Heath, Surrey, CR7 7HL
Shareholder: Shawnafi Dynesen
Officers: Shawnafi Dynesen [1979] Director/Entrepreneur [Swedish]

Index of Directorships

Abani, Natasha Ngozi
Pampered Me Ltd

Abani, Philomena Agnes
Pampered Me Ltd

Abbey, Thomas James
Cares Laboratory Limited

Abdallah, Mohamad
M.A. Industries Limited

Abdelaliem Rashwan, Lotfy Mahmoud
United Company Specialty Chemicals & Mineral Oils

Abdelalim Elzawily, Nader Mahmoud
United Company Specialty Chemicals & Mineral Oils

Abdelhamid, Mohamed
Blok Soap Ltd

Abid, Ahmad
Touch of Nature Limited

Abuqasem, Sief Addeen Mujahed Ibrahim
Supreme Wax Limited

Lee, Carl Richmond
R P Adam Limited

Rawding, Paul
R P Adam Limited

Adil, Ersin Akif
Estela Dermocosmetics Ltd

Aggrey-Fynn, Nana
Amita Cosmetics Ltd

Ahmet, Joan
Capricorn Detergents Limited

Ahmet, Nureddin
Capricorn Detergents Limited

Akkuratova, Anna
Ora-Heal Ltd

Akobeng, Catherine
Kokoa UK Limited

Alabi, Thitima
Oryza Naturale Limited

Alexander, Amy
Check You Limited

Alkassem, Hasan
Levant Soap Limited

Allen, Thomas
Madcow Brand Limited

Allijohn, Junior Everton
Arulabeauty Ltd

Allijohn, Symone Marie
Arulabeauty Ltd

Allison, David Paul
Shorrock Trichem Limited

Allman, Grant
Buypolar Ltd

Allsworth, Thomas Donald
Medichem Manufacturing Ltd

Alves Dos Reis Fielder, Ana Paula
Meaningful Earth Soap Co Ltd

Alyedreessy, Mona
Azara Beautique Ltd

Amoah, Lillian
Aventual Ltd

Anderson, Helena Alice Lucy
Narauli Ltd

Anderson, Nicola Lynn
Makin' Scents Ltd

Anderson-Taylor, Kirsty Emma
Golden Soaps Ltd

Andrews, Charlotte
Mayde Essence Ltd

Anestis, Schoinopoulos
Anastaz Beverly Hills Ltd

Angelico, Susan
KA Shere-Khan Limited

Angus, Murray
Java Coffee Co Ltd

Campbell, Stewart
The Antifoaming Agents Ltd

Antonio, Nathan
Ultra Bien Limited

Appleton, Anthony Joseph
Procter & Gamble Product Supply (U.K.)

Aprcovic, Ilija
GEA Farm Technologies (UK) Ltd

Archer, Gemma Louise
Superfine Manufacturing Ltd

Archer, Lyn
Superfine Manufacturing Ltd

Archer, Maureen
Superfine Manufacturing Ltd

Archer, Nigel John
Superfine Manufacturing Ltd

Armitage, Richard John
Cleenol Group Limited

Arnold, Andrew John
Serchem Limited

Arnold, Elizabeth Amelia
Serchem Limited

Arnold, Paul David
Serchem Limited

Arvanitopoulou, Paschalina
Firecraft Ltd

Ashby, Michaela Leanne
D'lishx0x0 Limited

Ashley, David James
3M UK Trading Limited

Ashton, Christopher Anthony
Autosmart Group Limited
Autosmart Holdings Limited

Ashton, Graham Alexander
Locks in Goodness Ltd

Ashton, Victoria Aviva
Locks in Goodness Ltd

Astley Weston, Julie Maria
Love To B Skincare Ltd

Asuoha, Baby Davies
Brush Europe Limited

Asuoha, Chukwudi
Brush Europe Limited

Atherton, Helen Rosemary
Dook Ltd

Atkinson, Richard
Dimex Limited

Atkinson, Sophie
Autosmart Group Limited
Autosmart Holdings Limited

Atughwe, Raymond
Globemeth Limited

Hinchliffe, Fiona
The Austonley Soap Co Ltd

Aveyard, David Peter
Christeyns UK Ltd

Avis, Kelly Ann
Crafty Lady Ltd

Avondo, Roberto
Chemtrading Limited

Aynsley, Adrian
Bramchem Ltd.

Babics, Mihaly
TWA Production Ltd.

Baggs, Lawrence James
Bio-Clean Limited

Bagshaw, Stephen Charles
Holchem Laboratories Limited

Baig, Mirza Yousaf
Businotech Limited
London Cosmetics (UK) Limited

Baillie, Jason Alan
AMB Hygiene Limited

Baines, Helen
Cocoa Lime Limited

Bains, Tania
Blok Soap Ltd

Balendres, Brenda
Seadpearl Ltd

Bambury, Jasmine
Rutherford Bambury Ltd

Barber, Stuart
Purealba Limited

Barnett, Sonia
Oooh Skincare Ltd

Barratt, Emily Lois
Emily's Soap Shop Limited

Barritt, Kelly Louise
Halritt Ltd

Bastable, Richard
Pure Solve UK Limited

Beard, Adam Graham
Ultimate Car Care Ltd

Beard, Michele Leagh
Tiger Lily Soapery Ltd

Beckman, Heinrich Kurt
Acdoco Limited

Beckmann, Heiner Kurt
Springdawn Bolton Limited

Beckmann, Nils
Acdoco Limited
Springdawn Bolton Limited

Belk, John Leonard
Dasic International Limited

Bell, Simon Lee
Holchem Laboratories Limited

Bell, Simon
Merlin Chemicals Limited

Bennett, Stephen Guy
Dimex Limited

Bentley, Michael Steven
Bramchem Ltd.

Bentley, Thomas James MacAulay
Stephenson Group Ltd

Bentley, Thomas Richard
Stephenson Group Ltd

Bethel, Andrew
Christeyns Food Hygiene Ltd

Beverley, Jeffrey
KA Shere-Khan Limited

Bianchi, Lucrecia Silvana
LU Aromatherapy Ltd

Bibi, Razna
Earth's Naturals Ltd
Touch Soap Ltd

Atkin, Joanne Elizabeth
The Bio-D Holdings (UK) Ltd

Atkin, Lloyd Spencer
The Bio-D Holdings (UK) Ltd

Bird, Jeremy Guy Nicholas
Astley Dye and Chemical Co Ltd

Birtles, Anna Vyacheslavovna
Spartisan Ltd

Bishop, Marta
Evocativ Limited

Bishop, Thomas
Evocativ Limited

Bispham, Beverley
Luvly Bubbly Limited

Blackburn, Janina
Completely Conkers Limited

Blackman, Evelyn Isabel
Loveve. Ltd

Blowes, Simon Christopher
London Soap Co Ltd

Bodragon, Christopher
Boweasel Ltd

Boey, Sharlene Suyin
Nomad Soapery Limited

Bond, Andrew
Nathalie Bond Limited

Bond, Natalie
Nathalie Bond Limited

Bongermino, Katia
Naturali360 Limited

Bonsu-Stewart, Rebecca
Sankofa Heritage Ltd

Booker, Darren Lee
Ideal Manufacturing Limited

Booth, Paul Richard
Syntec Manufacturing Limited

Bostoen, Paul Gerrard Victor Camiel
Christeyns UK Ltd

Botha, Natasha
Spa Mommy Limited

Boulos, Mark
LJSP Ltd

Boulton, Geoffrey
Future Developments (Manufacturing)

Boumecid-Thompson, Anissa
Thebubblebar Ltd

Bower, Simon Peter
Cater-Lyne Limited
Zenith Hygiene Group Limited

Bowhay-Singer, Rachael Jane
Chemisphere UK Limited

Bracher, Verity Kate
Meadow Farm Friends Ltd

Bradley, Christine
Scent By Hand Ltd

Brain, Christopher Keith
Autosmart Group Limited
Autosmart Holdings Limited

Branda, Gianluca
Procter & Gamble Product Supply (U.K.)

Brander, Christine Linda
Residual Barrier Technology Ltd

Bridge, Peter John
Coventry Chemicals Limited

Brindley, Gowan
Dino-Mite Ltd

Brinton, Joanne
Winchester Soap Co Ltd

Brockhus, Eric Anthonius
Molton Brown Limited

Broomberg, Ashley Dan
Clean Bidco Limited
Clean Topco Limited

Brown, Chantelle
Harmonious Brown Limited

Brown, Darren
Kush Moma Limited

Brown, Fiona Anne
Calman Enterprise Limited

Brown, Kim
Anyki Ltd

Brunton, Clare
Simply Ewe Limited

Buck, Hugh Alan, Dr
Yeardeal Limited

Buckthorp, Alexander George
Procter & Gamble Product Supply (U.K.)

Bulgakova, Natalia
Kindness Collective Limited

Burns, Niema
Ennebee Ltd

Bustamante, Eliseo
LU Aromatherapy Ltd

Butler, Ashley Charles
K C Butler & Son Limited

Butler, Jane
K C Butler & Son Limited

Bynoe, Justice Marie
Kalula Cosmetics Ltd

Cai, Huangjia William
W & J Global Ltd.

Caley, Judy
Caley's of Exeter Ltd

Cameron, Charmaine
Nu-E55ence Ltd

Campbell, Alan
Sheer Bliss Retail Ltd

Campbell, Kenneth William
Syntec Manufacturing Limited

Campbell, Maureen Marie
Harmony Bodycare Limited

Cardwell, Linda Ann
Dynamic Chemicals Limited

Cardwell, Robert Alan
Dynamic Chemicals Limited

Carr, Dean Alexander
Spectrum Industrial Limited

Carr, Harry James
Spectrum Industrial Limited

Carr, John
Chemiclean Products Limited

Carr, Margaret Rose
Spectrum Industrial Limited

Carr, Robert Leo
Stephenson Group Ltd

Carr, Wayne Evan
Spectrum Industrial Limited

Carson, Philip Mathew
Libra Speciality Chemicals Ltd

Carter, Nicholas Thomas
Arch UK Biocides Limited

Cartlidge, Alan
Handmade Naturals Ltd

Cartlidge, Rossitza Vassileva Roudeva
Handmade Naturals Ltd

Carver, Allen Rodney
Industrial Chemicals Limited

Carver, Charles Daryl
Industrial Chemicals Limited

Carver, John William
Industrial Chemicals Limited

Cassell, Josephine, Dr
Little Green Beehive Ltd

Chapman, Gary
ICP Direct Limited

Chapman, Michael James
Diversey Holdings Limited
Zenith Hygiene Group Limited

Chauhan, Elaxi
PRSS Solutions (UK) Limited

Ridge, Jason Paul
The Chemical Hut Ltd

Ridge, Paul William
The Chemical Hut Ltd

Chen, Meiling
SC567361 Ltd.

Childerstone, Jeremy Martin
Cleenol Group Limited

Chinnery, Samantha Ophelia
Magpie's Ocean Ltd

Chonzi, Stellah Linda
Sisi Cosmetics Ltd

Chopdat, Zakir Hussain
Ottimo Supplies Limited

Choudhury, Khandoker
TAC Perfumes & Cosmetics (UK) Ltd

Choudhury, Tasbirul Ahmed
TAC Perfumes & Cosmetics (UK) Ltd

Chowdhary, Saima
SKC Resources Ltd

Cita, Natalie
Mbikudi Ltd

Clancy, Steven Patrick
Holt Lloyd International Ltd

Clark Prakash, Preyanka Jayanti
Bloomtown Ltd

Duffy, Victoria Jayne
William Clements (Chemicals) Ltd

Rooney, Michael Patrick Thomas
William Clements (Chemicals) Ltd

Farley, Mary Patricia
William Clements (Chemicals) Ltd

Farley, Raymond Scott
William Clements (Chemicals) Ltd

Clements, Christina
Butter Bar Soapery Ltd

Clews, James Aaron
Stephenson Group Ltd

Climpson, Carl John
Travik Chemicals (UK) Limited

Climpson, Kim Joy
Travik Chemicals (UK) Limited

Climpson, Laura
Travik Chemicals (UK) Limited

Climpson, Robert James
Travik Chemicals (UK) Limited

Clough, Tony
Zenith Hygiene Systems Limited

Cole, Richard Anthony
Cole & Wilson, Limited

Reilly, Alan William
The Colhoon Corporation Ltd

Collier, Harold
Melpass Limited

Collier-Hunter, Charlotte Elsie Rose
Lamina Animal Limited

Collington, Kelsey
Driftwood Shaper Ltd

Collington, Robert
Driftwood Shaper Ltd

Collins, Anna
24 Cures Limited

Collins, Iain Malcolm
CB Services Limited

Collins, Tony
Nuts About Soap Limited

Colton, Deborah Ann
Nature Reflects Limited

Cook, Isobel Frances
Diversey UK Production Limited

Cook, Zoe Nalini
Mild + Wild Ltd

Cooke, Richard Edward
Natural By Nature Limited

Costello, Robin
Friendly Soap Limited

Cotovio, Patricia
Green Spa Therapy Ltd

Coulter, Anthony James Matthew
Powerclean Chemicals Limited

Coulter, Daren Russell Stephen
Powerclean Chemicals Limited

Coulter, George Robert
Shinerite Solutions Limited

Coulter, Graham Leslie Nigel
Powerclean Chemicals Limited

Coulter, Stephen Allan
Powerclean Chemicals Limited

Bridge, Peter John
The Coventry Group Limited

Langdon, Darren Paul
The Coventry Group Limited

Marsh, Paul
The Coventry Group Limited

Scott-Underdown, Michael Montgomery
The Coventry Group Limited

Quinlan, Stephen
The Coventry Group Limited

Cowell, David
Pluswipes Limited

Cox, Graham, Dr
Libra Speciality Chemicals Ltd

Cox, Philip Roger
X.R.O. Chemical Services Ltd

Crawford, Michael James
Elimin8 Limited

Cronnolley, Gary John
Tersus Niteo Limited

Culkin, Andrew James
Pluswipes Limited

Culmer, Medwin John
Bloomtown Ltd

Currie, John Leslie
NCH (UK) Limited
Pure Solve UK Limited

Cutler, Jessica Louise
Marsh Valley Ltd

Dabrowska, Magdalena
Pure Purpose Cosmetics Ltd

Forsyth, Jonathan Scott
The Dales Heritage Soap Co Ltd
The Dales Natural Soap Co Ltd

O'Shaughnessy, Shane
The Dandy Gent Manufactory Ltd

O'Shaughnessy, Sherri
The Dandy Gent Manufactory Ltd

Daniel, Georgina
T. & Toff Ltd

Danville, Sarah
Buypolar Ltd

Darlington, Caron Michelle
Shorrock Trichem Limited

Darville, Valerie Margaret Elizabeth
Chela Ltd
Ecosearch Limited
Fisher Research Ltd
Langhedge Limited

Davies, Gillian Elizabeth
Let It Bee Ltd

Davies, William George
Lower Swell Chemicals Limited

Davila, Manuel Julian
Soapworks Limited

Davis, Andrew Charles
A-Chem Plant & Equipment Ltd
Vehicle Cleaning Products Ltd

Davis, Ashleigh Victoria
A-Chem Plant & Equipment Ltd

Davis, James
A-Chem Plant & Equipment Ltd

Davis, Sharon
A-Chem Plant & Equipment Ltd
Vehicle Cleaning Products Ltd

Davison, Lisa St Claire
Innoscent Ltd

De Feo, Loretta
Dizziak Ltd

De Lange, Mark Christiaan
Royal Sanders (UK) Limited

Dela Cruz, Michelle
Glametuber Ltd

Deman, Mathias
Humble Bee Botanica Ltd.

Denner, Laura Elizabeth
Itaconix (U.K.) Limited

Denning, Malcolm
Shorrock Trichem Limited

Deshpande, Anish Prabhakar
Thistle & Berry Ltd

Destang, Keisha Chanel
Roots & Paradise Ltd

Detsiny, Hazel Karen
Unilever UK Limited

Devos, Elisabeth Josepha Margaretha Ghislenus
Christeyns UK Ltd

Dewey, Tara Isabel Josephine
Naked Cosmetics Ltd

Dharmsee, Rukhsana
Fairy Treats Ltd

Dibbo, Nigel Fraser
Sycamore (UK) Limited

Dilloway, Angela
Greener Solutions Ltd

Dimitrova, Doris
KrUde Cosmetics Ltd

Dixon, Elizabeth Amanda
Scorcher Idea Limited

Djin, Nana
Shea Life Limited

Dobrock, Ash Paul
Very Good Vegan Co Ltd

Dobrock, Hannah Faye
Very Good Vegan Co Ltd

Dodson, Charley Terri
Diamond Fizzles Ltd

Doherty, Thomas Raymond William
Ethicalsoap Limited

Donbavand, Timothy John
GEA Farm Technologies (UK) Ltd

Doran, Martin Simon
MDCO Ltd

Doran, Susan
MDCO Ltd

Dore, David James
Quill International Group Ltd

Dore, Nicholas David James
Quill International Chemicals Ltd

Dore, Susan Yvonne
Quill International Group Ltd

Dos Santos Rita de Jesus, Ieva
Leum Skin Care Ltd

Douglas, Jeroen
Soapworks Limited

Dragicevic, Martina
Molecula Ltd

Driscoll, Simon
Hydrophilic Ltd

Dritz, Shawn
Soap School Ltd

Drummond, Mairi
Trichem Scotland Limited

Drummond, Malcolm Robert
Trichem Scotland Limited

Drury, Edward John
John Drury & Co. Limited

Drury, Martin Robert
John Drury & Co. Limited

Drury, Richard Arnold
John Drury & Co. Limited

Drury, Edward John
John Drury Holdings Limited

Drury, Martin Robert
John Drury Holdings Limited

Drury, Richard Arnold
John Drury Holdings Limited

Dudley, Alan Robert
Safe Solutions (Safe4) Limited

Dudley, Leanne Yvonne
Carvansons Ltd

Duke, Lee Richard
Savon Paradis Ltd

Dupire, Isabelle
Nuts About Soap Limited

Duque, Astrid
Soapworks Limited

Dutton, Tom
McIntyre Group Ltd.

Dynesen, Shawnafi
Zyzven Naturals Cosmetics Ltd

Eckersley, Ian James
Shorrock Trichem Limited

Edgerton, Graham John
Molton Brown Limited

Crooks, Thomas James
The Edinburgh Natural Skincare Company (Retail Shops)

Edmondson, Warren
Zenith Hygiene Systems Limited

Edwards, Emma Victoria
Oleonix Solutions Limited

Edwards, Gareth William James
Acdoco Limited
Springdawn Bolton Limited

Edwards, Nicholas Quentin
Holchem Laboratories Limited

Edwards, Richard Mark
Oleonix Solutions Limited

Edwards, Simone
Nature Native Limited

Effendowicz, Christopher Michael
Droyt Products Limited

Ekpenyong, Alfred
Natural Jem Limited

Ellington, Phillip
Puddlemud Ltd.

Ellis, Bruce Edward
Holt Lloyd International Ltd

Elsheikh, Mohamed Ahmed Fadlallah, Dr
GM Globalhealth Ltd

Emmett, Stuart
Rutpen Limited

Epureanu, Dorin
La Boulle Ltd

Ersin, Sevin
Sevin London Limited

Estrada, Nadia Patricia
SC Johnson Professional Ltd

Etim-Ibom, Rose
R & T Natural Cosmetics Ltd

Eustace, Desmond Charles
Clover Chemicals Limited

Evans, Anthony Ian
Evans Vanodine International PLC

Evans, Christopher John
Evans Vanodine International PLC

Evans, Clinton James
Chimera UK Chemical Solutions Ltd

Evans, Derek Anthony
Evans Vanodine International PLC

Evans, Peter David
Evans Vanodine International PLC

Ewart, Nita
Edinburgh Soap Co Ltd

Ezeakunne, Joseph Chukwubuike
Times Capital Industry Limited

Fanous, Cherine Adel
Aromatic Flavours & Fragrances Europe

Fanous, Marie Nadia
Aromatic Flavours & Fragrances Europe

Farmer-Moruthoane, Sophaia Mamoloko
Wholesome Toiletries Ltd

Femi-Obasan, Enitan Adebola
Kleos Naturals Ltd

Fenwick, Paul William
Unilever UK Limited

Fernandez, Maria Del Carmen
Fernandez Cosmetics Ltd

Field, Rachel
Paws and Unwind Limited

Fielder, Benjamin Douglas
Meaningful Earth Soap Co Ltd

Finlay, David
Origin Pet Products Limited

Fisher McRoberts, Kirsty Patricia
Lady Smidgeton's Apothecary Ltd

Fisher, Anthony Clive Umfreville
Chela Ltd
Eco-Point Laboratories Limited
Ecosearch Limited
Fisher Research Ltd
Langhedge Limited

Fisher, Iwan Clive Umfreville
Chela Ltd
Eco-Point Laboratories Limited
Ecosearch Limited
Fisher Research Ltd
Langhedge Limited

Fishwick, Duncan
Shorrock Trichem Limited

Flannery, Lisa
Stephenson Group Ltd

Fleischer, Ashley Joan
Refresh Tea & Soap Co Ltd

Fletcher, Jane
TRU Products Limited

Fogarty, Colin Kenneth
Zenith Hygiene Systems Limited

Forshaw, Lorraine
Libra Speciality Chemicals Ltd

Fouracre, Michael
Chela Ltd

Fraisse, Jean Pierre
Fillcare Limited

Francis, Lee
Nuts About Soap Limited

Francis, Ringo Daisley
Zenith Hygiene Group Limited
Zenith Hygiene Systems Limited

Fraser, David John
Calman Enterprise Limited

Fraser, James Thomas
Steri-7 Brazil Limited
Steri-7 Worldwide Limited

Fraser, Mairi Lisa
Calman Enterprise Limited

Fraser, Sheila
Calman Enterprise Limited

Fujiwara, Ayaka
Genten Skincare Ltd

Fulton, John Thomas
Strathpeffer Spa Soap Co Ltd

Galbert, Sandrine
Macob Online Shopping Ltd.

Garthwaite, Nicholas James
Christeyns Food Hygiene Ltd
Christeyns UK Ltd
Clover Chemicals Limited
Cole & Wilson, Limited
Klenzan Direct Limited

Gasior, Michal
Body Candy Ltd.

Gates, George Christopher
Mitcheldean Soap Ltd

Gates, Sara Jayne
Mitcheldean Soap Ltd

Gatongi, Francis Nderitu
MWK Cosmetics (UK) Ltd

Gazzard, Matthew
TRU Products Limited

Ge, Lili
Chinese Gentry Limited

Geach, Nigel Anthony
Bonasystems Europe Ltd

Geary, Julita Joanna, Dr
All Natural Cosmetics Ltd
All Naturals Beauty Limited

Geddes, Craig Malcolm
Emollience Ltd

Geddes, David Williams
Emollience Ltd

Gilbert, Karen
Fragrant Alchemy Ltd

Gilland Robinson, Christine
Ko. Essentials Ltd.

Gilluley, Jacqueline Ann
Relax Candle and Bath Co Ltd

Warrington, Charlotte
The Ginchiest Artisan Soap Co Ltd

Girling, Gavin John
International Maintenance Chemicals Ltd

Glauber, Martin
Eurotank Limited

Gleghorn, Stuart John
Residual Barrier Technology Ltd

Bedford, Jennifer Ann
The Goat Soap Co Ltd

Gonzalez Exposito, Jared
Jared Gonzalez Ltd

Hoy, Sally
The Good Soap Co Ltd

Torres-Hernandez, Greg
The Good Soap Co Ltd

Good, Amanda Jayne
Stockcare Limited

Goodger, David
Ideal Manufacturing Limited

Gopalakini, Veena
Ayurveda Wellness Ltd

Gorden, Fraser William
Ultima Direct Limited

Zhou, Qindong
Daisy Gordon Limited

Gordon, Remecae
Rustic Blends Limited

Goss, Anthony Stuart
Lamella Structures Limited

Gottlieb, Zoltan
Zenken Limited

Gould, Clive Martin
Evonik Goldschmidt UK Limited

Gouldstone, Sally, Dr
Seilich Limited

Grahame, Angus Robert
Splosh Limited

Grant, Alan
Aromabar (Scotland) Ltd

Grant, Catherine
Aromabar (Scotland) Ltd

Gray, Pamela Anne
Pur Natural Soaps Ltd

Greatorex, Wendy Elaine
X.R.O. Chemical Services Ltd

Greaves, Richard Stephen
Cleenol Group Limited

Greaves, Samuel Charles
Cleenol Group Limited

Humphreys, Gillian
The Green Housekeeper Ltd

Van Heeswijk, Alice
The Green Housekeeper Ltd

Van Heeswijk, Philippa
The Green Housekeeper Ltd

Munier, Helen Louise
The Greener Good Ltd

Munier, Marc Andrew James
The Greener Good Ltd

Greensmith, Richard Mark
ERH Propack Limited

Greenway, Stephen Paul
Paramount Chemicals Limited

Greenwood, Ian
Ian Greenwood Engineering Ltd

Greer, Stefan Joshua
Ohana CBD Limited

Gregory, Ian Mark
Rapid Washrooms Limited

Gribbin, David John
PH Direct Limited

Griffiths, Hannah
Irae Limited

Griffiths, Mark
Irae Limited

Guest, Ian
Autosheen Ltd
ICP Direct Limited

Hadleigh, Thomas
Body Station Limited

Hale, Richard David
Filthy Kids Ltd

Halesworth, Kevin
Sechelle Manufacturing Limited

Hall, Daniel William
Swan Lake Candle Ltd

Halsey, Derrick William
Halritt Ltd

Hamilton, Helen Grainne
HGH Trading Ltd

Hamilton, Mica Grace Lillian
Spiritual Cleanse Ltd

Hamilton-Gillings, Ashleigh
Funkydz Ltd

Hamilton-Gillings, Juleigh Gail
Funkydz Ltd

Hanan, Bakhtiar
Zenith Hygiene Systems Limited

Handy, Christopher
RBL Laboratories Ltd

Handy, Paul Leon
RBL Laboratories Ltd

Hanks, Abigail Juliet
Welsh Valley Soapery Ltd

Hanks, Emma Louise
Welsh Valley Soapery Ltd

Hannaway, James Duncan
Cater-Lyne Limited
Zenith Hygiene Systems Limited

Johnson, Tracy Jane
The Happy Bee Co Ltd

Hardman, Samantha Jayne
Holchem Laboratories Limited

Harpham, Andrew Harpham Dennis
Carapoll Chemicals Ltd

Harris, Chad Andrian
Elizabeth Vintage Soap Ltd

Harris, Glenda
Elizabeth Vintage Soap Ltd

Harrison, Ian Whillas
Melpass Limited

Harrison, John Wyndham Fowler
SAS Environmental Services Ltd

Hartmann, Hannelore
Red Cottage Industries Ltd

Harwood, Reginald Frank
Ottimo Supplies Limited

Hatfull, Leigh
Kallisti Ltd

Hayman, Richard James
Ebiox Limited

He, Zhanhong
Sanofi International Biotech Co Ltd.

Head, Emilia Sophia Mary Primrose
Emilia's Handmade Bath and Body Ltd

Healey, Sarah Jane
Hunca Munka Limited

Healy, Nicola
Willis Doyle Limited

Heathcote James, Emma Julie
Little Soap Co Ltd

Heathcote, Steven Trevor
Little Soap Co Ltd

Heathcote-James, Emma Julie
Sustain Global Limited

Henry, Desmond De'oliver
Oooh Skincare Ltd

Hernandez Guaitolini, Sabrina Sonia
SGHP Ltd

Hetherington, Eleanor Lunaria
Magpie's Ocean Ltd

Hey, Paul
Ecolab Limited

Higgin, Andrew
Omnova Performance Chemicals Ltd

MacDonald, Angus Francis
The Highland Soap Co. Limited

MacDonald, Archibald Sven
The Highland Soap Co. Limited

Parton, Emma
The Highland Soap Co. Limited

Hill, Jennifer Anne
Field International UK Limited

Hinds, Dee
Coco Timyal Limited

Hinkle, Michael K
Afco C & S Limited

Hodgkinson, Andrea Marie
Lankem Ltd.

Hodgkinson, Sean Graham
Lankem Ltd.

Holah, John Trevor, Dr
Holchem Laboratories Limited

Bagshaw, Stephen Charles
The Holchem Group Limited

Bell, Simon Lee
The Holchem Group Limited

Edwards, Nicholas Quentin
The Holchem Group Limited

Hallows, Katherine Emma
The Holchem Group Limited

Hardman, Samantha Jayne
The Holchem Group Limited

Holah, John Trevor, Dr
The Holchem Group Limited

Middleton, Stuart
The Holchem Group Limited

Holford, David John
Wild Planet Products Ltd

Holford, Eileen Clare
Wild Planet Products Ltd

Holland, Martin
Fresh from Nature Limited

Holloway, Michael
Peak Soap Ltd

Davies, Simon Howard
The Home of The Green Gobblin Ltd

Firth, Delvyn Bradley
The Home of The Green Gobblin Ltd

Kimble, Carolyn Patricia
The Home of The Green Gobblin Ltd

Horton, Ruth
ZOK International Group Ltd

Horton-Mansfield, Julia
Pembrokeshire Seaweeds Ltd

Houghton, Ginina
Aromatherapy Infusions Ltd

Hoy, Alexander Henry
Arch UK Biocides Limited

Huang, Shizhong
UK Better Cleaner Industry Co., Ltd

Hubbins, Dean Alvin
Soap & Soak Limited
Soapnsoak Limited

Hubbins, Luke
Soap & Soak Limited

Huckert, Anne Stephanie Rita
Hutrade Ltd.

Hugill, Joseph Mark
Revert Limited

Hullegie, Bart Otger
Royal Sanders (UK) Limited

Humphrey, Sophie Louise
Soapberries Ltd

Humphrey, Valerie Anne
Soapberries Ltd

Humpula, Jiri
P & H Natural Skincare Ltd

Humpulova, Pavla
P & H Natural Skincare Ltd

Hunneman, Graham Nigel
Christeyns Food Hygiene Ltd

Hunniford, Brian Alexander
Archem (N.I.) Ltd

Hunniford, Lynne Diane Dorothy Joan
Archem (N.I.) Ltd

Hussein, Ghazi Abbass Mohammed Ali, Dr
GM Globalhealth Ltd

Hutchinson, Diane
Icilda's Ltd

Ibom, Tracy
R & T Natural Cosmetics Ltd

Imoru, Anna
Hunam Limited

Imran, Shaista Hina
MOL Soap Ltd.

Indzhov, Vladislav Mihaylov
Elinor-UK Ltd

Ipek, Kemal
Silk Detergent Limited

Ireland, Sarah Louise
Sarah Ireland Perfumes Ltd

Irfan, Mohammed
Fragrance Tree Ltd

Irvine, Michael Hamilton
Kitchenmaster (N.I.) Limited

Isaacs, Elliot James
Pangaea Laboratories Limited

Bloomfield-Johnson, Shemaraiah
The Italist Skincare Ltd

Mowatt, Suneil
The Italist Skincare Ltd

Ivy, Jessica
Dino-Mite Ltd

James, Jennifer
Zenith Hygiene Systems Limited

James, John Lyndon
Paragon PE Ltd

Jameson, Samantha Miranda
Soapsmith Limited

Janes, Sarah Jane
Soap School Ltd

Janmohamed, Mohsin
Academy Hair and Beauty (UK) Ltd

Jarmey, Michael
Wash Bomb Ltd

Jarvis, Adam
Greatest of All Time Soapworks Ltd

Jarvis, Sarah
Greatest of All Time Soapworks Ltd

Jenkins, Richard Mark
Techtron Limited

Jenkins, Sharron
Kalabash Limited

Jenkins, Steven Andrew
2J's Medical Supplies Ltd

John, Mazel Caryl
GoodNaturedSkincare Ltd

Johnson, Mark
Molton Brown Limited

Johnson, Olubunmi Oyetoun
Orikii Naturals Ltd

Jones, Christopher Glyn
Delf (UK) Limited

Jones, Gillian Lavinia, Dr
Rural Skills Centre Limited

Jones, Ian
Perboscolo Ltd

Jones, Jane, Dr
Delf (UK) Limited

Jones, Kate Harriet
Rural Skills Centre Limited

Jones, Nia
Spirit of The Isle Ltd.

Jones, Rachel Nadine
Aglow Limited

Jones, Tony Wyn
Spirit of The Isle Ltd.

Jover Goma, Placid Oriol
Unilever UK Limited

Kalkowska, Patrycja
Cosmetic Hooligans Ltd

Kalli, Michael
Ideal Manufacturing Limited

Kalli, Phillip
Ideal Manufacturing Limited

Kalomoiri, Natalia
Pebble Soap Ltd

Kalopungi, Charles
Aqua Chemicals Limited

Kalukenda, Sara Ntumba
Mbikudi Ltd

Kearns, David Thomas
Libra Speciality Chemicals Ltd

Keil, Gregor
Arch UK Biocides Limited

Kekiene, Aiste
Lathersmith Ltd

Kelly, Anthony William
Arch UK Biocides Limited

Kelly, Christina
CKC Aromatherapy Beauty Products Ltd

Kelly, Robert Anthony
Wizard Soap Co Ltd

Kemeny, John
Cueball Cosmetics Ltd

Kendall, Elizabeth Brock
Strathpeffer Spa Soap Co Ltd

Kenmuir, Grace Brown
Portland Janitorial Products Ltd

Kenmuir, Neil Shannon Baird
Portland Janitorial Products Ltd

Kenmuir, Paul Baird
Portland Janitorial Products Ltd

Kenny, Charlene
Lather Cute Soap Limited

Kerouac, Geoffrey David
Friendly Soap Limited

Khan, Muhammad Mohsin
Lofty Gardens Ltd

Khatun, Sojia
Soap & Soak Limited
Soapnsoak Limited

Kilci, Mustafa Nejat
Ersag UK Limited

Kilgallon, Daniel John
Christeyns UK Ltd

Kilpatrick, Timothy Fraser
Newton Formulations Limited

King, Sasha
Insensed Ltd

Kirby, Christopher
Naturally Nourishing Ltd

Kirk, Karen
Syntec Manufacturing Limited

Kirkwood, Georgina Grace
Anahita Limited

Klymczuk, Natasha
Paws and Unwind Limited

Knight, Kieron Patrick
Revert Limited

Knox, James Christopher
Gard Chemicals Limited
Larragard Limited
Main Chemical Co Limited

Knox, Sarah Kate
Larragard Limited
Main Chemical Co Limited

Korkus, Andrew
NS Industries Ltd

Korytakova, Veronika
B.Me Skincare Ltd
Savon de V Ltd

Krajewska, Ilona Anna
Proskin Europe Ltd

Krajewski, Rafal Tomasz
Proskin Europe Ltd

Krauss, Johann Gerhard
Acdoco Limited
Springdawn Bolton Limited

Kristian, Jan
Chemisphere UK Limited

Kruger, Anya
Anyki Ltd

Kundrak, Peter
Exterin Ltd

Kwiecinski, Tomasz
Holistic Plant Technologies Ltd

Lafbery, Derek John
Zenith Hygiene Systems Limited

Lambart, Paul
R-MC Power Recovery Limited

Landreth-Smith, Joseph
Ko. Essentials Ltd.

Landreth-Smith, Megan
Ko. Essentials Ltd.

Lang, Barbara
MSL Limited

Lang, Gillies
MSL Limited

Langdon, Darren Paul
Coventry Chemicals Limited

Laskaris, Panagiotis
Fysifarm Limited

Laurie, Stephen
Calman Enterprise Limited

Jefferson, Toby Marcus
James Law (Chemicals) Limited

Wilkinson, Sean
James Law (Chemicals) Limited

Lawrence, Sarah
Gosling Soap Ltd

Lee, Carl Richmond
Adam Investment Co Ltd
Ecolab Limited

Lee, Nikki, Dr
Little Green Beehive Ltd

Lees, Jane
Millchem (UK) Limited

Lees, Jevan Maurice
Millchem (UK) Limited

Lees, Sheila
Millchem (UK) Limited

Leigh, Stephen Paul
Prime Industries Ltd

Lemay, James
Omnova Performance Chemicals Ltd

Levy, Alexander
Safeway Wood Care Limited

Levy, John Irvin
NCH (UK) Limited

Lewis, Emma Jayne
Smelliz Ltd

Lewis, Joel Howard
Shorrock Trichem Limited

Lewis, Owen Richard
Pangaea Laboratories Limited

Lim, Charissa Salvacion Simangan
Bare & Bloom Works Handmade Bath and Body Treats

Lindberg, Cecilia Monika Jenny
Soapaffection Ltd

King, Andrew
The Little Goat Soap Co Ltd

King, Joanne
The Little Goat Soap Co Ltd

White, Maxine Sharon
The Little Wax Workshop Ltd

Littlebury, Nicholas Stephen
Gemini Cosmetics Ltd

Llewellyn Williams, Gareth David
Seren Soaps Limited

Llewellyn Williams, Jillian, Dr
Seren Soaps Limited

Lock, Richard Antony David
Libra Speciality Chemicals Ltd

Lockley, Andrew Thomas
Pluswipes Limited
Sani Professional Limited

Longshaw, Roy
Prime Industries Ltd

Lucas, John Stephen
Food Tech Hygiene Limited
Specialised Aerosols Co Ltd

Lucas, Kevin Paul
Food Tech Hygiene Limited
Specialised Aerosols Co Ltd

Lucas, Marene
Specialised Aerosols Co Ltd

Lucas, Noel Heeley
Specialised Aerosols Co Ltd

Lucas, Robert Stanley
Cut from The Wild Limited

Luchowa, Zeena
Wild Stem Soaps Limited

Luu, Anh
Evonik Goldschmidt UK Limited

Lymn, Edward George
Rapid Washrooms Limited

Lyth, Mark Anthony
Completely Conkers Limited

M'baye, Tidiane, Lord
Coco Timyal Limited

MacDonald, Alexander Arthur
Zenith Hygiene Group Limited

MacDonogh, Stephen James
Renbow Haircare Limited

Mainwaring, Paul
Aromatic Scents Ltd

Makangu, Hermine
Mbikudi Ltd

Lawson-Brown, Jonathan Frederick
Tony Maleedy Hair Ltd.

Maleedy, Anthony Thomas
Tony Maleedy Hair Ltd.

Malet, Ryan James
Letlalo Ltd

Malik, Mohammad Irfan
3M UK Trading Limited

Mancuso, Angelo
Shifting London Ltd

Mangan, Claire Amy
Deliciously Me Ltd

Mansfield, Anthony Brian
Decontamin8 (Europe) Limited
Decontamin8 Limited

Mansfield, John Phares
Pembrokeshire Seaweeds Ltd

Marosi, Szonja Fruzsina
Zenken Limited

Marsh, Paul
Coventry Chemicals Limited

Marshall, Samuel Kyle
Marsh Valley Ltd

Martin, Elizabeth
Elizabeth Martin Creative Studio Ltd

Martin, Benjamin
Mano Pack Limited

Martin-Gilmore, Bruno
Nature B Limited

Matterson, Nicholas Noel Hardwick
SC Johnson Professional Ltd

Mattinson, Tracey
Dalton Luxury Ltd

Matvejevs, Ilja
Hempia Limited

Maxwell, Bruce James Peter
Dri-Pak Limited

Maxwell, Carolyn Mary
Dri-Pak Limited

Maxwell, Jillian
Dri-Pak Limited

Maxwell, Peter Stuart
Dri-Pak Limited

Butts, Christina Juliet
Christina May Limited

Butts, Courtenay Arthur Robert
Christina May Limited

Butts, Oliver Courtenay Richard
Christina May Limited

Mazurek, Wojciech
Stepan UK Limited

Rattigan, David Thomas
Robert McBride Ltd

Smith, Christopher Ian Charles
Robert McBride Ltd

Vos, Rik Jean Pierre Dora Albert De
Robert McBride Ltd

McCaffrey, Paul David
Paul McCaffrey Systems Ltd

McCaffrey, Josephine Anne
Paul McCaffrey Systems Ltd

McCaig, Bryce
MSL Limited

McClennan, Lee
Hocktester Ltd

McCloy, David Michael
Kitchenmaster (N.I.) Limited

McComish, Ian
Bespro Chemicals Ltd

McCormick, Darren Johnston
Shinerite Solutions Limited

McCourt, Sandra
Mauchit Ltd

McCracken, Alistair Samuel David
Droyt Products Limited

McCracken, Glyn Robert
Chemisphere UK Limited

McGee, Maria Teresa, Dr
Marble Hill Soaps Limited

McGee, Michelle
Denykem Limited

McGuigan, Kevin Generald
Techtron Limited

McGuinness, Emma
Belkor Bay Limited

McIntosh, David Dennis
Residual Barrier Technology Ltd

McIntosh, Gordon Henry
Calman Enterprise Limited

McKay, Craig
Biologico Cosmetics Limited

McMillan, David Brian
Inter Bio Chemicals Ltd

McNally, Gavin Patrick
Royal Sanders (UK) Limited

Meehan, Michael Christopher
Holt Lloyd International Ltd

Mensah, Charlotte Irene
Amira Products Ltd

Merali, Shabbir
Toilet Safe UK Limited

Micklethwaite, Andrew
Star Brands (Holdings) Limited

Middleton, Sarah Kay
Scinn Limited

Middleton, Stuart
Holchem Laboratories Limited
Merlin Chemicals Limited

Mihut, Beatrice Mariana
Adamy Cosmetics Ltd

Mills, Stephanie Rachel Anne, Dr
Little Lodge Bees Ltd

Mills, William Stuart
Little Lodge Bees Ltd

Mitchell, Ian James
Ian Mitchell Distribution Ltd

Mitchell, Leah
Ultra Bien Limited

Molli Boulock, Richard
Haromatic Ltd

Moon, John Andrew
Totem Properties Limited

Moon, Susan Anne
London Soap and Chemical Co. Ltd
Totem Properties Limited

Moore, Beatrice
Amita Cosmetics Ltd

The Top UK Soap and Detergent Manufacturers

Moore, Nicola Jane
Jackanoryjones Limited

Moore, Steven Karl
Jackanoryjones Limited

Morris, Clive Andrew
Medichem Manufacturing Ltd

Mortimer, Andrew John
Fillcare Limited

Mosley, Darren James
Easy Newco Limited

Moss, Christina
Bloom and Blossom Limited

Moss, Stephen David
Bonasystems Europe Ltd

Mouyokolo, Gladys Gladys
Arize and Dazzle Limited

Muhammad, Raechel
Lana-Rae Ltd Ltd

Mullane, Mark Gary
Texatherm Systems Limited

Mullane, Patricia Ann
Texatherm Systems Limited

Munden, Sebastian John
Unilever UK Limited

Munro, Neil William
Smartic Truckwash Ltd

Munro, William Donald
Smartic Truckwash Ltd

Murakami, Yoshihiro
Molton Brown Limited

Murphy, Alison
McIntyre Group Ltd.

Murphy, Sarah Jayne
Yogi Fresh Limited

Murray, Lee Daryl
Saanro International Limited

Muschner, Jenny
Salopian Ltd

Muschner, Jorg Alexander Richard
Salopian Ltd

Naik, Kalpana Rajesh
Best-Chem Limited
MSH Chemical Manufacturing Ltd

Naik, Rajesh
Best-Chem Limited
MSH Chemical Manufacturing Ltd

Naik, Suraj
Momar Limited

Naisbitt, Peter Alexander
Field International UK Limited

Phillips, Max
The Natural Soap Co Ltd

Phillips, Sara
The Natural Soap Co Ltd

Navaresi, Francis
Annael Ltd

Navaresi, Joanne
Annael Ltd

Naysmith, John
Syntec Manufacturing Limited

Neicho, Martin
Gently Handcrafted Ltd

Neicho, Monica
Gently Handcrafted Ltd

Nelson, Natalee
Madalyn and Rose Ltd

Nimmo, Jane Elvere
Let It Bee Ltd

Nnochiri, George Cinadu
Nuts About Soap Limited

Noonan, Anne Patricia
Omnova Performance Chemicals Ltd

Nouri, Monika
Poppy Products Limited

Novo, Rob
Zep UK Limited

O'Donnell, Jonathon Micheal
R-MC Power Recovery Limited

O'Kane, Brian A
Kitchenmaster (N.I.) Limited

O'Neill, Tracey Ann
GEA Farm Technologies (UK) Ltd

O'Sullivan, Evbi
Berry Inc Ltd
Evbioo Ltd

Ocampo, Edman Relox
Ed N' Grace Ltd

Odam, Elizabeth Louise
Murray-Smith Consulting Ltd

Ogario, Norris
OC Transformation Limited

Ogario, Rachael
OC Transformation Limited

Ogunlesi, Simon Kayode
Vuitton Group Ltd

Okoji, Ndoh Akpan
Koorax Ltd

Oladejo, Adeyinka Samuel
Samola Industries Limited

Oliver, David Lee
Shorrock Trichem Limited

Onuba, Nnenna
21 Road Limited

Carolus, Elisa Rosa Marije
The Original Soapchair Co Ltd

Gilmour, Douglas Fullarton
The Original Soapchair Co Ltd

Ovens, Hayley
Mazu Seaweed Limited

Ovens, Justin
Mazu Seaweed Limited

Owens, Kieran Dean
Ultima Direct Limited

Ozdemir, Rustem
Silk Detergent Limited

Pade, Henrik Nygaard
Clean Bidco Limited
Clean Topco Limited

Ballesteros, Marie Margaret
The Paisley Soap Co Ltd

Palmer, Stacey Jamie
Soaps By Stacey Limited

Papadopoulos, Amina
Fysha Ltd

Parker, James
Bubble Shack Ltd

Parkinson, Anita Jayne
Duchess Naturals Limited

Partridge, Naomi Joy
Ko. Essentials Ltd.

Partridge, Raymond Keith
Diversey Limited

Partridge, Thomas Michael
Ko. Essentials Ltd.

Pascoe, Gloria
Born To Be Natural Ltd

Pascoe, Malcolm James
Born To Be Natural Ltd

Pascu, Adina
Procter & Gamble Product Supply (U.K.)

Pastoll, Errol, Dr
Ora-Heal Ltd

Patel, Abdul Ebrahim
Freshorize Ltd

Patel, Himanshu
Cleanux Chemicals Ltd

Patel, Rakesh
Zenith Hygiene Systems Limited

Pathak, Nina
Midland Chemicals Limited

Pathak, Sunil
Midland Chemicals Limited

Patience, Talon
Pebble Soap Ltd

Fraser, Elise Anne, Dr
The Peaceful Potager Limited

Pearce, David James
Easy Newco Limited

Pearson, Cynthia Jean
Unitor Limited

Pearson, Dean
Pangaea Laboratories Limited

Pearson, John Dudley D'Urben
Unitor Limited

Peart-Johnson, Joseph
Wholesome Toiletries Ltd

Pedler, Cherry Elizabeth
Ideation Solutions Limited

Perman, Timothy James
TRU Products Limited

Perrin, Marie Ruth
Chemisphere UK Limited

Perring, Marie
Vienne Luca Limited

Petkov, Jordan Todorov
Arch UK Biocides Limited

Pettitt, Alison Jane
Cater-Lyne Limited
Zenith Hygiene Group Limited
Zenith Hygiene Systems Limited

Pfeffer, Uziel
Sycamore (UK) Limited

Philippou, Antony
Chela Ltd

Phillips, Steven
Bonasystems Europe Ltd

Piekarska, Michalina Elzbieta
Polka Lab Limited

Pilkington, Frederic Alexander Broughton
Nomad Soapery Limited

Pilling, Brandon
Acdoco Limited
Astley Dye and Chemical Co Ltd
Pilling Trading Limited
Springdawn Bolton Limited

Pilling, Elizabeth
Astley Dye and Chemical Co Ltd
Pilling Trading Limited

Pinnington, Giles
Vanillin Limited

Pisano, Anthony, Dr
Mimi Pisano Limited

Plant, Christopher
Piesse and Kinney Limited

Polegri, Paolo
Zep UK Limited

Woodger, Victoria Helen
The Pretty Little Treat Company (Yorkshire)

Price, Russell Lawrence
NCH (UK) Limited

Pronk, John Otto Eduard
Apvodo Ltd.

Angus, Murray
The Proton Group Limited

Shaw, David
The Proton Group Limited

Purdie, Gavin Ernest
Purdie's of Argyll Ltd

Quaddus, Samina
Detergents Ltd

Quinlan, Stephen
Coventry Chemicals Limited

Quinn, Melanie Gail Campbell
Windy Mill Ltd

Majoros, Agnes Renata
The Quint Essence Lab Ltd

Varro, Attila
The Quint Essence Lab Ltd

Qureshi, Myra Husain
Conatural Ltd

Radley, Deborah Jane
Goats on the Coast Ltd

Radley, Stuart James
Goats on the Coast Ltd

Ramnathkar, Tejal Ajay
Washworks Bodycare Limited

Ranno, Consolazione
Sikania Ltd

Rasool, Kasam
Diamond (Edibles) Limited

Rawding, Paul
Adam Investment Co Ltd
Ecolab Limited

Ray, Didier
Stepan UK Limited

Redman, Patrick Garfield
Diversey Limited

Redrobe, Sharon, Dr
Sustain Global Limited

Reilly, Alan William
Wagonwash Limited

Reilly, Karen Nichola
Bonham Soaps Limited

Reilly, Peter
Zep UK Limited

Rhodes, Simon Timothy
Dee Doo Limited

Rhodes, Suzan
Dee Doo Limited

Rhodes, Terence Richard
Zamo Household Products Ltd

Rice, James
Newry Chemicals Ltd

Rice, Margaret
Newry Chemicals Ltd

Richards, Natalie Sarah
Mild + Wild Ltd

Richardson, Philip William
Melpass Limited

Richardson, Sandra
Respect Soaps Limited

Ricketts, Jemma
Enchanted Plants Ltd

Ripley, Levi
Lick Labs Limited

Ritchie, Fiona
Ochil Skincare Co Ltd

Burton, Andrea
The Rite Solution Limited

Burton, Ian Anthony
The Rite Solution Limited

Burton, Luke Michael
The Rite Solution Limited

Roberts, David Thomas
Rutpen Limited

Roberts, Julie Susan
Christeyns UK Ltd
Clover Chemicals Limited

Roberts, Martin Cameron
Total Liquid Solutions Ltd

Robertson, Barbara Ann
St Andrews Soap Co Ltd

Robson, Chandler Conner
Team Titan Performance Ltd

Rochford, John
Safe Solutions (Safe4) Limited

Roe, Jamie Andrew
Suds & Salve Ltd

Rogers, Thomas Karl
Eco Earth Limited

Rose, Amber Marie
Amsar Soap Co Ltd

Rosewarne, Ross Anthony
Lick Labs Limited

Ross, Derek Blair
Montague Lloyd Limited
Scottish Fine Soaps Limited

Ross, Robert Collumbine
Scottish Fine Soaps Limited

The Top UK Soap and Detergent Manufacturers

Ross, Robert Columbine
Montague Lloyd Limited

Royle, Debra
Cliffe House (Organics) Ltd

Royle, Graham
Libra Speciality Chemicals Ltd

Royle, Peter Andrew
Cliffe House (Organics) Ltd

Royle, Thomas Michael
Cliffe House (Organics) Ltd

Ruan, Qingye
UK Pandora Fairy Skin Beautiyfying Co.,

Russell, Chinwe Mercy
Sheabynature Ltd

Ryan, Mark
Natural British Limited

Saik, Kawther
Elegant Soap Co Ltd

Salawu, Awulatu Enitan
Natural Jem Limited

Salifu, Haja Nana
Dagarti CIC

Salifu, Haja
Nana's Studio Ltd

Salur, Fulya
SE & SA Limited

Satchell, David Christopher
Eucaderm Limited

Saunders, Reece
Eljay Group Ltd

Saunders, Ryan
Eljay Group Ltd

Sawyer, Graham
De Montfort Marketing Limited

Sawyer, Maria Louise
De Montfort Marketing Limited

Scaramuzza, Catarina
CS Holistic Therapy Products Ltd

Scarffe, Rory
Industrial Chemical Experts Ltd

Schnidrig, Astrid
Arch UK Biocides Limited

Schofield, Jeffrey
Midland Chemicals Limited

Schofield, Mary
Lemon Spring Ltd

Scott-Underdown, Michael Montgomery
Coventry Chemicals Limited

Seddon, Stuart
Soapworks Limited

Sedman, Jonathan Paul
Black and Silver Equestrian Ltd

Seewald-Butzerin, Alexandre
Axwood Limited

Semerciyan, Simla
3M UK Trading Limited

Senturk, Gizem Ezgi
SE & SA Limited

Serra, Massimo
Farasha-Cosmetics Ltd

Shah, Dinesh Chhabildas
Eden Classics Limited
Freestyle Beauty Products Ltd
Universal Toiletries Corporation Ltd

Shah, Jayshree Dinesh
Eden Classics Limited
Freestyle Beauty Products Ltd
Universal Toiletries Corporation Ltd

Shah, Karan
Freestyle Beauty Products Ltd
Universal Toiletries Corporation Ltd

Shaikh, Shahishtaanjum Irfan
Soul of Ayurveda Ltd

Sharma, Rajinder Kumar
Nimble Babies Limited

Shaw, David
Java Coffee Co Ltd

Shaw, John Roger
Itaconix (U.K.) Limited

Shemesh Idelson, Efrat
Zomi Ltd

Shepherd, Daryl Paxton
Universal Chemicals Limited

Shepherd, Malcolm David
Universal Chemicals Limited

Shepherd, Ryan David
Universal Chemicals Limited

Sheth, Neha Vijay
Felicity Solutions Ltd

Shipman, Jonathan David
Bar.None Limited

Shode, Olufemi Olukayode, Dr
Yess Essentials Limited

Shode, Oluyemisi Olabisi, Dr
Yess Essentials Limited

Shorrock, Keith Entwistle
Shorrock Trichem Limited

Shorrocks, Janet Marie
Soapy Skin Limited

Short, Annabelle
Dijon Soaps Limited

Barker, Aimee Sarah
The Shrieking Soap Shack Ltd

Shrigley-Feigl, Francis Henry
Piesse and Kinney Limited

Siddall, Philip Graham
Star Brands (Holdings) Limited
Star Brands Limited

Siddons, Stacey
Bean and Boy Ltd

Silcox, Nigel Patrick
Clean Sciences Limited

Sim-Morbey, Amanda Jane
Island Soapery Ltd

Simpson-White, Faye Leanora
Beardog and Roo Ltd

Sinclair, Rachel Isabella
Soap Sensations Ltd

Singer, Edward Cameron
Apex Industrial Chemicals Ltd

Singleton, Sarah
Azure Liquid Solutions Limited

Sitlani, Vijay Indroo
Procter & Gamble Product Supply (U.K.)

Slater, Thomas Agnew Hamilton
Montague Lloyd Limited
Scottish Fine Soaps Limited

Smales, Stephen David
Stepan UK Limited

Smith, Fiona
Saltaire Soap Ltd

Smith, Jackie
Ohana Soaps and More Limited

Snoekx, Eline
Humble Bee Botanica Ltd.

Williams, Beatrice Emma
The Soap Arcade Limited

Khoo, Daniel
The Soap Cellar Limited

Coleman, Victoria
The Soap Collection Limited

Wilde, Kate
The Soap Collection Limited

Mills, Benjamin Charles Lewis
The Soap Foundry Limited

Ismail, Muhammad Mobeen-Ul-Anwar
The Soap Legacy Ltd

Patel, Husnabanu
The Soap Legacy Ltd

Munier, Helen Louise
The Soap People Ltd

Rogerson, Faye
The Soap Shop Ltd

Jeena, Marria
The Soap Souk Ltd

Waring, Simon Banks
The Soap Story Limited

Waring, William Banks
The Soap Story Limited

Beddows, Hazel Margaret
The Soapy Goat Ltd

McCrystal Edge, Gemma Rita
The Soapy Goat Ltd

Sowden, Michael John
Cornwall Soapbox (Mevagissey) Ltd

Sowden, Suzanne Eileen
Cornwall Soapbox (Mevagissey) Ltd

Spence, Ian Dale Benham
So.Soap Co Ltd

Spence, Patricia Ann
So.Soap Co Ltd

Spina, Carlo Alberto
West Trading Ltd

Day, Olga
The Springer Soap Co Ltd

Spurling, Stuart Anthony
Malibu Health Products Limited

Stadward, Rebecca Jane
Season Clean Ltd

Stanley, Colin John
Kitchenmaster (N.I.) Limited

Starkey, Paul
Coventry Chemicals Limited

Staton, Michael Alexander
Pluswipes Limited

Stephen, Philips
Bonasystems Worldwide Ltd

Stepney, Pamela
4th Floor Products Limited

Stepney, Richard Ian
4th Floor Products Limited

Stevens, Hannah
Wren and Willow Limited

Stevens, Kevin Shaun
Bristol Soap Limited

Stewart, Sarah Christina
Smelliz Ltd

Stockwin, Allan David
Safe Solutions (Safe4) Limited

Stokes, Kerry
Soap & Soak Limited

Stone, Robert Michael
Gondar Soaps Ltd

Stoner, Amanda Jane
Denykem Limited

Stoner, Paul
Denykem Limited

Storf, David
Forward Chemicals Ltd

Storf, Richard Charles
Forward Chemicals Ltd

Story, John Michael
Stephenson Group Ltd

Strachan, Jonathan David
Unilever UK Limited

Strang, Edwin John
Industrial Chemicals Limited

Stubbs, Colin Timothy
Diversey Holdings Limited
Diversey Industrial Limited
Diversey Limited

Stubbs, Peter Richard
Chromasol Limited

Subramaniam, Karunakaran
Anuvaayum Ltd

Sukdao, Wesley Timothy
Emma Victoria Cosmetics Ltd

Sumner, Jonathan
LJSP Ltd

Sumner, Robert Bird
LJSP Ltd

Surdo, John-Paul
Diversey Limited
Zenith Hygiene Group Limited

Sutherland, Linda Gail
Hebridean Soap Co Ltd

Swan, Nicholas Alistair
Residual Barrier Technology Ltd

Swinney, Paul Christopher
Scorcher Idea Limited

Swithenbank, Lisa
Smellifiscent Ltd

Sy, Von Ryan Chua
Nimble Babies Limited

Tait, Mark Alexander
Sheer Bliss Retail Ltd

Talai, Farzaneh
E-Sensual Oil Soap By Farah Ltd

Taylor, Barbara Izabella
Decon Laboratories Limited

Taylor, Craig
Get The Scent Limited

Taylor, Jessica
47 Skin Ltd

Taylor, John
Chemisphere UK Limited

Taylor, Robert Nicholas
Decon Laboratories Limited

Taylor, Stephen Roger
Sechelle Manufacturing Limited

Taylor-Dix, Yvonne
Von Bons Bath Bombs Limited

Teasdale Brown, Marten Llewellyn
Pluswipes Limited

Teasdale-Brown, Marten Llewellyn
Sani Professional Limited

Teneqja, Valdet
Alkleen Ltd

Adjei, Emma
The Therapy Factory Ltd

Thomas, Isamba Tausi
Wildcraft Ltd

Thomas, Jasmin
Ohana CBD Limited

Thomas, Joanne Patricia
Grassroots Health Ltd

Thomas, Richard Neil
Lamella Structures Limited

Thomas, Stephen James
Dasic International Limited

Thomas, Titty Pappachen
Heavenly Fragrance (UK) Ltd

Thomlinson, Nicholas Howard
Bonasystems Europe Ltd

Thompson, Samuel David Andrew
Kirkwood Chemicals Ltd

Thornton, Geoff Thomas Glenn
Thornton Baron Ltd

Thorp, Simon James
Datesand Limited

Tillbrook, Dean Thomas William
Grassroots Health Ltd

Atkins, Charles David
Kathryn Tilly Limited

Atkins, Kathryn Sophie
Kathryn Tilly Limited

Timmis, Jonathan
ERH Propack Limited

Tobias, James Mark
Clover Chemicals Limited

Toms, David
Cares Laboratory Limited

Torres Benitez, Gloria Magali
Everfolk Limited

Tothova, Timea
Soap Lab Limited

Trew, Neil
OCD Finish Limited

The Top UK Soap and Detergent Manufacturers

Tripp, Richard Terence
Rutpen Limited

Tuckey, Callum
Auto. B Limited

Turner, Alexandra Louise
Washworks Bodycare Limited

Turner, Jason John
Grumpy Gorilla Ltd

Tylko, Joanna
Gio Natura Ltd

Tzortzis, Akis Zafirios
Carzel Limited

Ukmata, Ardian
Alkleen Ltd

Usman, Godman
Maribella London Limited

V.David, Krisztin
Glamour Natural Cosmetics Ltd

V.David, Tamas
Glamour Natural Cosmetics Ltd

Van Aken, Peter Jozef
Arch UK Biocides Limited

Vasilkovaite, Beata
Mama Bee Soaps Ltd

Vaughan, Melanie Susan
Biggin Bees Limited

Hedger, Claudia Elizabeth
The Vegan Soap Co Ltd

Vijayam, Upendra Shenoy Umesh
Ayurveda Wellness Ltd

Vundum, Marina Emma Lucy
Essential Spirit Limited

Wainwright, Dominic Neil
Hitchin Soap Co Ltd

Walczak, Mariusz
Danchemtech Ltd

Wallen, Andrew Wray
Melpass Limited

Wallen, James Wray
Melpass Limited

Wallen, Richard Wray
Melpass Limited

Walsh, Jacqualine
Kitchenmaster (N.I.) Limited

Wang, Yinghui
Nimble Babies Limited

Ward, Paul
Paragon PE Ltd
Paragon Technical PE Services Ltd

Hall, Ami-Jayne
The Waterside Soap Co Ltd

Watson, Adam
Savage Alchemy Limited

Webb, Dawn
Fresh from Nature Limited

Weber, Andrea
Candy & Mischief Ltd

Wells, Susan Jane
Old Park Farm Estate Limited

Wheeler, David George
Rutpen Limited

Whelan, Claire Margaret
Mrs Whelan Ltd

White, Deloris Elaine
Deloris White Limited

White, David Charles
Diversey UK Production Limited

White, Laurel
Sweet Orange Soapery Ltd

Whittle, Kevin David
Rutpen Limited

Whowell, John Luke
Carvansons Ltd

Wightman, Gary Kenneth
Procter & Gamble Product Supply (U.K.)

Wilcock, Chloe
Goatally Soaps Ltd

Wilcock, David James
Goatally Soaps Ltd

Willatt, Daniel
Natural By Nature Limited

Williams, Beatrice Emma
You're Gorgeous Handmade Soap Ltd

Williams, Charles Edwin
Chemex (North West) Limited

Williams, Daniel
Cahercon Group Limited

Williams, Daphne Veronica
Rowanhays Ltd

Williams, David Alfred
Future Developments (Manufacturing)

Williams, Marie Ann
Reesoaps.co.uk Ltd

Williams, Paul
Future Developments (Manufacturing)

Wilson, Dorothy
Ottimo Supplies Limited

Wilson, Harry Edward
Ottimo Supplies Limited

Wilson, Janice
Northumbrian Botanicals Ltd

Wilson, Robert
Durabond Chemicals Limited

Wilson, Scott Alan Grant
Christeyns UK Ltd

Wilson, William Brown
Montague Lloyd Limited
Scottish Fine Soaps Limited

Winks, Kedric
Ghastly Games Limited

Winning, James Provan
Syntec Manufacturing Limited

Winters, Joanne
Making Scents Ltd

Withey, John Damon
CClear Limited

Withey, Sandra Lynn Eunice
CClear Limited

Wittouck, Jozef Maria Jaak
Christeyns UK Ltd
Clover Chemicals Limited

Wittouck, Jozef
Christeyns Food Hygiene Ltd

Wood, Claire
Datesand Limited

Wood, Jonathon Richard
Datesand Limited

Wood, Laura
Bayer-Wood Technologies Ltd

Wood, Nicholas Andrew
Datesand Limited

Wood, Roderick Charles Rowland
Bayer-Wood Technologies Ltd

Woodhead, David Alexander
Selden Research Limited

Woodhead, Denis Edwin
Selden Research Limited

Woodhead, Mark Andrew
Selden Research Limited

Woodhead, Peter Philip
Selden Research Limited

Woodhead, Sandra Buchanan
Selden Research Limited

Woodley, Elaine
Dogbreath Brewery Ltd

Woodley, Timothy
Dogbreath Brewery Ltd

Woodward, Marc John
Unilever UK Limited

Wordsworth-Goodram, Gillian Margaret
Wordsworth Handcrafted Soap Co Ltd

Worsley, Wilfred Paul
Chemisphere UK Limited

Wozniak, Aleksandra
Gondar Soaps Ltd

Turner, Lisa
The Wrinkly Elephant Co Ltd

Turner, Stuart Paul
The Wrinkly Elephant Co Ltd

Yates, Emma Victoria, Dr
Emma Victoria Cosmetics Ltd

Ye, Qiaoyin
UK Nuduun Personal-Care Supply Co.,

Yearsley, Robert William
Hygenol Cleaning Supplies Ltd

Forsyth, Jonathan Scott
The Yorkshire Dales Soap Co Ltd

Young, Christopher John
Procter & Gamble Product Supply (U.K.)

Yule, Julia
Bloom and Blossom Limited

Yussouf, Saba
Clensure Global Ltd

Standard Industrial Classification
excluding
Manufacture of soap and detergents

01110 Growing of cereals (except rice), leguminous crops and oil seeds
Paul McCaffrey Systems Ltd

01190 Growing of other non-perennial crops
Peaceful Potager Limited

01280 Growing of spices, aromatic, drug and pharmaceutical crops
Seilich Limited

01500 Mixed farming
Little Lodge Bees Ltd

01629 Support activities for animal production (other than farm animal boarding)
Rural Skills Centre Limited

03210 Marine aquaculture
Pembrokeshire Seaweeds Ltd

08930 Extraction of salt
Anyki Ltd

10320 Manufacture of fruit and vegetable juice
Kleos Naturals Ltd

10390 Other processing and preserving of fruit and vegetables
Biggin Bees Limited
SE & SA Limited

10410 Manufacture of oils and fats
Diamond (Edibles) Limited
Kleos Naturals Ltd

10511 Liquid milk and cream production
Goats on the Coast Ltd

10512 Butter and cheese production
Goats on the Coast Ltd

10519 Manufacture of other milk products
Goats on the Coast Ltd

10520 Manufacture of ice cream
Ideation Solutions Limited
Unilever UK Limited

10710 Manufacture of bread; manufacture of fresh pastry goods and cakes
Very Good Vegan Co Ltd

10831 Tea processing
Zyzven Naturals Cosmetics Ltd

10840 Manufacture of condiments and seasonings
Jared Gonzalez Ltd

10860 Manufacture of homogenized food preparations and dietetic food
Haromatic Ltd

10890 Manufacture of other food products n.e.c.
Dri-Pak Limited
Felicity Solutions Ltd
Happy Bee Co Ltd
Nana's Studio Ltd
Pembrokeshire Seaweeds Ltd

10910 Manufacture of prepared feeds for farm animals
GM Globalhealth Ltd

13300 Finishing of textiles
Anyki Ltd

13921 Manufacture of soft furnishings
Lamina Animal Limited

13990 Manufacture of other textiles n.e.c.
Auto. B Limited

14120 Manufacture of workwear
Madcow Brand Limited

14190 Manufacture of other wearing apparel and accessories n.e.c.
Dino-Mite Ltd

16240 Manufacture of wooden containers
Paul McCaffrey Systems Ltd

16290 Manufacture of other products of wood; manufacture of articles of cork, straw and plaiting materials
Paul McCaffrey Systems Ltd

17220 Manufacture of household and sanitary goods and of toilet requisites [12]
Cahercon Group Limited
Chinese Gentry Limited
Evocativ Limited
Lick Labs Limited
Mild + Wild Ltd
Original Soapchair Co Ltd
SC567361 Ltd.
Sanofi International Biotech Co Ltd.
Toilet Safe UK Limited
UK Better Cleaner Industry Co., Ltd
UK Nuduun Personal-Care Supply Co.,
United Company Specialty Chemicals & Mineral Oils

17230 Manufacture of paper stationery
Crafty Lady Ltd

18202 Reproduction of video recording
Anastaz Beverly Hills Ltd

19201 Mineral oil refining
Holt Lloyd International Ltd

20130 Manufacture of other inorganic basic chemicals
Aqua Chemicals Limited
Ideal Manufacturing Limited
Industrial Chemicals Limited
M.A. Industries Limited
Madcow Brand Limited
Molton Brown Limited
Team Titan Performance Ltd

20140 Manufacture of other organic basic chemicals
Aqua Chemicals Limited
Body Candy Ltd.
Daisy Gordon Limited
Italist Skincare Ltd
Lana-Rae Ltd Ltd
Macob Online Shopping Ltd.
Mauchit Ltd
McIntyre Group Ltd.

20200 Manufacture of pesticides and other agrochemical products
Clean Sciences Limited

20301 Manufacture of paints, varnishes and similar coatings, mastics and sealants
Boweasel Ltd
Holt Lloyd International Ltd
Safeway Wood Care Limited
Supreme Wax Limited

20412 Manufacture of cleaning and polishing preparations [48]
3M UK Trading Limited
R P Adam Limited
Archem (N.I.) Ltd
Auto. B Limited
Autosheen Ltd
Autosmart Group Limited
Autosmart Holdings Limited
Boweasel Ltd
K C Butler & Son Limited
Carapoll Chemicals Ltd
Cater-Lyne Limited
Chimera UK Chemical Solutions Ltd
Chromasol Limited
Clean Bidco Limited
Clean Sciences Limited
Clean Topco Limited
Cleanux Chemicals Ltd
Diversey UK Production Limited
Ebiox Limited
Evans Vanodine International PLC
Evocativ Limited
Freshorize Ltd
Java Coffee Co Ltd
Larragard Limited
Madcow Brand Limited
Main Chemical Co Limited
Robert McBride Ltd
OCD Finish Limited
Old Park Farm Estate Limited
Ottimo Supplies Limited
Paramount Chemicals Limited
Proton Group Limited
Quill International Chemicals Ltd
SC567361 Ltd.
Saanro International Limited
Safeway Wood Care Limited

The Top UK Soap and Detergent Manufacturers

Sanofi International Biotech Co Ltd.
Season Clean Ltd
Star Brands (Holdings) Limited
Star Brands Limited
Supreme Wax Limited
Techtron Limited
Tiger Lily Soapery Ltd
Travik Chemicals (UK) Limited
Trichem Scotland Limited
United Company Specialty Chemicals & Mineral Oils
Wash Bomb Ltd
Zamo Household Products Ltd

20420 Manufacture of perfumes and toilet preparations [112]

Anuvaayum Ltd
Anyki Ltd
Archem (N.I.) Ltd
Aromabar (Scotland) Ltd
Aromatherapy Infusions Ltd
Aromatic Scents Ltd
Aventual Ltd
Axwood Limited
Ayurveda Wellness Ltd
Berry Inc Ltd
Biologico Cosmetics Limited
Bloomtown Ltd
Body Candy Ltd.
Body Station Limited
CS Holistic Therapy Products Ltd
Caley's of Exeter Ltd
Carapoll Chemicals Ltd
Carzel Limited
Clover Chemicals Limited
Cocoa Lime Limited
Cosmetic Hooligans Ltd
Eco Earth Limited
Ed N' Grace Ltd
Eden Classics Limited
Elinor-UK Ltd
Essential Spirit Limited
Evans Vanodine International PLC
Evocativ Limited
Farasha-Cosmetics Ltd
Fillcare Limited
Freestyle Beauty Products Ltd
Freshorize Ltd
Fysifarm Limited
Gio Natura Ltd
Glamour Natural Cosmetics Ltd
Greatest of All Time Soapworks Ltd
Haromatic Ltd
Heavenly Fragrance (UK) Ltd
Highland Soap Co. Limited
Holistic Plant Technologies Ltd
Icilda's Ltd
Insensed Ltd
Sarah Ireland Perfumes Ltd
Itaconix (U.K.) Limited
Ko. Essentials Ltd.
LJSP Ltd
LU Aromatherapy Ltd
Lana-Rae Ltd Ltd
Lathersmith Ltd
Leum Skin Care Ltd
Lick Labs Limited
Little Green Beehive Ltd
Lofty Gardens Ltd
MWK Cosmetics (UK) Ltd
Madalyn and Rose Ltd
Magpie's Ocean Ltd

Making Scents Ltd
Maribella London Limited
Christina May Limited
Mbikudi Ltd
Robert McBride Ltd
Meadow Farm Friends Ltd
Molecula Ltd
Molton Brown Limited
Natural Soap Co Ltd
Naturali360 Limited
Nature B Limited
Old Park Farm Estate Limited
Orikii Naturals Ltd
Ottimo Supplies Limited
P & H Natural Skincare Ltd
Paisley Soap Co Ltd
Polka Lab Limited
Pretty Little Treat Company (Yorkshire)
Purdie's of Argyll Ltd
Quint Essence Lab Ltd
Reesoaps.co.uk Ltd
Relax Candle and Bath Co Ltd
Renbow Haircare Limited
Rustic Blends Limited
Rutherford Bambury Ltd
SE & SA Limited
Salopian Ltd
Saltaire Soap Ltd
Sanofi International Biotech Co Ltd.
Savage Alchemy Limited
Savon de V Ltd
Seilich Limited
Sheabynature Ltd
Shifting London Ltd
Sikania Ltd
Simply Ewe Limited
Smelliz Ltd
Soap Cellar Limited
Soap Legacy Ltd
Soap People Ltd
Soap Souk Ltd
Soapberries Ltd
Soapy Skin Limited
Spirit of The Isle Ltd.
Strathpeffer Spa Soap Co Ltd
Superfine Manufacturing Ltd
TAC Perfumes & Cosmetics (UK) Ltd
Thebubblebar Ltd
Tiger Lily Soapery Ltd
Travik Chemicals (UK) Limited
UK Pandora Fairy Skin Beautiyfying Co.,
Universal Chemicals Limited
Universal Toiletries Corporation Ltd
Very Good Vegan Co Ltd
Washworks Bodycare Limited
Yess Essentials Limited

20530 Manufacture of essential oils [20]

Anastaz Beverly Hills Ltd
Aromatherapy Infusions Ltd
Aromatic Scents Ltd
Buypolar Ltd
Cocoa Lime Limited
Eden Classics Limited
Evbioo Ltd
Felicity Solutions Ltd
Freestyle Beauty Products Ltd
Freshorize Ltd
Haromatic Ltd
Heavenly Fragrance (UK) Ltd
Macob Online Shopping Ltd.
Making Scents Ltd

Old Park Farm Estate Limited
Seilich Limited
Soap Cellar Limited
TAC Perfumes & Cosmetics (UK) Ltd
Therapy Factory Ltd
UK Pandora Fairy Skin Beautiyfying Co.,

20590 Manufacture of other chemical products n.e.c. [40]

R P Adam Limited
Apex Industrial Chemicals Ltd
Archem (N.I.) Ltd
Aromatic Flavours & Fragrances Europe
Aromatic Scents Ltd
Carapoll Chemicals Ltd
Chemiclean Products Limited
Chinese Gentry Limited
Clover Chemicals Limited
Datesand Limited
Diversey Industrial Limited
Durabond Chemicals Limited
Eco Earth Limited
Elinor-UK Ltd
Ersag UK Limited
Evans Vanodine International PLC
Gio Natura Ltd
Glamour Natural Cosmetics Ltd
Daisy Gordon Limited
Holt Lloyd International Ltd
Industrial Chemicals Limited
Itaconix (U.K.) Limited
Java Coffee Co Ltd
LJSP Ltd
Larragard Limited
Main Chemical Co Limited
Mauchit Ltd
McIntyre Group Ltd.
Midland Chemicals Limited
NCH (UK) Limited
Powerclean Chemicals Limited
Proton Group Limited
Residual Barrier Technology Ltd
SAS Environmental Services Ltd
Safe Solutions (Safe4) Limited
Selden Research Limited
Stepan UK Limited
Superfine Manufacturing Ltd
Techtron Limited
Texatherm Systems Limited

21100 Manufacture of basic pharmaceutical products [10]

CKC Aromatherapy Beauty Products Ltd
Farasha-Cosmetics Ltd
GM Globalhealth Ltd
Hutrade Ltd.
Ideal Manufacturing Limited
Kalula Cosmetics Ltd
Little Green Beehive Ltd
Ochil Skincare Co Ltd
Mimi Pisano Limited
Zomi Ltd

21200 Manufacture of pharmaceutical preparations

GM Globalhealth Ltd
Stockcare Limited

23190 Manufacture and processing of other glass, including technical glassware

KA Shere-Khan Limited

23420 Manufacture of ceramic sanitary fixtures
Original Soapchair Co Ltd

25620 Machining
Diversey Industrial Limited

25710 Manufacture of cutlery
KA Shere-Khan Limited

25990 Manufacture of other fabricated metal products n.e.c.
Rapid Washrooms Limited

28990 Manufacture of other special-purpose machinery n.e.c.
Clensure Global Ltd
Quill International Group Ltd
R-MC Power Recovery Limited

29320 Manufacture of other parts and accessories for motor vehicles
3M UK Trading Limited

31090 Manufacture of other furniture
Lamina Animal Limited
Narauli Ltd

32120 Manufacture of jewellery and related articles
Driftwood Shaper Ltd
KA Shere-Khan Limited
Mbikudi Ltd
Nana's Studio Ltd
Piesse and Kinney Limited

32130 Manufacture of imitation jewellery and related articles
Crafty Lady Ltd

32409 Manufacture of other games and toys, n.e.c.
Ghastly Games Limited
Lather Cute Soap Limited

32500 Manufacture of medical and dental instruments and supplies
Ebiox Limited
Zomi Ltd

32990 Other manufacturing n.e.c. [12]
Annael Ltd
Nathalie Bond Limited
CKC Aromatherapy Beauty Products Ltd
LU Aromatherapy Ltd
Lana-Rae Ltd Ltd
Malibu Health Products Limited
Narauli Ltd
Nature Reflects Limited
Oooh Skincare Ltd
Smellifiscent Ltd
UK Pandora Fairy Skin Beautiyfying Co.,
Very Good Vegan Co Ltd

33120 Repair of machinery
GEA Farm Technologies (UK) Ltd

33200 Installation of industrial machinery and equipment
CB Services Limited
Danchemtech Ltd

36000 Water collection, treatment and supply
Apvodo Ltd.

38110 Collection of non-hazardous waste
Shorrock Trichem Limited
Vuitton Group Ltd

43290 Other construction installation
Apvodo Ltd.

43390 Other building completion and finishing
Danchemtech Ltd

46120 Agents involved in the sale of fuels, ores, metals and industrial chemicals
Chemical Hut Ltd

46160 Agents involved in the sale of textiles, clothing, fur, footwear and leather goods
Team Titan Performance Ltd
UK Better Cleaner Industry Co., Ltd
UK Nuduun Personal-Care Supply Co.,

46170 Agents involved in the sale of food, beverages and tobacco
SE & SA Limited

46180 Agents specialised in the sale of other particular products
Team Titan Performance Ltd

46190 Agents involved in the sale of a variety of goods
Apvodo Ltd.
Hempia Limited
MDCO Ltd
Pampered Me Ltd
Universal Toiletries Corporation Ltd

46410 Wholesale of textiles
Chromasol Limited

46420 Wholesale of clothing and footwear
Shifting London Ltd

46450 Wholesale of perfume and cosmetics [49]
All Naturals Beauty Limited
Aromabar (Scotland) Ltd
B.Me Skincare Ltd
Berry Inc Ltd
Biologico Cosmetics Limited
Bloomtown Ltd
Chinese Gentry Limited
Cleanux Chemicals Ltd
Conatural Ltd
Cosmetic Hooligans Ltd
Dee Doo Limited
Elinor-UK Ltd
Emilia's Handmade Bath and Body Ltd
Emma Victoria Cosmetics Ltd
Ersag UK Limited
Estela Dermocosmetics Ltd
Evbioo Ltd
Fysifarm Limited
Genten Skincare Ltd
GoodNaturedSkincare Ltd
Harmonious Brown Limited
Heavenly Fragrance (UK) Ltd
Hempia Limited
Highland Soap Co. Limited
Holistic Plant Technologies Ltd
Icilda's Ltd
Sarah Ireland Perfumes Ltd
Kalabash Limited
Ko. Essentials Ltd.
Kokoa UK Limited
Lady Smidgeton's Apothecary Ltd
Loveve. Ltd
MWK Cosmetics (UK) Ltd
Magpie's Ocean Ltd
Meadow Farm Friends Ltd
Molecula Ltd
Natural British Limited
Nu-E55ence Ltd
Orikii Naturals Ltd
Quint Essence Lab Ltd
R & T Natural Cosmetics Ltd
SGHP Ltd
Sankofa Heritage Ltd
Sheabynature Ltd
Sikania Ltd
Sisi Cosmetics Ltd
TAC Perfumes & Cosmetics (UK) Ltd
Universal Toiletries Corporation Ltd
Zyzven Naturals Cosmetics Ltd

46460 Wholesale of pharmaceutical goods
Academy Hair and Beauty (UK) Ltd

46499 Wholesale of household goods (other than musical instruments) n.e.c
Ersag UK Limited

46610 Wholesale of agricultural machinery, equipment and supplies
GEA Farm Technologies (UK) Ltd

46690 Wholesale of other machinery and equipment
CB Services Limited

46730 Wholesale of wood, construction materials and sanitary equipment
Original Soapchair Co Ltd

The Top UK Soap and Detergent Manufacturers

46750 Wholesale of chemical products
Chemical Hut Ltd
Chemiclean Products Limited
Chromasol Limited
Danchemtech Ltd
Evonik Goldschmidt UK Limited
R-MC Power Recovery Limited
Ultimate Car Care Ltd

46760 Wholesale of other intermediate products
Chemiclean Products Limited

46900 Non-specialised wholesale trade
Datesand Limited
Portland Janitorial Products Ltd
Shorrock Trichem Limited
TWA Production Ltd.
You're Gorgeous Handmade Soap Ltd

47190 Other retail sale in non-specialised stores
Butter Bar Soapery Ltd
Thistle & Berry Ltd

47250 Retail sale of beverages in specialised stores
Refresh Tea & Soap Co Ltd

47710 Retail sale of clothing in specialised stores
Bloomtown Ltd

47750 Retail sale of cosmetic and toilet articles in specialised stores [53]
24 Cures Limited
4th Floor Products Limited
All Naturals Beauty Limited
Arize and Dazzle Limited
B.Me Skincare Ltd
Biologico Cosmetics Limited
Butter Bar Soapery Ltd
Conatural Ltd
Deliciously Me Ltd
Dook Ltd
Emma Victoria Cosmetics Ltd
Fysifarm Limited
Genten Skincare Ltd
Handmade Naturals Ltd
Harmony Bodycare Limited
Hempia Limited
Highland Soap Co. Limited
Hydrophilic Ltd
Icilda's Ltd
Sarah Ireland Perfumes Ltd
Kallisti Ltd
Kalula Cosmetics Ltd
Kleos Naturals Ltd
Kokoa UK Limited
Lady Smidgeton's Apothecary Ltd
Little Lodge Bees Ltd
London Soap Co Ltd
MWK Cosmetics (UK) Ltd
Mama Bee Soaps Ltd
Maribella London Limited
Meadow Farm Friends Ltd
Natural By Nature Limited
Nature B Limited
OC Transformation Limited

Oooh Skincare Ltd
Orikii Naturals Ltd
Purdie's of Argyll Ltd
R & T Natural Cosmetics Ltd
Rustic Blends Limited
SGHP Ltd
Savage Alchemy Limited
Savon de V Ltd
Shea Life Limited
Sisi Cosmetics Ltd
Soapy Goat Ltd
Thebubblebar Ltd
Thistle & Berry Ltd
Thornton Baron Ltd
UK Better Cleaner Industry Co., Ltd
UK Nuduun Personal-Care Supply Co.,
Yogi Fresh Limited
Zomi Ltd
Zyzven Naturals Cosmetics Ltd

47789 Other retail sale of new goods in specialised stores (not commercial art galleries and opticians)
Enchanted Plants Ltd

47820 Retail sale via stalls and markets of textiles, clothing and footwear
Nana's Studio Ltd

47890 Retail sale via stalls and markets of other goods [16]
CS Holistic Therapy Products Ltd
Dino-Mite Ltd
Duchess Naturals Limited
Greener Good Ltd
Halritt Ltd
Humble Bee Botanica Ltd.
Insensed Ltd
Loveve. Ltd
Oooh Skincare Ltd
Pampered Me Ltd
Peaceful Potager Limited
Refresh Tea & Soap Co Ltd
Smellifiscent Ltd
Soap People Ltd
Spartisan Ltd
T. & Toff Ltd

47910 Retail sale via mail order houses or via Internet [41]
24 Cures Limited
Aromabar (Scotland) Ltd
Berry Inc Ltd
Butter Bar Soapery Ltd
CS Holistic Therapy Products Ltd
Dee Doo Limited
Dino-Mite Ltd
Evbioo Ltd
Everfolk Limited
Genten Skincare Ltd
Halritt Ltd
Handmade Naturals Ltd
Harmonious Brown Limited
Holistic Plant Technologies Ltd
Insensed Ltd
Kallisti Ltd
Ko. Essentials Ltd.
Lamina Animal Limited
Leum Skin Care Ltd
Loveve. Ltd

Elizabeth Martin Creative Studio Ltd
Molecula Ltd
OC Transformation Limited
Peaceful Potager Limited
Quint Essence Lab Ltd
R & T Natural Cosmetics Ltd
Reesoaps.co.uk Ltd
Refresh Tea & Soap Co Ltd
Scent By Hand Ltd
Sikania Ltd
Smellifiscent Ltd
Soap People Ltd
Spa Mommy Limited
Spartisan Ltd
T. & Toff Ltd
Thebubblebar Ltd
Thistle & Berry Ltd
Thornton Baron Ltd
Ultima Direct Limited
Ultimate Car Care Ltd
Yess Essentials Limited

47990 Other retail sale not in stores, stalls or markets
3M UK Trading Limited
GoodNaturedSkincare Ltd
Greener Good Ltd
Humble Bee Botanica Ltd.
Residual Barrier Technology Ltd
United Company Specialty Chemicals & Mineral Oils

49410 Freight transport by road
Industrial Chemicals Limited

55100 Hotels and similar accommodation
Vuitton Group Ltd

56102 Unlicenced restaurants and cafes
Grassroots Health Ltd

56103 Take-away food shops and mobile food stands
Calman Enterprise Limited

56290 Other food services
Dogbreath Brewery Ltd

62012 Business and domestic software development
Elizabeth Martin Creative Studio Ltd

62020 Information technology consultancy activities
Globemeth Limited
HGH Trading Ltd

63110 Data processing, hosting and related activities
Aventual Ltd

64204 Activities of distribution holding companies
Yogi Fresh Limited

68100 Buying and selling of own real estate
Vuitton Group Ltd

68209 Other letting and operating of own or leased real estate
Arulabeauty Ltd
Denykem Limited

69201 Accounting and auditing activities
Zenken Limited

69202 Bookkeeping activities
Windy Mill Ltd

70100 Activities of head offices
21 Road Limited
Colhoon Corporation Limited

70229 Management consultancy activities other than financial management
21 Road Limited
Grassroots Health Ltd
Murray-Smith Consulting Ltd

71121 Engineering design activities for industrial process and production
SAS Environmental Services Ltd

71200 Technical testing and analysis
Techtron Limited

72110 Research and experimental development on biotechnology
Residual Barrier Technology Ltd

72190 Other research and experimental development on natural sciences and engineering
Academy Hair and Beauty (UK) Ltd
SKC Resources Ltd

74100 Specialised design activities
GEA Farm Technologies (UK) Ltd
Greener Good Ltd

74300 Translation and interpretation activities
Aventual Ltd

74909 Other professional, scientific and technical activities n.e.c.
Ebiox Limited
Hutrade Ltd.
SGHP Ltd
SKC Resources Ltd

75000 Veterinary activities
Datesand Limited

77390 Renting and leasing of other machinery, equipment and tangible goods n.e.c.
CB Services Limited
SAS Environmental Services Ltd

77400 Leasing of intellectual property and similar products, except copyright works
CClear Limited

79120 Tour operator activities
Ayurveda Wellness Ltd

80100 Private security activities
Globemeth Limited

81222 Specialised cleaning services
Dalton Luxury Ltd

81299 Other cleaning services
AMB Hygiene Limited
Unitor Limited

82990 Other business support service activities n.e.c.
Anuvaayum Ltd
Handmade Naturals Ltd
Humble Bee Botanica Ltd.
Kalabash Limited
Sheabynature Ltd
Windy Mill Ltd

85320 Technical and vocational secondary education
Calman Enterprise Limited

85520 Cultural education
Mbikudi Ltd
Sankofa Heritage Ltd

85590 Other education n.e.c.
Rural Skills Centre Limited

86900 Other human health activities
Ayurveda Wellness Ltd
Felicity Solutions Ltd
Nature B Limited
SKC Resources Ltd
Therapy Factory Ltd

90030 Artistic creation
21 Road Limited
Driftwood Shaper Ltd

94200 Activities of trade unions
Amita Cosmetics Ltd

96020 Hairdressing and other beauty treatment [13]
Amita Cosmetics Ltd
Arize and Dazzle Limited
Buypolar Ltd
Eucaderm Limited
GoodNaturedSkincare Ltd
Harmony Bodycare Limited
Italist Skincare Ltd
Kalula Cosmetics Ltd
Kokoa UK Limited
La Boulle Ltd
Roots & Paradise Ltd
Sisi Cosmetics Ltd
Soap Cellar Limited

96040 Physical well-being activities
Therapy Factory Ltd

96090 Other service activities n.e.c.
Hutrade Ltd.
Savon Paradis Ltd
Deloris White Limited

Printed in 8pt Nimbus Sans L

Designed by URW++ Design and Development GmbH

Dellam Publishing Limited

2 Heath Drive, Sutton, Surrey, SM2 5RP

Fax: 020 8770 7478   email: enquiries@dellam.com

SAN: 0177881   EAN/GLN: 5030670177882

www.ingramcontent.com/pod-product-compliance
Lightning Source LLC
Chambersburg PA
CBHW081123080526
44587CB00021B/3721